Elisha Forerunner of Jesus Christ

Bible Commentary on 2 Kings 2-9

Daniel Arnold

Published in French in 2002 :
Elisée précurseur de Jésus-Christ. Commentaire de 2 Rois 2-9
Editions Emmaüs, route de Fenil 40, CH-1806 Saint-Légier,
Switzerland

English translation: Henriette L. Ludwig
Published in English in February 2015, CreateSpace
ISBN 978-1-5084-2942-5

All Scripture quotations are taken from the NKJV unless otherwise
stated.

TABLE OF CONTENTS

ABBREVIATIONS

BA	Bible Annotée, Frédéric GODET
BFC	Bible en Français Courant
CBQ	Catholic Biblical Quarterly
DRB	Darby Bible
JBL	Journal of Biblical Literature
JER	Bible de Jerusalem
JSOT	Journal for the Study of the Old Testament
KJ	King James
LSG	Bible Louis Segond
LXX	Greek version of the Septuagint
NASB	New American Standard Bible
NBC	New Bible Commentary, H. L. ELLISON
NCB	Nouveau Commentaire Biblique, W. S. LA SOR
NDB	Nouveau Dictionnaire Biblique
NEB	New English Bible
NIV	New International Version
NKJV	New King James Version
RSV	Revised Standard Version
SEM	Bible du Semeur
SER	La Bible Segond révisée (Colombe)
TOB	Traduction œcuménique de la Bible
TWOT	Theological Wordbook of the Old Testament
VT	Vetus Testamentum

PREFACE

Elisha is an utterly unique man. No prophet performed as many miracles as he did, in such an unusual manner, and with such ease. Elisha is like a magician who carries out all sorts of tricks with the sole purpose of stunning his audience. Why make an iron axe head float on water when a simple offering taken among the sons of the prophets would have allowed a worker to repay a lost tool (2 Kings 6:5-7)? Why show his servant the presence of celestial armies when they never intervene in the story (2 Kings 6:17)? Why strike enemy soldiers blind and deliver them to the King of Israel, only to feed and release them afterwards (2 Kings 6:18-23)?

The objects used in these miracles further enhance the impression of "magic" in Elisha's acts. Why ask for salt in a new bowl to purify a spring (2 Kings 2:19-22)? Why ask for a harp player in the middle of the desert before consulting God (2 Kings 3:3-15)? Why stretch out on top of a corpse to restore it to life (2 Kings 4:34-35)? How is one to understand the ineffectiveness of the staff placed on the face of a small boy (2 Kings 4:29-31)?

The ease with which Elisha solves numerous difficulties is as astounding as his technique. He never fails, and the rare setbacks he encounters do not seem to trouble him. Elisha knows the enemy's best-kept secrets. He announces the future and sees the invisible world. He transcends the world of humans.

The believer is perplexed by Elisha. What can we learn from this extraordinary person? The spiritual lessons are not evident, and it comes as no surprise that pastors prefer Elijah to Elisha as a sermon topic.

The links between Elijah and Elisha are also surprising. On the one hand, Elisha is Elijah's successor and resembles him in many ways. Like Elijah, for example, he parts the waters of the Jordan (2 Kings 2:8, 14); he multiplies material goods and brings back to life the only child of a woman who shelters him (2 Kings 4; 1 Kings 17:14-24). On the other hand, Elisha is Elijah's opposite. He is almost never bothered by the king of Israel (the king's only bout of anger against him quickly dissipates: 2 Kings 6:31-32). He does not need to flee, but can live among his people. He is not a solitary prophet, but a social one who lives in the middle of Israel. He is not a fugitive, but has a main house in the capital and a second residence in Shunem. How are the links between Elijah and Elisha to be understood? Why is there continuity and at the same time discontinuity? The question is important due to the fact that the prophetic succession from one to the other is the only one of its kind in Israel's history. Never before or since did a prophet name his successor. Why are Elijah and Elisha different?

Many mysteries are related to Elisha, but most of them are explained when his ministry is viewed in the light of the Messiah. Elisha foreshadows the ministry of Jesus Christ in a typological fashion. *Elijah* is thus a forerunner of John the Baptist and represents the prophets of the Old Testament on the Mount of Transfiguration; *Elisha* announces the New Testament. The former is filled with Old Testament justice, the latter radiates New Testament grace. The link between Elijah and Elisha is characteristic of the links which both unify and separate the Old and New Testaments.

This commentary follows the commentary by the same author on Elijah, entitled *Elijah between Judgment and Grace, Commentary on 1 Kings 17 to 2 Kings 2*. The two books complement each other, yet are independent of one another. Each one stands on its own. Some repetition is necessary; occasionally some references permit the reader to go deeper into material elaborated in the first book. The parallels between the two prophets are specifically developed in this book, because the ministry of Elisha is in part defined by the links to the ministry of his predecessor.

This commentary is preceded by two chapters which develop the characteristics of Elisha and the context of his ministry. At the end of the book there is a condensed commentary on the story of the end of the house of Ahab (2 Kings 9-10), an analysis of the section of Scripture relating to the death of Elisha (2 Kings 13:14-21), and a study of the influence of Elisha on the authors of the New Testament.

INTRODUCTION

THE CHARACTER OF ELISHA

The Prophet of Grace

Elisha represents grace as much as Elijah represents judgment. Elijah began his ministry by depriving Israel of water (1 Kings 17:1), but Elisha begins his by giving water back (2 Kings 2:19-22). Elijah stopped the water from above (lack of rain), but Elisha purifies the water from below (cleansing of a spring). Elijah pronounced his judgment on the sins of Israel (they were deprived of rain because they worshiped a rain deity), but Elisha lifts the curse which Joshua had pronounced at Jericho (Jos 6:26). Throughout his ministry Elisha aids both individuals as well as communities, poor and rich, men and women, Jews and pagans. The narrator usually provides *two* examples from each area.

1. Among the individuals who are particularly blessed by the prophet we find two women and two men in the following order: one poor and one rich woman, one rich and one poor man. A poor widow receives the means to pay her creditors who are about to take her children and sell them into slavery (2 Kings 4:1-7); the child of a rich woman of Shunem is brought back to life (later she recovers all of her belongings which she had abandoned during a famine: 2 Kings 4:8-37; 8:1-6); Naaman, a pagan general, is cured of leprosy (2 Kings 5); a poor workman recovers a borrowed tool which he had lost (2 Kings 6:1-7).
2. Twice a Jewish community is miraculously fed (2 Kings 4:38-41, 42-44). The first time Elisha neutralises the evil and the second time he multiplies the good. The former case involves a hot liquid (soup) and the latter warm, solid food (loaves of bread taken from a sack).
3. Two Jewish cities are delivered from their misfortune. The inhabitants of Jericho receive a permanent supply of pure water and the famished inhabitants of Samaria are provided

with an abundance of nourishment (2 Kings 2:19-22; 6:24-7:20)

4. Elisha delivers Israel from two military conflicts: the first time during a raid led against Moab in the south, the second during a raid of the Syrians from the north. One battle is offensive and the other is defensive (2 Kings 3; 6:24-7:20).

5. Twice Elisha blesses pagans who have come to see him for different reasons: Naaman the general seeks his aid to heal his leprosy, whereas the Syrian army besieges Dothan with the intention of arresting Elisha. Naaman is healed; the Syrian soldiers are fed by the king of Israel after being captured, and are then set free without harm. First, Elisha removes an illness (leprosy) from one who seeks his aid, and then he refrains from doing evil to his attackers (2 Kings 5; 6:8-23).

Elisha releases men from illnesses, poverty and their enemies. Regarding illnesses, he triumphs over death resulting from a sudden illness (2 Kings 4:8-37), then permanently cures a serious illness (leprosy, 2 Kings 5). The first case concerns a boy brought by his mother; in the second an adult is counselled by a slave girl. Regarding material wealth, Elisha multiplies the meagre resources of a widow, and another time he helps a workman recover a borrowed tool so he can return it to its owner (2 Kings 4:1-7; 6:1-7). The woman risks losing her children, the workman and his colleagues feel that other houses should be built to shelter everyone.

Elisha is the prophet of grace, to the degree that all armed conflicts in which he is involved end with hardly any loss of human life.

1. During the siege of Dothan Elisha captures Syrian troops and brings them to Samaria without any damage, then orders the king to feed and release them (2 Kings 6:8-23).

2. During the siege of Samaria the Syrians run off in fright during the night, without killing a single enemy nor losing a single soldier, leaving all of their belongings behind (2 Kings 24:7-20). The only person to die in this story is the royal equerry, who is trampled by the crowd. However, Elisha had warned him of the misfortune which awaited him.

3. The military campaign against Moab could have ended in disaster, but Elisha provides the army with water and contributes to its victory over the enemy (2 Kings 3). The narrator never mentions either death or blood in this conflict except for one optical illusion which the Moabites experience. They think they see the blood of the Israelites whom they suppose have killed one other. The misfortunes inflicted on Moab appear to be limited to the loss of material goods (overthrown cities, fields made unfit for planting, wells filled with earth, fruit trees felled). The only death mentioned is that of the son of the king who is sacrificed by his father.

Elisha is consequently never "responsible" for the death of any soldiers.

Elisha's brilliant path seems to be overshadowed by two judgments: the first is pronounced against the children of Bethel and the second against his servant Gehazi (2 Kings 2:23-25; 5:20-27). The children of Bethel die, and Gehazi is permanently stricken with the leprosy that Naaman had. These two stories show that the contrast between Elijah and Elisha is only partial. Elijah is the prophet of judgment, yet his ministry reflects grace in several instances, for example when he brings an infant back to life. In the same way, Elisha is the prophet of grace, yet his ministry is marked by judgments, particularly in the case of the children of Bethel. Elijah and Elisha contrast each other without ever opposing each other.

Elisha loves life and is grieved by death. He anoints Hazael with his tears, because he knows that the Syrian will inflict great suffering on the Israelites (2 Kings 8:12). To better separate Elisha from the acts of this cruel man, the narrator avoids the term "anointing" (even though he implies that act). Jehu, the other bloodthirsty avenger, is indirectly anointed by Elisha, who sends one of his servants to perform the symbolic gesture (2 Kings 9:1-10).

Finally, we note that Elisha's entire ministry is characterised by a time of grace towards the house of Ahab. Ahab had been condemned to death, but the Almighty postponed the sentence. During Elisha's ministry the narrator *never* mentions this imminent judgment. Elisha embodies the time of grace to such an extent that the judgment appears forgotten. It is only at the end of his ministry that Elisha anoints the two kings already mentioned in the time of Elijah (1 Kings 19:15-17). Immediately after the anointment of these two vengeful kings Elisha disappears from the narrative.

The Prophet of the People

Elisha is a social prophet whereas Elijah was a solitary prophet. Elisha is called to the ministry while he is working in the fields as part of a team of twelve labourers (1 Kings 19:19). Before following Elijah he wishes to take leave of his parents, to whom he is quite attached: *"And he left the oxen and ran after Elijah, and said, 'Please let me kiss my father and my mother, and then I will follow you.'"* (1 Kings 19:20). He also invites everyone to share a last meal which he prepares from his oxen (1 Kings 19:21).

Later on, shortly before his master's ascension, Elisha refuses to leave him, even though Elijah repeatedly tells him to go (2 Kings 2:2, 4, 6). The contrast between the social character of Elisha and the asocial character of Elijah is particularly evident in this story. The more Elijah insists on being alone, the more Elisha refuses to leave him. The sons of the prophets do not speak a word with Elijah, but communicate only with Elisha, even though it is Elijah who leaves them.

Elisha crosses the Jordan after the ascension of Elijah and returns to the world of men to live with them. He stays in five different cities: Jericho (2 Kings 2:15-22), Shunem (2 Kings 4:8-10), Gilgal (2 Kings 4:38), Dothan (2 Kings 6:13) and several times in Samaria (2 Kings 2:25; 5:3, 9; 6:32). He has a house in the capital (2 Kings 5:9; 6:32) and a permanent lodging in Shunem (2 Kings 4:10). Elisha is engaged in community projects and accompanies the labourers to the banks of the Jordan, probably for several months, the time required to build new dwellings (2 Kings 6:2-3).

Elisha is attached to people. He lives in cites and not in the desert like Elijah. Elisha does travel sometimes, but only to go from one city to the other (and once to live at a construction site: 2 Kings 6:1-4). The narrator mentions his arrivals (2 Kings 4:8,

11, 38), but never his departures, except when he accompanies people (the workers going to the Jordan and the Syrian soldiers being led to Samaria: 2 Kings 6:4, 19). There is also the departure of Elisha when he is called (1 Kings 19:19-21), the only departure which is described in detail. Elisha leaves his father and mother in order to *follow* Elijah. This is not solitude, but an expression of affection towards a new "family" (if one can use this term for Elijah the loner).[1] Elisha is almost always surrounded by collaborators. His main servant is Gehazi (2 Kings 4:8-37; 5:20-27; 8:4-5). During the siege of Dothan another man assists him (2 Kings 6:15-17). During the siege of Samaria the ancients keep him company in his room (2 Kings 6:32). In the desert, when he is accompanying the soldiers of the coalition, Elisha requests the presence of a musician (2 Kings 3:15). When Elisha separates from Gehazi for an urgent mission in Shunem the mother of the child insists on going with him (2 Kings 4:30). But even when physically separated from Gehazi Elisha knows what his servant is doing at every moment (2 Kings 5:26).

Elisha is always approachable when someone looks for him, unlike Elijah who escapes from all pursuit. The widow who risks losing her two children can reach him without difficulty on two occasions (2 Kings 4:1, 7). The Shunammite who builds a special room for the prophet knows where to find him when he is not at her home (2 Kings 4:22-25). Even the little Jewish girl who is a prisoner of the Syrians knows where the itinerant prophet is staying (2 Kings 5:3).

Elisha can be found not only by the common people, but also by the kings of Israel. During the siege of Samaria king Joram knows where to look for Elisha in order to arrest him (2 Kings 6:31-32). When Elisha is dying, king Joash can make a courtesy call (2 Kings 13:14). The ease with which the kings of Israel, Judah and Edom, in the middle of the desert with their armies during their campaign against Moab, find Elisha is even more

---

[1] We would point out that although Elijah wants to be alone, he does not ask Elisha to leave just before being carried away, but rather to *remain* (2 Kings 2:2-6). It is Elijah who wishes to leave so as to separate himself from Elisha.

astonishing (2 Kings 3:9-11). Finally, even the enemies of Israel rapidly discover his residence when they want to arrest him (Dothan: 2 Kings 6:13-14). From the start to the end of his ministry Elisha lives in the midst of the people, and anybody who seeks him quickly finds him.

The only exception to Elisha's commitment to community is his voyage from Jericho to Bethel (2 Kings 2:23-25). There, *everything* is done the other way around. Elisha travels alone, does not speak to the adolescents, does not stop in the city, but rather leaves it to go elsewhere (the narrator points this out), and most of all he bears malediction instead of benediction. Elisha is not respected by the people and is not integrated into their community. He makes difficult progress (the adolescents mock the perspiring man who has been climbing up from the Jordan plain), and he then proves his authority by sending punishment upon the sinners. In this story Elisha resembles Elijah more than himself. Here even the animals intervene more than men do. The meaning of this particular text is explained in the commentary (see pp. 66-70). Basically it emphasises the link which ties Elijah to Elisha.

The Prophet of Perfection

Elisha personifies perfection. His interventions *permanently* solve problems. The spring of Jericho remains purified *"to this day"*, i.e. until the time of writing (2 Kings 2:21-22). The coalition army not only escapes death, but lastingly weakens Moab (the cities are reduced to rubble, the fields are made unfit for planting, the wells are filled with earth, fruit trees are chopped down: 2 Kings 3:24-25). The widow terrorised by her creditors receives enough money, not only to pay her debts, but also to live on afterwards (*"Then she came and told the man of God. And he said, 'Go, sell the oil and pay your debt; and you and your sons live on the rest'"* 2 Kings 4:7). The amount of bread multiplied exceeds the need (*"So he set it before them; and they ate and had some left over"*, 2 Kings 4:44). Naaman is completely healed of his leprosy (*"and his flesh was restored like the flesh of a little child, and he was clean."* 2 Kings 5:14). The departure of the Syrian army provides Israel with abundant goods (2 Kings 7:15-16). The Shunammite recovers her property after a famine of seven years: *"all that was hers, and all the proceeds of the field from the day that she left the land until now."* (2 Kings 8:6). The king of Israel has an opportunity to conquer the Syrians permanently (but, unfortunately, does not take advantage of it: 2 Kings 13:19). Even death does not seem to have a hold on Elisha, as his bones restore a dead soldier to life (2 Kings 13:21).

The fullness of Elisha's ministry is more evident when compared with the temporal situations which accompany the ministry of his predecessor. For *Elijah* permanent solutions do not seem to exist, as they are always left for the next day. The judgments during the time of Ahab are slow in coming. To begin with, the sentence against the heathen king is limited to an absence of rain (1 Kings 17:1). Afterwards, when the rain returns despite the lack of profound repentance, God asks Elijah on Mount Horeb to postpone Ahab's punishment (1 Kings 19:9-18).[2] Later on the punishment pronounced for the murder of Naboth is immediately deferred after the king's repentance (1 Kings 21:28-29). On a personal level Elijah often receives his subsistence a day at a time (1 Kings 17:2-16). He is guided by the Almighty one step at a time (1 Kings 17:3, 9). Although promised by God, the rain comes after a long prayer (1 Kings 18:1, 41-45). It is therefore not surprising that Elijah is known for his perseverance (James 5:17-18).

Elisha, on the other hand, has everything and gives everything. He himself is almost never inconvenienced by others, except for the adolescents who perish immediately (2 Kings 2:23-25) and by a king who orders his arrest but immediately changes his mind (2 Kings 6:32-33). The communion between Elisha and God is so profound that the prophet generally does not need to pray. On the other hand, Elijah must pray, often with perseverance. Elisha contents himself with *speaking to people*, and his word is fulfilled. Only one story mentions prayer to God: during the siege of Dothan Elisha prays that the eyes of his assistant would be opened and those of the Syrians closed, then opened again in Samaria. The

---

[2]   See D. Arnold, *Elijah between Judgment and Grace*, pp. 123-130.

narrator describes God's intervention as simply as possible, indicating that any request by Elisha is immediately fulfilled (*"the Lord opened the eyes"*, *"the Lord struck them with blindness"*, *"the Lord opened"*: 2 Kings 6:17, 18, 20).[3]

The permanent "solutions" are not restricted to health, but also deal with the rare judgments linked to the ministry of Elisha: the mocking adolescents of Bethel are immediately torn to pieces by two bears (2 Kings 2:24); the leprosy falls on Gehazi and his descendants forever as soon as he steps over the threshold (2 Kings 5:27); the unbelieving equerry dies the next day, at the moment the starving people are rushing out to gather food (2 Kings 7:1, 17-20).

The Timeless Prophet

The perfection of Elisha's interventions places him in a sense outside of time. Contrary to Elijah's ministry which varies in the course of time, Elisha's ministry is stable from beginning to end. No progression is possible because Elisha walks in perfection from the start. Where Elijah must pass over mountains and valleys to reach some distant peak, Elisha strolls effortlessly along the crest of high plateaus. Where there is no more progression, time is obliterated.

There are few chronological references, and the stories follow one another without temporal links. The name of the king of Israel is given once at the time of the first armed conflict (2 Kings 3). Afterwards, during the sieges of Dothan and Samaria (2 Kings 6:8-7.20), and when the Shunammite goes before the king to retrieve her possessions (2 Kings 8:1-6), the narrator simply mentions *"the king of Israel"* without giving his name.[4] Certainly the death of Joram recounted in Chapter 9 identifies the "anonymous" king of the preceding chapters as Joram. Still, the author could have regrouped all of the stories on

---

[3] The author also tells us that Elisha withdraws to his room to pray as soon as he has brought the child of the Shunammite back to life. (2 Kings 4:33).

[4] In these passages (2 Kings 6:8-8:6), the expression *"king of Israel"* is used seven times and the word *"king"* (without qualification) 19 times to designate the king of Israel.

Elisha. The prophet actually lived under six different kings. During the reigns of the first two (Ahab and Ahaziah) Elisha lived in the background, in Elijah's service. After Elijah's departure he begins his ministry of deliverance. All of Elisha's miracles are reported between the ascension of Elijah and the death of Joram (2 Kings 2-8), with the exception of his two posthumous miracles (2 Kings 13:14-21). What happened during the 28-year reign of Jehu, the sixteen years under Joahaz and the first years of Joash? There are three possibilities:

1. The narrator gave priority to the thematic arrangement in regrouping all of the stories of the miracles.[5]
2. The narrator reported only the miracles which took place during Joram's reign, as he was interested only in the house of Ahab.
3. Elisha did not perform any miracles during more than forty-five years (the reigns of Jehu and Joahaz), in order to emphasise the ministry of the Messiah, who retired to heaven for a long period after having carried out his earthly ministry (see item 3, p. 212).

We should also note that Gehazi becomes leprous *"forever"* in chapter 5 (v. 27), but can freely present himself to the king in chapter 8 (v. 4-5). Was Gehazi's leprosy benign or non-transmissible? Did Gehazi repent and did God cleanse him of his leprosy? Does the second precede the first in chronological order?

It is difficult to find a final answer to all of these questions. The author of Kings, who is generally fastidious about chronological questions,[6] leaves Elisha in a temporal flux. He thus reinforces the idea that Elisha's ministry is unusual,

---

[5] The thematic arrangement is obvious (see diagram on p. 43), but this does not prove that the narrator did not respect the chronological order. Certain authors had numerous stories with which to compose their narratives. (cf. John 21:25 *"And there are also many other things that Jesus did, which if they were written one by one, I suppose that even the world itself could not contain the books that would be written."* For these historian-narrators, it was relatively easy to follow a thematic order and at the same time respect the chronological order.

[6] The books of 1+2 Kings contain more chronological references than any other books of the Bible.

timeless, on the edge of unfolding history. Elisha is an exceptional prophet who dominates time; he is an earthly sign of eternity.

The Prophet of Knowledge

Elisha's perfection appears particularly in the area of knowledge. Elisha knows everything his servant Gehazi says and does when he is away (2 Kings 5:26). He knows the secret strategies developed by the Syrians to stop the king of Israel (2 Kings 6:8-12). He also sees the invisible army of the Lord camping around Dothan (2 Kings 6:16-17).

Elisha not only knows things hidden in the present, but also astounding events of the future. He predicts the coming of water in the middle of the desert and the annihilation of enemy forces set to make mincemeat of the coalition army (2 Kings 3:16-19). He oversees the unlimited multiplication of oil to save a poor widow from her merciless creditor (2 Kings 4:4). He promises the impending birth of a son to a childless woman whose husband is old (2 Kings 4:16). He announces the purification of soup (2 Kings 4:41) and the multiplication of food (2 Kings 4:43). He guarantees the healing of a leper by a simple bath in the Jordan (2 Kings 5:10). He proclaims the sudden end of extreme famine, as well as a very low price of two food items (2 Kings 7:1). He also announces to an incredulous equerry his imminent death (2 Kings 7:2). He informs king Joash of a triple victory over the Syrians (2 Kings 13:19).

Whereas Elijah was guided step by step by God, Elisha needs no instruction, having perfect knowledge of God's will. God never speaks to him, although his predecessor was instructed by God *fourteen* times: seven times for a journey[7] and on seven

---

[7] To go to the torrent of Kerith (1 Kings 17:3), to Zarephath (1 Kings 17:9), before Ahab to announce the return of the rain (1 Kings 18:1), to Damascus to anoint Hazael (1 Kings 19:15), to the vine of Naboth to reprimand Ahab (1 Kings 21:18), to the servants of Ahaziah (2 Kings 1:3), to Ahaziah (2 Kings 1:15). Therefore, twice to speak to Ahab, twice to speak to Ahaziah, and once to anoint a pagan king.

other occasions.[8]

Elisha predicts the near future to his contemporaries, but he also prophesies the future of later generations. His life and ministry announce the life and ministry of the Messiah, but before we delve into this typological teaching (pp. 24-29) we should emphasise other characteristics of Elisha's ministry, starting with the symbolic dimension of his miracles.

The Prophet of Signs

Elisha uses specific objects in seven miracles:
1. Elijah's mantle to separate the waters of the Jordan (following his predecessor's example);
2. salt in a new bowl to purify a spring (2 Kings 2:20);
3. his prone body to bring a dead person back to life (2 Kings 4:34-35);
4. flour to neutralise poisoned soup (2 Kings 4:41);
5. the waters of the Jordan to heal a leper (2 Kings 5:10);
6. a piece of wood to make an iron axe head float (2 Kings 6:6);
7. an arrow shot towards the east and arrows beaten on the ground to defeat the Syrian army (2 Kings 13:15-19).

He also calls for a musician so he can discern the Lord's counsel (2 Kings 3:15), and contact with his bones brings a dead soldier back to life (2 Kings 13:21).

Some might believe this to be magic, but objects in Scripture never have intrinsic force. The Lord is all-powerful, and the material world is subject to Him. Attention should be drawn to the fact that Elisha never uses the same objects, which in part eliminates any idea of magic. Elisha does not follow any ritual nor does he recite any magic spells. His word alone, always different and always appropriate, is the determining element.

---

[8] The order to eat the cake prepared by the angel (1 Kings 19:5, 7), the order to leave the cave on Mount Horeb (1 Kings 19:11), the question on the reason for Elijah's presence at Horeb (1 Kings 19:9, 13), the question of Ahab's repentance (1 Kings 21:28), the revelation by a soft murmur (1 Kings 19:12). Three orders, three questions and one non-verbal revelation. Bergen (*Elisha and the End of Prophetism*) interprets the "silences" of the Lord towards Elisha negatively (see footnote 16 p. 30).

The objects have only a pedagogical function, serving as symbols to illustrate certain principles. This is how we must understand Elisha's staff placed on the body of a child (2 Kings 4:29-31) and the earth of Israel which Naaman requests (2 Kings 5:17). The mantle is a sign of authority; salt illustrates sterility (and not purification as proposed by some authors); the waters of the Jordan symbolise the Promised Land, and above all God's alliance with his people; striking arrows on the ground indicates the extent of a military victory. This is not the time to explain the meaning of each object, but only to draw attention to this symbolic dimension. The meaning of each object will be explained in the commentary.

Elisha wants to *teach* through his miracles, and it is vital to understand this teaching. It stands in relation to the ministry of Jesus Christ, because all of Elisha's acts are oriented towards him.

The Prophet of "Gratuity"

Elisha accomplishes wonder after wonder, but some of his actions seem overdone and unnecessarily miraculous. The material needs of the widow or the labourer who lost his axe could have been resolved in a simpler way. Why make an axe blade float (2 Kings 6:6), a premiere in human history and a miracle unequalled since, when financial aid would have sufficed? The same applies to the widow who was unable to pay her creditor (2 Kings 4:1-7). Why not ask the sons of the prophets to show their solidarity towards the wife of one of their deceased comrades? Elisha could have used his influence with the king (just as he later proposed to the Shunammite: *"What can I do for you? Do you want me to speak on your behalf to the king or to the commander of the army?"* 2 Kings 4:13). In Israel creditors did not have unlimited rights, and had to respect the poor (cf. Deut 24:10-13, 17-22). Why does Elisha use such exceptional means to help the poor?

On the other hand, the miracles performed on pagans seem to be poorly exploited. The healing of Naaman, the Syrian general, does not change the tense relations between Israel and its northern neighbour in any way. After Naaman's healing the king of Syria continues to harass the Israelites (2 Kings 6:8-9, 24). Certainly a leper is healed, but only one leper among the many contemporaries of Elisha who suffered from the same illness (2 Kings 7:3). In the same way the famous and miraculous capture of the Syrian army after the siege of Dothan (2 Kings 6:8-23) does not lessen the aggressiveness of the Syrians who continue their attacks, perhaps with the very soldiers who had been so graciously freed by Elisha (2 Kings 6:24). Regarding the siege of Dothan, we could also question the usefulness of showing Elisha's servant the celestial army (2 Kings 6:16-17).

Elisha's miracles do not change the history of Israel. They are like a sword thrust in water, lost efforts without a future. What is the reason for this waste of power producing results which in the end are insignificant? The answer lies in the nature of Elisha's ministry. The prophet is not called to reform the country, but to announce by different signs the one who will reform the world. The ministry of Elisha must be marked by generosity and gratuitous effort, because the Messiah whom he announces is the champion of grace.

The Prophet as a Prime Minister

Throughout his ministry Elisha acts with the authority of a prime minister, at times even that of a king.

1. Elisha begins by crossing the Jordan from east to west without getting wet, in order to reach the Promised Land (2 Kings 2:14). His gesture recalls the conquest of the Promised Land under Joshua. Elisha however is alone, whereas Joshua was accompanied by all of the people. Elisha is just a scout who is preparing the terrain. His behaviour is not that of a spy who needs to hide (like the men sent by Joshua to explore Jericho), but that of a diplomat or prime minister who handles the important points before the people's coming. The conquest Elisha prepares will be different from that of Joshua, because the Promised Land will be of a different kind.

2. Jericho is the first city of his itinerary, just as in the conquest of the Promised Land (2 Kings 2:19-22). He stops there, not to destroy like Joshua did, but to restore life. He purifies the polluted spring which has prevented life. Joshua had

cursed the city forever (Jos 6:26), but Elisha permanently removes the malediction, as the waters remain pure afterward (*"to this day"*, v. 22).

3. Elisha goes to Bethel, one of the cultural centres of the land. He reprimands the mockers who not only ridicule him but also make fun of his master, Elijah (the expression *"Go up, you baldhead"* is undoubtedly a reference to the ascension of Elijah, see commentary p. 68). Elisha demands respect for honour and sacred things (Elijah and Elisha are the spokesmen of God), the priority of his ministry being spiritual. Bethel was one of the two religious centres of the country (1 Kings 12:28-33).

4. During the campaign against Moab Elisha is engaged in a war of conquest to take back lost territory from the enemy. He holds the position of chief counsellor, being consulted when nothing else works (2 Kings 3:10-12). He saves the coalition and counsels the leaders on what must be done to defeat the enemy (2 Kings 3:16-19).

5. Elisha saves the poor and sets things straight for widows and orphans (2 Kings 4:1-7), as God has done (Deut 10:18; Ps 68:6; 146:9; Jer 49:11) and as any good master should do (Deut 24:17; Is 1:23; Jer 22:3).

6. He rewards the faithful and gives them privileges. He proposes to speak *"to the king or to the commander of the army"* on the Shunammite's behalf (2 Kings 4:13), demonstrating a ministerial influence. When the king hears of favours which Elisha has granted to an individual, that person subsequently receives the king's full support. In favour of the Shunammite, the king orders a chamberlain to *"appoint a certain officer for her, telling him to "restore all that was hers, and all the proceeds of the field from the day that she left the land until now."* (2 Kings 8:6).

7. Elisha helps communities survive food shortages (2 Kings 4:38-44) just as a responsible government should to aid the people who have been hit by catastrophe.

8. In the area of health he offers healing to a leper (2 Kings 5). Elisha does not accept money for this, as he is not a physician. He simply leads the patient to the place of healing (in this case, the Jordan represents the God of Israel), like a minister who refers the physically ill to places of treatment. Elisha

receives Naaman "coldly", as the Syrian is no king but only a *general*. Elisha behaves toward him with the dignity of a prime minister. The refusal of money also seems to indicate that the prophet has no material worries, although there are probably other reasons behind this refusal (see commentary p. 128).

9. Elisha also participates in land development. He accompanies a group of labourers who are establishing a new village (2 Kings 6:1-4).

10. Elisha counsels the king in military matters (2 Kings 6:21-23), stops enemy infiltrations (2 Kings 6:9) and repels military aggressions (2 Kings 6:18-23). When the Syrians lay a long siege to Samaria, the king of Israel is irritated with Elisha, as if the prophet were responsible for the crisis (2 Kings 6:31).

11. Elisha also decides political changes on national and international levels. He anoints Hazael, future king of Syria (2 Kings 8:11-13) and orders one of the sons of the prophets to go and anoint Jehu, future king of Israel (2 Kings 9:1-3).

12. Elisha has such far-reaching influence that when a miracle happens the author is more apt to attribute it to Elisha than to the Lord. In the Book of Kings the fulfilment of a prophecy is a major topic. The author often uses the expression *"according to the word of the Lord"* to emphasise the fulfilment of a prophecy. The expression *"according to the word ..."* appears seven times in connection with Elijah and seven times in connection with Elisha. In Elijah's case it is the word *of the Lord* six times (1 Kings 17:5, 16; 22:38; 2 Kings 1:17; 9:26; 10:17)[9] and once the word *of Elijah* (1 Kings 17:15). In the Elisha series, the word *of the Lord* only occurs twice (2 Kings 4:44; 7:16). Elsewhere it is the word *of Elisha* (twice: 2 Kings 2:22; 6:18) and the word of *the man of God* (three times: 2 Kings 5:14; 7:17; 8:2).

Elisha acts like a prime minister because the man whom he precedes – namely Jesus Christ – will handle the affairs of his heavenly Father. *"The Father loves the Son, and has given all things into His hand"* (John 3:35). *"Jesus, knowing that the*

---

[9] In these six references, it is specified three times that it is the word which *"the Lord* has spoken *through Elijah"* (1 Kings 17:16; 2 Kings 1:17; 10:17).

Father had given all things into His hands, and that He had come from God and was going to God" (John 13:3).

The Prophet Who is the Forerunner of Jesus Christ

Elisha is the only prophet called to a prophetic ministry by another prophet. He has a predecessor, but no successor. At his death the time of miracles and grace ends. No one takes up the mantle of the prophet to continue his ministry; Gehazi had shown that he did not qualify.

No one takes up the ministry, because the prophet of *perfection* had perfectly completed his ministry, one of witness. Elisha is not a saviour (if that had been the case, he would have failed in his mission, because after his death, life goes on as before). Elisha is a *witness for the Saviour*, as the forerunner of the Messiah. In his person and by his acts he announces Jesus Christ, the one who will bring salvation to the world.

Elisha's many miracles provide a preview of the Messiah's acts. The multiplication of the bread is the most obvious *christological* event (2 Kings 4:42-44). Elisha asks his assistant to feed a large crowd with a few loaves. "Impossible", he says, to which Elisha replies that not only shall everyone be fed, but that there will be food left over. It makes no difference that there are twenty loaves instead of five loaves and two fish (cf. Matt 14:15-21). Elisha precedes Jesus, who certainly does more as he is the master and Elisha the servant. Thus Jesus feeds more men with fewer loaves. He feeds not only five men with one loaf, but one thousand families[10] (Matt 14:21) and he repeats the miracle a second time (Matt 15:32-38).[11]

---

[10] For Elisha: $100 : 20 = 5$; and for Jesus: $5000 : 5 = 1000$. With the two multiplications of loaves by Jesus, the numbers account only for the men (*anêr*), i.e. the heads of a family. Matthew states that the women and children were not counted (Mat 14:21; 15:38). There were thus five thousand plus four thousand *families* present, e.g. some twelve thousand persons.

[11] The miracle of the multiplication of loaves holds a key position both in Kings as well as the other Gospels. In Kings, the miracle is situated at the centre of the series on Elisha (see diagram p. 43) and in the New

This superiority of the Son of God over the prophet is found in other accounts. Elisha brings back to life the only son of a Shunammite woman (2 Kings 4:8-37), whereas Jesus brings several people back to life, one of whom is the only son of a woman of Nain (Luke 7:11-17). Some think that the two places are one and the same, Nain being the abbreviation of Shunem.[12] In Elisha's case the prophet must stretch himself twice over the full length of the body of the deceased in order to restore life, whereas Jesus just touches the coffin to revive a young man. Elisha's miracle is exceptional (there are only two resurrections in the Old Testament), but that of Jesus is even more so. Regarding the resurrection of the dead we must also note that the body of Elisha, in the tomb, restores a man back to life (*"So it was, as they were burying a man, that suddenly they spied a band of raiders; and they put the man in the tomb of Elisha; and when the man was let down and touched the bones of Elisha, he revived and stood on his feet"*. 2 Kings 13:20-21), but when Jesus died, *"the graves were opened; and many bodies of the saints who had fallen asleep were raised;"* (Matt 27:50-53). Through his death Jesus gives life back to all who place their faith in him.

As far as healings are concerned we note that although Elisha heals a leper (the only mention of such a healing in the Old Testament), Jesus heals many of them, even ten at a time during one encounter (Luke 17:12). On this occasion Jesus also sends the lepers away from his presence (not to the Jordan as in Naaman's case, but to the high priests: Luke 17:14), and they are healed on the way there. The only one who goes back to Jesus to thank him is a Samaritan, a stranger like Naaman. The geographical region is the same: Elisha stayed in Samaria and *"as Jesus went to Jerusalem ... he passed through the midst of Samaria and Galilee."* (Luke 17:11). Elisha announces the mercy of Christ to pagans in a more general way. The free healing of Naaman, commander in chief of the enemy armies, or

---

Testament, it is the only miracle reported by all four evangelists (Matt 14:15-21; Mark 6:35-44; Luke 9:12-17; John 6:5-14).

[12] The New Bible Dictionary, 1996, p. 799; Jacques Ellul: *Politique de Dieu, politiques des hommes*, p. 11; R.D. Nelson: *First and Second Kings*, p. 176.

the liberation of the Syrian soldiers captured by Elisha foreshadow the giving of grace to all men of all nations.

Regarding miracles of nature, the axe head floating on water announces in a sense Jesus' walking on the water. Both men are capable of defying the law of gravity, but Jesus can do it for a longer time (he walked on water for about five or six kilometres: John 6:19), and repeated the operation a second time when he let Peter come and join him again in the boat (Matt 14:28-29). The axe head floats to the surface of the water (2 Kings 6:6), whereas Jesus stands on the water.

We can recognise three more common traits between the two men: their immense knowledge, divine protection and the prophets who preceded them.

1. *Immense knowledge.* Elisha seems to know everything clearly with one exception: he confesses not to know the needs of the Shunammite *"for her soul is in deep distress, and the LORD has hidden it from me, and has not told me."* 2 Kings 4:27). Jesus knows everything, also with one exception: he admits not knowing the day of his return (*"But of that day and hour no one knows, not even the angels of heaven, but My Father only."* Matt 24:36). The Lord never speaks directly to either Elisha or Christ concerning their call to their ministry, nor to guide or instruct them, as their communion with the Lord is so deep that the two men know his will perfectly.

2. *Divine protection.* Jesus, like Elisha, passes through hostile crowds who want to arrest him (Luke 4:28-30 and John 7:30; 2 Kings 6:18-20). Jesus, like Elisha, speaks of a heavenly army ready to defend him. In one case, it is a dozen legions of angels (Matt 26:53), in another, a huge group of horses and chariots of fire (2 Kings 6:16-17). Neither of the two men calls on these armies.

3. *The forerunners.* The link between Elijah (forerunner of Elisha) and John the Baptist (forerunner of Jesus) is close: *"And if you are willing to receive it, he (John the Baptist) is Elijah who is to come".* (Matt 11:14). Each forerunner is followed by a more powerful successor (2 Kings 2:9-10;

John 3:27-31), and the transfer of power takes place at the Jordan.[13]

In conclusion Elisha accomplishes numerous miracles; he saves the weak; he gives hope to the faithful; he triumphs over evil. But everything does not stop at his death, as indicated by the fact that a man is brought back to life simply by contact with his bones (2 Kings 13:21). Elisha is more than just a *transitional* fireworks display. Through his acts he renders the clearest witness to the ministry of Christ.

Elisha is the prophet of *grace, perfection* and *knowledge,* because he announces him who is full of grace and mercy, filled with divine wisdom and knowledge, the perfect man, without sin, who by the gift of his life redeems humanity from eternal perdition. Elisha is the prophet *of the people,* as Jesus Christ, God in the flesh, lived among men (John 1:14). Elisha is the *timeless* prophet, because his witness is not limited to his own generation; he announces to following generations the one whose life will mark humanity for eternity. Elisha is the *Prime minister* prophet, as the Messiah is the Son of God, destined by the Father to bring redemption to the world and also to rule the world. *"For He has put all things under His feet. But when He says 'all things are put under Him,' it is evident that He who put all things under Him is excepted. Now when all things are made subject to Him, then the Son Himself will also be subject to Him who put all things under Him, that God may be all in all."* (1 Cor 15:27-28).

Christ and Elisha act in complete sovereignty and their word is invariably fulfilled. They receive no directives from God because they know his divine will perfectly and always carry it out. Each one lives among men, but sometimes uses intermediaries to communicate with them. The diagram on the following page illustrates the "divine" position of the two men. Of course Elisha is not God, but he announces the ministry of the One who is God made man. *"He is the image of the invisible God, the firstborn over all creation. For by Him all things were created that are in heaven and that are on earth, visible and*

---

[13] Ellul p. 10.

invisible, whether thrones or dominions or principalities or powers. All things were created through Him and for Him. And He is before all things, and in Him all things consist." (Col 1:15-17).

God	Elisha	Jesus
	Does not receive orders from God, but carries out his will perfectly	He does not receive orders from his Father, but carries out his will perfectly

Elijah	Gehazi	The apostles
He is an intermediary between God and men	Is the intermediary between Elisha and men	They are the intermediaries between Christ and men
He receives orders from God, but sometimes hesitates to carry them out	He receives orders from Elisha, but sometimes hesitates to carry them out. Woe to him if he denies his master	They receive orders from Christ. Woe to him who denies his master

The People	The People	The People

If Elisha accomplishes so many miracles, it is to announce the all-powerful ministry of Jesus. If Elisha uses so many objects for his miracles, it is for pedagogical reasons. He wants to show that we should not stop at the result of the miracle, but seek to comprehend its meaning. Elisha illustrates and announces the

Messiah so that every miracle, even every detail, is rich in meaning.[14]

Elisha highlights Christ, but Christ also highlights Elisha. To read the ministry of this prophet in the light of the gospel is a source of great blessing. Once you have started, you can hardly stop.[15] The mysterious acts of Elisha become clear; there is meaning and unity. Jesus throws true light on the Old Testament.[16]

---

[14] Elisha announces the ministry of Jesus, but he is not himself the Messiah. Certain aspects of Christ's ministry are not announced, particularly the entire extent of his suffering (see p. 152). Other prophets took care of this, starting with Elijah.

[15] The last chapter of the appendix to "Reflections of Elisha in the New Testament" (pp. 215-221) provides a glimpse of these sometimes unsuspected riches.

[16] Unfortunately many commentators do not present any culminating point of Elisha's ministry, and several suggest one which is not cantered on the person of Jesus Christ. Rick Dale Moore presents five positions which reject the historical validity of his miracles (*God saves: lessons from the Elisha stories,* JSOT Supplement Series 95, 1990). In the same way Hermann Gunkel attributes the origin of Elisha's story to the *veneration of the prophets:* the community of the sons of the prophets, who, astonished by Elisha, embellished the acts of the prophet. But Moore rejects this idea because according to him, not all of the stories are to Elisha's advantage. For example the story of the malediction of the children of Bethel or the judgment of Gehazi. Burke O. Long thinks that a *prophetic conflict* lies at the origin of these texts: the miracles of Elisha serve to authenticate Elisha in relation to the other prophets. This standpoint is not based directly on the stories about Elisha, but is the result of a particular approach to biblical prophecy. Several criticisms of the first view also apply to the second. Leah Bronner defends the idea of a *conflict with Baal.* She supports the thesis that all of the stories about Elijah and Elisha are polemic and are used to discredit Baal worship (*The Stories of Elijah and Elisha as Polemics Against Baal Worship*). If certain texts from the Elijah cycle can be understood as such, then the generalisation is delusive, particularly regarding the stories of Elisha (for a more detailed evaluation, see D. Arnold: *Elijah between Judgment and Grace,* p. 61, note 11). Robert LaBarbera prefers the idea of a *class conflict*: the poor originated these stories of Elisha to show how God defends the poor who are oppressed by kings and the rich. But not all of the rich are bad (for example Naaman) and not all of the poor are good (for example the cannibal women: 6:28-29). Finally, Moore suggests that the best context would be that of a *theological conflict initiated by the Aramean domination.* Faced with the Syrian (or Aramean) menace, the loyalists faithful to the Almighty had sought to refresh the faith of their contemporaries by explaining the saving

power of the Almighty. It is true that Elisha plays a part in different military conflicts in favour of Israel, but his help is not limited either to military conflicts or to the Israelites. His aid contains a universal dimension which perfectly illustrates the ministry of Jesus. Hebrews and pagans, the rich and poor all receive help.

As for Wesley J. Bergen (*Elisha and the End of Prophetism*, JSOT Supplement Series 286, 1999), he develops a negative criticism of Elisha's ministry, as the title of his book indicates. "The Elisha narrative provides a negative judgment on prophetism and confines prophets to a rather limited scope of action in the narrative world... The narrative never provides for the reader an explicit condemnation of prophets or prophetic activity. Elisha is consistently regarded as a true prophet of YHWH, and his power is never questioned. There will always be, however, fragments of doubt as to the nature of the connection between YHWH and Elisha." (p. 11). "The voice of YHWH is never heard by the reader." (p. 13). Even worse: (p. 105) "This usurpation of the role of God is not likely to endear Elisha to readers." The usefulness of his ministry is doubtful: "On the surface, Elisha should be ushering in a new era of peace and prosperity for Israel. Baal appears nowhere in the story to challenge the supremacy of YHWH. Jezebel has quietly disappeared, and the kings are portrayed in a surprisingly positive light. Elijah's victory appears complete, and Elisha remains to bask in this success. Yet these factors all reappear at the end of Elisha's mission. Thus they have not been missing; it is more that they appear to have been ignored or repressed", as is shown at the end of his ministry (p. 14, cf. p. 43-45). Bergen recognises that the world of the prophet is presented differently than the greater context of the narrative. It is as if we are entering a different reality, which operates with different rules than the reality of the rest of Genesis –2 Kings." This remark is pertinent (p. 43), but the refusal to read the story of Elisha in the light of the Messiah leads Bergen to consider that the ministry of Elisha is like a storm in a teacup.

THE CONTEXT OF ELISHA'S MINISTRY

The Political and Spiritual Context

Contrary to his predecessor, Elisha carries out his ministry within a relatively favourable political environment. Whereas political authorities pursued Elijah throughout his ministry, Elisha is respected by the kings. We can point out following:

1. At the beginning of his ministry kings *Joram* (Israel) and *Jehoshaphat* (Judah) consult him during the campaign against Moab and follow his recommendations (2 Kings 3).
2. At the end of Elisha's life *Joash,* king of Israel, visits the sick prophet and bemoans his nearing end (2 Kings 13:14).
3. Elisha is sufficiently confident of his influence on the king of Israel and his general to propose mediation to the Shunammite (2 Kings 4:13).
4. At Naaman's visit he reprimands the king of Israel, who is mistakenly scandalised by Syrian's bearing (2 Kings 5:8).
5. After the Syrian army's capture during the siege of Dothan, the king of Israel asks Elisha for advice. He then carries out Elisha's words to the letter, even though they are in complete opposition to his own plans (2 Kings 6:21-23).
6. During the siege of Samaria the king, in a fit of rage, orders Elisha's arrest, but then rapidly changes his mind (2 Kings 6:31-32).
7. Elisha's reputation is such that the king loves to hear of his "exploits", and the simple mention of his name draws royal favour on those who are near him (2 Kings 8:4-6).

The ministry of Elisha seems to be restricted to the reign of Joram, whose death is mentioned in 2 Kings 9 (this standpoint is defended in the commentary on Chapter 13, point 3, p. 212), but it is possible that the author regrouped all of Elisha's actions (see "The Timeless Prophet" pp. 16-18). The stories of 2 Kings 3:1-8:6 could also be from the reigns of the other four monarchs:

Joram (852-841), Jehu (841-814), Joahaz (814-798), Joash (798-782). Whatever the case, Elisha seems to have always been treated with respect by the political authorities. *Joram* heeded his counsel (2 Kings 3) and *Joash* wept at his death (2 Kings 13:14). *Jehu* and *Joahaz* are not mentioned, but Jehu the reformer must certainly have appreciated Elisha, as this king opposed Baal worship. Moreover, Elisha anointed him by means of an intermediary (2 Kings 9:1-10).

The lessening of political pressure on Elisha is probably a late fruit of Elijah's ministry. The latter had fought kings Ahab and Ahaziah, and had ended with sending fire from heaven on two groups of fifty soldiers (2 Kings 1); this no doubt impressed them—if not Ahaziah, then at least his brother Joram.

The *spiritual context* also is more favourable than during Elijah's day. Admittedly the four kings of Israel who reigned between the beginning of Elisha's ministry and his death (Joram, Jehu, Joahaz, Joash) received a negative spiritual assessment (2 Kings 3:2-3; 10:29; 13:2; 13:11), as these kings all followed the steps of Jeroboam I, accepting a cult rival to that of Jerusalem, but none of them encouraged Baal worship like Ahab had done nor even consulted Baal like Ahaziah. On the contrary they opposed the worship of that idol. To start off, *Joram* overthrew *"the sacred pillar of Baal that his father had made"* (2 Kings 3:2), and then just tolerated Baal. *Jehu,* his successor, fought Baalism to the point of eradicating it in the northern kingdom for two generations (2 Kings 9-10). *Joahaz* and *Joash* were therefore no longer confronted with this idolatry.[1]

The political and spiritual environment of Elisha resembles the one during which the Messiah practised his ministry. The Romans tolerated other religions and the *Pax Romana* permitted Jesus and the apostles to circulate freely within the empire. The religion practised in Palestine was based on Yahweh, but was corrupted, less by political considerations as in Elisha's time, but more by legalistic premises and the hypocrisy of the scribes and Pharisees.

---

[1] The cult of Baal reappears in the time of the prophet Hosea, whose ministry lasted during the last two decades of the northern kingdom.

The Context of the Book of 1-2 Kings

The Connections between Elisha and Elijah

The ministry of Elisha contrasts with that of Elijah. The two prophets form a pair, but in a particular way. They resemble each other but are not identical, in the way that the right foot is different from the left, or like a photo and its negative. Similarities and contrasts abound. Elisha is the colour photo and Elijah its negative. The themes of judgment and grace are reflected in inverse proportion. We can list the following similarities:

1. The two names are so similar that "There are no two Bible names more often confused than those of Elijah and Elisha" (H. L. Ellison p. 43). Nevertheless, the two names have different meanings. Elijah signifies "my God is the Almighty" and Elisha means "God is salvation".

2. Jesus compares the aid provided by Elijah to the widow Zarephath and that given to Naaman by Elisha (Luke 4:24-27; 1 Kings 17:8-24; 2 Kings 5). Two pagans are blessed. One is a poor woman who lives in a neighbouring country to the west of and friendly to Israel, and the other is a rich man who lives in enemy territory east of Israel. Elijah goes to a foreign place to perform a miracle with physical matter (flour and oil in unlimited supply) and Elisha heals Naaman, who has undertaken a long voyage to be cured of an illness which was incurable at that time.

3. The story of the widow of Zarephath is also echoed in the tale of a young Jewish widow (1 Kings 17:8-24; 2 Kings 4:1-7). Two poor widows have their oil multiplied but must exercise their faith. The women are mothers and risk losing their children: one because of an illness (the child dies) and one because of ruthless creditor who wants to sell her two children into slavery. Elijah goes abroad to Zarephath, whereas Elisha is visited by the Jewess whose origin is not mentioned. The foreigner gives all she has, unburdening to the utmost, whereas the Jewess seeks everything she can get, taking a maximum burden. The former must start by giving everything she possesses before receiving her food bit by bit,

and the latter receives all of her money in one instance, without having to give anything.

4. The story of the widow of Zarephath is reflected a third time in the story of the Shunammite (1 Kings 17-24; 2 Kings 4:8-37). Two women receive a prophet and give him a room in an upper storey. Their only sons die, but return to life after a prophet lies along their bodies in the upper chamber where the prophet lives. Elijah must lie upon the entire length of the child's body, whereas Elisha places three objects on the child's body (his staff, and then his body twice); Elisha also places three parts of his body on the child (mouth, eyes, hands). Elijah invokes God so that the *"child's soul"* should come back to it, whereas Elisha places his mouth on the mouth of the child who sneezes seven times. The woman of Zarephath is a widow, poor, a foreigner, but has a child; the Shunammite is married, rich, Jewish, but has no child. The poor one gives all she has and the rich one makes what she does not have (a room for Elisha). When misfortune occurs, there is a double confrontation in the first story (the woman to Elijah and Elijah to God), and twice a refusal to speak by the woman in the second story (she says that "all is well" in order to avoid explanations). Elijah is near the woman when the misfortune happens, but Elisha is absent when the death occurs.[2]

5. The stories of the judgments pronounced by Elijah are also reflected in the ministry of Elisha. The two prophets ask God to punish the impious, and God grants their request with a twofold witness: fire descends from heaven twice on the aggressive soldiers, and two female bears kill the mocking adolescents (2 Kings 1:9-12; 2:23-25). Elijah intercedes twice and obtains a double divine intervention, whereas Elisha speaks once and receives one divine intervention. Elijah asks for this judgment at the end of his ministry, but

---

[2] Rudolf Kilian (*Die Totenerweckungen Elias und Elisas – eine Motivwanderung?* in *BZ*, 1966, pp. 44-56) mentions several similarities and contrasts between the two stories. Unfortunately, he analyses these parallels under the aspect of fictional literature, seeking above all to prove that the story of Elijah is earlier than that of Elisha. This prevents him from meditating on the historical reality and on the meaning which Elisha wished to give to his acts by partly copying those of Elijah.

Elisha asks for it at the beginning. Elijah specifies the type of judgment; Elisha only pronounces a curse and accepts the divine judgment given. With Elijah the judgment comes from heaven as a physical phenomenon, whereas with Elisha the judgment comes from the earth and the animal world.

6. Both prophets announce judgments (1 Kings 21:17-29; 2 Kings 7:1-2, 16-20). Elijah foretells the death of the royal house of Ahab and Elisha predicts the death of a simple equerry. The sin of Ahab is his injustice and that of the equerry is his lack of faith. Ahab repents and his punishment is amended, whereas the servant remains in his sin and dies the following day.

7. Elijah applies Mosaic law and kills four hundred and fifty prophets of Baal (cf. Deut 13), whereas Elisha applies the law of retaliation by preventing the king of Israel from killing the Syrian troops (the Syrian soldiers do not want to kill Elisha at Dothan, but only capture him; Elisha eagerly turns the tables on them; see commentary p. 151).[3]

In a more general way, we note that Elijah is the prophet of judgment and Elisha the prophet of grace (see p. 9-12); Elijah is the solitary prophet and Elisha the prophet of the people (see pp. 12-14); Elijah evolves during the course of his ministry, but Elisha is at the peak of perfection right from the start (see p. 14-16).

Elisha is very different from Elijah, and yet he is his successor. The same Spirit fills both prophets (even if the second has received a double portion). In order to understand Elisha well and to appreciate his true value it is important to read his story in the light of Elijah, as Elisha gives the old order a new

---

[3]   The stories of the Elijah series where Elijah does not intervene (1 Kings 20 and 1 Kings 22) are also reflected in the stories of Elisha, particularly the last battle of the army in the Elijah series and the first battle in the stories of Elisha (1 Kings 22:1-40; 2 Kings 3). Both times Israel initiates combat: the first time against Syria to reconquer a territory and the second time against Moab to keep a vassal under submission. The king of Judah, Jehoshaphat, present each time, requests the counsel of a prophet. During the battle he barely escapes being killed. We must again note the importance of blood in the two accounts. The blood of Ahab which flows into a pond (1 Kings 22:35-38) and the blood of the people which supposedly has flown so much that it forms a pool (2 Kings 3:22-23).

orientation. He is the forerunner of a new era. The differences between Elijah and Elisha put Elijah in contrast with certain characteristics of the new covenant.

The General Context of 1-2 Kings

Two themes run throughout the book[4] of Kings: (1) the patience of God which defers the punishment of the sins of the kings and of the people; (2) the preservation of the Messianic bloodline.

The Patience of God towards His Sinful People

Contrary to the periods of Moses, Joshua and the Judges, during which God rapidly meted judgment on his people, the period of Kings is marked by the slowness of divine intervention. God often postpones the punishment of the sinful nation to another generation. The sin of Solomon, for example, causes a schism during the reign of his son (1 Kings 11:11-12); the sin of Jeroboam I is followed by the disappearance of his dynasty during his son's reign (1 Kings 15:29-30; cf. 1 Kings 14:9-11); Ahab's sin is given the same verdict (1 Kings 21:29); in Manasseh's case, the deportation of the northern kingdom is predicted four generations before the end (2 Kings 21:10-15; 23:25-26).[5]

The Preservation of the Messianic Bloodline in the South

The divine alliance with the house of David, established when David took the Ark of the Covenant to Jerusalem around 1000 B.C. (2 Sam 7:11-16), significantly characterises the divine actions which follow. God had promised David that one of his descendants would always sit on the throne of Israel: *"And your house and your kingdom shall be established forever before you. Your throne shall be established forever."* 2 Sam 7:16). The covenant primarily concerns the Messiah, who will be a descendant of King David and reign for evermore.

---

[4]   In the Hebrew canon, 1–2 Kings are only one book. The division into two parts stems from the Greek translation of the Septuagint (LXX).

[5]   For a more complete discussion, see D. Arnold: *Elijah between Judgment and Grace,* pp. 69-72.

The covenant with the house of David guarantees the continuity of that dynasty despite the uncertainties of history. *"The sins of the kings shall be punished, but the alliance shall never be revoked: I will be his Father, and he shall be My son. If he commits iniquity, I will chasten him with the rod of men and with the blows of the sons of men. But my mercy shall not depart from him, as I took it from Saul, whom I removed from before you."* (2 Sam 7:14-15).

The author of Kings emphasises the *continuity* of the house of David. The sin of Solomon causes his kingdom to fall apart but not to disappear completely. Ten tribes are torn from the house of David and given to Jeroboam, son of Nebat, but the tribe of Judah remains under the authority of Rehoboam, son of Solomon.[6] The house of Judah is humiliated but not destroyed, and the humiliation is only temporary *"And I will afflict the descendants of David because of this, but not forever."* 1 Kings 11:39). To ensure that the fundamental message of Ahijah to Jeroboam Is well understood, the author does not hesitate to repeat it often:

> *"Then Ahijah took hold of the new garment that was on him, and tore it into twelve pieces. And he said to Jeroboam, "Take for yourself ten pieces, for thus says the LORD, the God of Israel: 'Behold, I will tear the kingdom out of the hand of Solomon and will give ten tribes to you (but he shall have one tribe for the sake of My servant David, and for the sake of Jerusalem, the city which I have chosen out of all the tribes of Israel),"* (1 Kings 11:30-32).

> *"However I will not take the whole kingdom out of his hand, because I have made him ruler all the days of his life for the sake of My servant David, whom I chose because he kept My commandments and My statutes. But I will take the kingdom out of his son's hand and give it to you – ten tribes. And to his son I will give one tribe, that My servant David may always have a lamp before Me in Jerusalem, the city which I have chosen for Myself, to put My name there."* (1 Kings 11:34-36).

---

[6]   The history of the tribe of Simeon, whose "inheritance was within the inheritance of the children of Judah" (Jos 19:1), was linked with the history of Judah since the conquest of the country (cf. Judg 1:3).

The author later inserts three other remarks to emphasise the permanence of the house of David. The sin of Abijam (913-911 B.C.) does not cause the dynasty to disappear: *"Nevertheless for David's sake the LORD his God gave him a lamp in Jerusalem, by setting up his son after him and by establishing Jerusalem; because David did what was right in the eyes of the LORD, and had not turned aside from anything that He commanded him all the days of his life, except in the matter of Uriah the Hittite."* (1 Kings 15:4-5). Furthermore, during the first siege of Jerusalem by the Assyrians in 701 B.C., the author twice confirms that the city is spared *"for My servant David's sake"* (2 Kings 19:34; 20:6).

The contrast to the *northern kingdom* is striking, where the sins of the kings of Israel result in a rapid succession of dynasties. Nine dynasties reigned during two centuries (from 930 to 722), whereas the house of David remained on the throne of Judah for more than four hundred years, from David's accession to the fall of Jerusalem (1010 to 586).

The case of king Joash of Judah is particularly interesting. In 841 Jehu kills the kings of Israel (Joram) and Judah (Ahaziah). He then organises a far-reaching reform in the northern kingdom, massacring the priests of Baal as well as all of the royal family. In the same year, in the kingdom of Judah, Athaliah, mother of the deceased king and daughter of Jezebel, kills all of the royal descendants except one baby named Joash, son of Ahaziah (2 Kings 11:1-3). For seven years the infant is hidden by his aunt and by the high priests before being placed on the throne of Judah. From the time of Athaliah the descendants of David remain on the edge of extinction, but the thread of the divine covenant is not torn even if it is greatly stretched. God promised that a descendant of David would one day reign for eternity, and that his word would be fulfilled. True, for six years no descendant of David occupied the throne, but this situation was temporary. God's promise to David concerns eternity. A momentary interruption of the reign does not annul God's promise.

We must view the fall of Judah in 586 and the deportation of the people to Babylon in the same light. No descendant of David occupies the throne of Judah because the kingdom has disappeared, but this situation is transitory. The author ends his book on a hopeful note. King Jehoiachin of Judah, a captive in Babylon for thirty-seven years, finally leaves prison in 562, and is treated with honour by the king of Babylon, Evil-Merodach. The last verses of the Book of Kings suggest that the history of the house of David has not come to a close:

> "*He* [the King of Babylon] *spoke kindly to him, and gave him a more prominent seat than those of the kings who were with him in Babylon. So Jehoiachin changed from his prison garments, and he ate bread regularly before the king all the days of his life. And as for his provisions, there was a regular ration given him by the king, a portion for each day, all the days of his life.* (2 Kings 25:28-30).

The Contribution of the Elisha Account to the Message of 1–2 Kings

The exile had disoriented and discouraged the Jews. The author of Kings explains the *reasons for the destruction* which had come after four centuries of monarchy. The repeated sins of the kings and the people had exhausted the immense patience of the Almighty. But the author also provides *reasons to hope*. The exile is deserved, but life does not end there. The alliance with the house of David and the messianic promises maintain hope for the nation's re-establishment. The liberation of the king of Judah recounted in the last verses of the book is a promise of hope.

The ministry of Elisha also stimulates the people's hope. Divine blessing is possible even in times of apostasy. Elisha carried out his ministry of grace in a kingdom of iniquity (the northern kingdom), during the reign of the most abominable house (that of Ahab). Nevertheless, despite the sin, the Almighty shows grace without precedent, and gives mercy to rich and poor, Israelites and strangers, adults and children, men and women. No category was excluded because God took every *individual* into account.

Following Elisha's ministry a Jew can await redemption from the Almighty, in favour of the faithful. As already indicated his ministry presages the work of the Messiah. Of course, a Jew under the old covenant could only partially discern divine redemption, as he lacked the manifestation of the Son of God in the flesh. Nevertheless he could feel that an exceptional work of grace was on the horizon, the more so because Isaiah, Jeremiah and other prophets had announced the coming of the Messiah in their writings.

The Structure of the Stories of Elisha and the Book of Kings

The Stories about Elisha

An Intricate Link

The stories about Elisha create a harmonious ensemble. The main part begins at the announcement of Elijah's departure (2 Kings 2:1) and lasts until the flight of Elisha's messenger (2 Kings 9:10).[7] This unit is composed of alternating short stories (3 to 6 verses) and longer accounts (16 to 30 verses).[8] There is a total of *seven* short stories and *seven* long ones, the number of perfection, the number seven being a characteristic of the whole book.[9] The fourteen sections of the Elisha cycle form a chiastic structure by the regrouping of several short sections and two long sections (see table p. 41).[10] Furthermore, the longer stories contain three parts each, which are themselves linked by the reflection of the first part in the third.[11]

---

[7] Elisha does, however, appear in two brief episodes before and after this central part: the prophet is briefly introduced when he is called, five chapters earlier (1 Kings 19:19-21), and he briefly reappears at the end of his life four chapters later (2 Kings 13:14-21). This introduction and ending mark the limits of Elisha's ministry, which not only covers the reigns of six kings (Ahab, Ahaziah, Joram, Jehu, Joahaz, Joash), but also one third of the book 1–2 Kings.

[8] "The juxtaposition of long and short stories gives variety to the way Elisha is presented" Bergen p. 66.

[9] The number seven is found in each section of 1–2 Kings (see D. Arnold: *Elijah between Judgment and Grace*, pp. 74-76).

[10] Two short stories follow each another twice (2 Kings 2:19-22, 23-25; 2 Kings 4:38-41, 42-44) and once two long stories follow each another (2 Kings 6:8-23 and 2 Kings 6:24-7:20).

[11] The long stories sometimes have an even more elaborate structure.

LONG
and *short*
stories

The Structure of the Elisha Account

A.1   SUCCESSION AMONG THE PROPHETS (2:1-18)
   - The dialogues between Elisha and the sons of the prophets about the Elijah's departure (2:1-7)
   - Elijah's ascension and the question of his succession (2:8-14)
   - The question of the sons of the prophets to Elisha regarding Elijah's departure (2:15-18)

a1   The purified waters (benediction of the people: 2:19-22)
a2   Punishment of the mockers (malediction of the people: 2:23-25)

B.2   ARMED CONFLICT AGAINST MOAB (3)
   - Israel's catastrophic military engagement (3:1-9)
   - Elisha's intervention (3:10-19)
   - Military success for Israel and collapse of Moab (3:20-27)

b3   A prophet's wife is helped (4:1-7)

C.3   BLESSING FOR A HIGH-RANKING JEWESS (4:8–37)
   - Elisha helps a woman with Gehazi's aid (4.8-17)
      - Elisha does not know the reason for the woman's troubles (4.18-28)
   - Elisha helps a woman without Gehazi's aid (4.29-37)

c4   The sons of the prophets are healed (4:38-41)
c5   The sons of the prophets are fed (4:42-44)

C.4   BLESSING FOR A HIGH-RANKING STRANGER (5)
   - A little girl's faith and the king of Israel's blindness (5:1-8)
      - Naaman's commitment (5:9-19)
   - Gehazi's guilty behaviour (5:20-27)

b6   A prophet's son is helped (6:1-7)

B.5   FIRST ARMED CONFLICT WITH THE SYRIANS (6:8-23)
   - Aggression against Elisha who protects the king of Israel (6:8-14)
      - Elisha encourages his servant, who can see the heavenly army (6:15-17)
   - Elisha captures the Syrians, but protects them from the king of Israel (6:18-23)

B.6   SECOND ARMED CONFLICT WITH THE SYRIANS
       (6:24-7:20)
   - The people suffer famine, a child dies and Elisha is threatened (6:24-7:2)
      - The adventure of the lepers (7:3-15)
   - The people live in abundance, a servant dies and the word of Elisha is confirmed (7:16-20)

a7   Return to the country is possible (blessing and curse of individuals (8:1-6)

A.7   SUCCESSION AMONG THE KINGS (8:7-9:10)
   - Anointment of Hazael (8:16-24)
      - Double transition of the kings of Judah: Jehoram and Ahaziah (8:16-29)
   - Anointment of Jehu (9:1-10)

The Duality of the Stories, the Themes and the Persons

Duality is a main characteristic of the Elisha cycle. All of the stories have their counterpart, the entire cycle being organised as a chiasm.

Certain stories are "echoed" twice or even thrice, and are either of the same kind or an antithesis of the story which precedes or follows.[12]

People often appear in pairs. Some of these pairings have already been mentioned at the beginning of this commentary (the two rich and the two poor people, e.g. the Shunammite and Naaman; the widow and the workman from the Jordan, see p. 9). Other "pairs" are more subtle:

1. The two servants of Elisha: Gehazi and *"the servant of the man of God"* in Dothan (6:15-17).
2. The two kings of Israel whom the prophet helps at the beginning and at the end of his ministry: Joram and Joash (3 and 13:14-19).
3. The two kings anointed by Elisha: Hazael and Jehu (8:7-15; 9:1-10).

The miracles of Elisha are also often grouped in pairs. We find:

1. Two resurrections (4:33-37; 13:20-21). Each time, the body of Elisha is involved.
2. Two purifications of a liquid: the spring of Jericho and the soup of Gilgal (2:19-22; 4:38-41). Both liquids are purified with white food (salt and flour).
3. Two multiplications of food: oil and loaves of bread (liquid for a woman and solid for a community of men: 4:1-7; 4:42-44).
4. The physical properties of the waters of the Jordan are changed: separation of the waters with the mantle of Elijah and an axe head floats on water with the help of a staff (2:14; 6:6).

---

[12] 2:19-22 and 2:23-25; 3 and 4:1-7; 4:1-7 and 4:8-37; 5 and 6:1-7; 6:8-23 and 6:24-7:20; 6:24-7:20 and 8:1-6. These parallels are dealt with in detail in the commentary.

The objects involved in the miracles also form pairs. In addition to the salt and flour mentioned above, there are:

1. A useless staff and a useful piece of wood (4:29-31; 6:6-7).
2. To collect different liquids (water or oil), it is necessary to dig several holes in the ground or gather a large number of empty jars (3:16-20; 4:3-4).

Many other elements are grouped in pairs:

1. Elisha is involved in two construction projects (4:9-10; 6:1-7)
2. Both the Syrian general Naaman and the king Ben-Hadad offer a magnanimous gift to Elisha for their healing (5:5; 8:8-9).
3. Two miracles happen at the Jordan, but the waters are once beneficial and once harmful (5:10; 6:5).
4. Elisha is involved in two natural famines (in addition to the one caused by the Syrians during the siege of Samaria: 4:38 and 8:1).
5. Elisha is twice sought by an aggravated king, by the king of Syria and by the king of Israel (6:13-14; 6:31-32).
6. Elisha prophesies two useless healings: the incredulous Hebrew equerry sees the healing but does not take advantage of it, and Ben-Hadad is healed of his illness, but still dies (7:2; 8:10).
7. In Dothan Elisha prays that his companion may momentarily see a certain sight, then he prays that the Syrians may be temporarily stricken with limited blindness (6:17, 18).
8. Elisha asks two people to go away from him in order to receive healing: Naaman and the Shunammite (5:10; 8.1). Gehazi is involved in these two stories.
9. Two bears come out of the forest to punish the youths of Bethel.
10. Elisha often uses an object to symbolise a truth, but twice he uses two objects: once to accomplish a miracle (a new bowl and salt to purify the spring of Jericho: 2:20) and once to communicate with king Joash (a bow and arrows: 13:15-19).
11. During the first and last miracles, the exterior and the interior of Elisha's body are involved: the mantle of the prophet parts the waters of the Jordan and the bones of the prophet restore a man to life (2:14; 13:21).

12. Sound is used twice to chase away the enemy: once it is the gentle melody of a harp which inspires the prophet with the strategy to be followed, and once the terrifying sound of the heavenly armies that shocks the Syrians into stopping their siege (3:15; 7:6-7).

13. The army of the Almighty intervenes twice during the siege of an Israelite city by the Syrian army: the first time the heavenly army is partly visible (the servant of Elisha can see it), but it does not change the course of events; the second time it is partially audible (the Syrians hear it, but not the Israelites) and it causes the hasty flight of the enemy (6:17; 7:6-7).

Sevenfold Mention of Certain Elements

The structure of the story of Elisha described above is further enriched by numerous elements which appear in sevens.

1. The cities visited by the prophet: Jericho, Bethel, Shunem, Gilgal, Dothan, Samaria, Damascus.[13]

2. The objects used for a miracle: Elijah's mantle (2:14), salt in a new bowl (2:20-21), Elisha's body (4:34-35), flour (4:41), the waters of the Jordan (5:14), a piece of wood (6:6), the prophet's bones (13:21).[14]

3. The persons indicated by name whom the prophet encounters: Elijah, Joram, Jehoshaphat, Gehazi, Naaman, Hazael, Joash. There are two Jews (Elijah, Gehazi; master and servant), two kings of Israel (Joram, Joash; beginning and end of Elisha's ministry), two Syrians (Naaman, Hazael; general and lieutenant), and one king of Juda (Jehoshaphat).

4. The kings mentioned in the stories of Elisha: Joram, Jehoshaphat, Mesha, Ben-Hadad, Hazael, Jehu, Joash.[15]

---

[13] Two other cities are also mentioned in the cycle of Elisha, but they were not visited by the prophet: Baal-Schalischa (4:42) and Ramoth (9:1).

[14] One could possibly count the "musician" (3:15)—who is a person and not an object or part of a body—instead of counting the "bones" of the prophet, as this miracle takes place at his suggestion.

[15] Note that the king of Edom is never mentioned by name (3:9). Regarding the number of miracles see footnote 11, p. 59.

The Structure of 1-2 Kings

The stories of Elijah and Elisha are located at the centre of the book of Kings and the transition between Elijah and Elisha (2 Kings 2:1-18) is in the middle of the book.

The General Structure of 1-2 Kings[16]

A.1	The united kingdom of Solomon, descendant of David (1 Kings 1-11)
B.1	Beginning of the northern kingdom (1 Kings 12-14): important prophets
C.1	First *transition*: seven reigns from Abijam to Omri (1 Kings 15:1-16:28)
D	The house of Ahab: the ministries of Elijah and Elisha (1 Kings 16:29-2 Kings 10:27)
C.2	Second *transition*: fourteen reigns from Jehu to Ahaz (2 Kings 10:28-16:20)
B.2	End of the northern kingdom: the prophetic explanations (2 Kings 17)
A.2	The sole kingdom of Judah: the last seven kings (2 Kings 18-25)

---

[16] For more details, see D. Arnold: *Elijah between Judgment and Grace,* pp. 74-76.

Detailed Structure of the Ministries of Elijah and Elisha

1.1	Beginning of the house of Ahab, in blood (1 Kings 16:29-34)
2.1	A 3 1/2-year drought (1 Kings 17-19).
3.1	Two invasions of the Syrians (1 Kings 20)
4.1	Unjust death of a faithful one (1 Kings 21)
5.1	War of conquest with the support of Jehoshaphat, king of Judah (1 Kings 22:1-40) *Transition: reign of Jehoshaphat, king of Judah (1 Kings 22:41-51)*
6.1	The last acts of Elijah: a healing refused (cf. the final end is announced) and God's judgment upon two groups of adults; one group is spared (1 Kings 22:52-2 Kings 1:18)
7	The transition from Elijah to Elisha (2 Kings 2:1-18)
6.2	The first acts of Elisha: deliverance granted (e.g. an eternal source of good) and earthly punishment carried out on a group of adolescents by two bears (2 Kings 2:19-25)
5.2	War of conquest with the support of Jehoshaphat, king of Judah (2 Kings 3)
4.2	The well-being of the faithful (2 Kings 4:1-6:7)
3.2	Two invasions by the Syrians (2 Kings 6:8-7:20)
2.2	A seven-year drought (3 1/2-times two): 2 Kings 8:1-15 *Transition: reign of Jehoram, king of Judah (2 Kings 8:16-24)* *Transition: reign of Ahaziah, king of Judah (2 Kings 8:25-29)*
1.2	End of the house of Ahab, in blood (2 Kings 9:1-10:27)

COMMENTARY

ELISHA, THE SUCCESSOR OF ELIJAH (2 KINGS 2:1-18)

The story of the carrying away of Elijah is focused on the link which unites Elijah to Elisha. In the first words of 2 Kings 2, the narrator announces the ascension of Elijah: *"And it came to pass, when the LORD was about to take up Elijah into heaven by a whirlwind"* (v. 1). In doing so he removes all suspense connected to Elijah's destiny. This direct jump start is astounding, because in the Elijah cycle the narrator had taken pains to surround the prophet with an aura of mystery. Every step of the prophet was unforeseeable. Elijah himself lived one day at a time, often not knowing what the next would bring. Everything changes with the story of his ascension.

In the story Elijah ceases to be the main actor, firstly because he leaves the earth, and then because he leaves his ministry to a man who will be anointed with a double portion of the Spirit and will thus make people quickly forget him. The author reinforces this dismissal in his manner of recounting the event. The plot of the narration centres around Elisha and not Elijah.

The story that follows reinforces this impression. Everyone knows about the ascension: the sons of the prophets of Bethel and the sons of the prophets of Jericho are informed of Elijah's departure and repeat this to Elisha, who also knows the news (2 Kings 2:3-5). On the other hand, the extent of Elisha's ministry remains a mystery until the very end.

At first, Elijah wants to *separate* himself from his servant, but Elisha solemnly refuses. Three times a verbal exchange takes place between the two men (2 Kings 2:2, 4, 6). The reader may ask why Elisha should be sent off. Had he perhaps displeased his master? Elisha's insistence on *following* Elijah also raises questions. Why does he wish to accompany Elijah at all costs? Why disobey him? Would this disobedience be sanctioned by

Elijah (because in the past, two prophets had been stricken dead for not following orders, e.g. for being unfaithful: 1 Kings 13:21-24; 20:35-36)? Amazingly enough, the opposite happens: Elijah suddenly proposes to reward Elisha with the most generous possible. Elijah signs a sort of blank cheque: *"And so it was, when they had crossed over, that Elijah said to Elisha, 'Ask! What may I do for you, before I am taken away from you?'"* (2 Kings 2:9).

Elisha's reply involves his ministry. He wishes to have a double portion of the spirit of Elijah. How should this request be understood? Does Elisha want to be the successor of Elijah or does he want to surpass him? How will the Spirit be manifested in Elisha? What similarities and what differences will we be able to observe? The narrator also emphasises another line of questioning which is not linked to the meaning of the request, but to its granting. Can Elisha receive what he asks? Elijah himself does not know. We must wait until Elijah's departure to find out: *"Nevertheless, if you see me when I am taken from you, it shall be so for you; but if not, it shall not be so."* (2 Kings 2:10). The story line centres on the conditions surrounding the ascension and not the ascension itself. The narrator draws our attention to the succession between Elijah and Elisha.

Elisha sees his master rise up to heaven, receives his mantle and carries out the same miracle which he himself has just seen happen. He separates the waters of the Jordan in full view of the sons of the prophets, and thus proves that he is the worthy successor of Elijah. The servant has fully followed his master and carries out the same miracles as he.

The story of Elijah's ascension basically centres on *Elisha*. Elijah nonetheless plays an important role. As to the structure, the story fits perfectly into two cycles: that of Elijah (see *Elijah between Judgment and Grace* p.63) and that of Elisha. We have chosen to comment on this story both in the book on Elijah as well as in the one on Elisha. The detailed analysis of verses 1 to 14 is almost identical in both books. Verses 2 to 18 form an intricate chiasm.

A.1	Dialogues between Elisha and the sons of the prophets concerning the departure of Elijah (2:2-6)
B.1	Presence of fifty sons of prophets on the bank of the Jordan (2:7)
C.1	Elijah parts the waters of the Jordan (2:8)
D.1	Elisha wishes to be the successor of Elijah (2:9)
E.1	Elisha must see Elijah depart in order to be his successor (2:10)
F	Elijah and Elisha are separated by the chariot and horses of fire (2:11)
E.2	Elisha sees Elijah depart (2:12)
D.2	Elisha gathers up the Elijah's mantle (2:13)
C.2	Elisha parts the waters of the Jordan (2:14)
B.2	Presence of fifty sons of prophets on the bank of the Jordan (2:15)
A.2	Dialogues between Elisha and the sons of prophets concerning Elijah's departure (2:16-18)

Elisha Insists on Following Elijah (2:1-6)

¹ And it came to pass, when the LORD was about to take up Elijah into heaven by a whirlwind, that Elijah went with Elisha from Gilgal.

²Then Elijah said to Elisha, "Stay here, please, for the LORD has sent me on to Bethel." But Elisha said, "As the LORD lives, and as your soul lives, I will not leave you." So they went down to Bethel. ³Now the sons of the prophets who were at Bethel came out to Elisha, and said to him, "Do you know that the LORD will take away your master from over you today?" And he said, "Yes, I know; keep silent"

⁴Then Elijah said to him, "Elisha, stay here, please, for the LORD has sent me on to Jericho." But he said, "As the LORD lives, and as your soul lives, I will not leave you!" So they came to Jericho. ⁵Now the sons of the prophets who were at Jericho came to Elisha and said to him, "Do you know that the LORD will take away your master from over you today?" So he answered, "Yes, I know; keep silent!"

⁶Then Elijah said to him, "Stay here, please, for the LORD has sent me on to the Jordan." But he said, "As the LORD lives, and as your soul lives, I will not leave you!" So the two of them went on.

Elijah ascends to heaven, but his work does not end with his departure. A successor will continue his ministry and give it a new direction. The account of the "taking up of Elijah" is also the story of the "sending out of Elisha". The text deals with both prophets and puts them side by side to better emphasise the contrasts between them.

Elisha reappears at the announcement of Elijah's departure (v. 1). The man is introduced in 1 Kings 19:15-21, but disappears from the story right afterwards. Other prophets appear, but the name of Elisha is not mentioned again. Not until the departure of Elijah can Elisha enter into action. If Horeb is the site of Elisha's calling, then the Jordan marks where he is sent out.

The relationship between the two men is ambiguous. Elijah asks Elisha not to accompany him, either to Bethel or to Jericho, nor over the Jordan, and each time the latter replies solemnly that he will follow him to the end (*"As the LORD lives, and as your soul lives,"* v. 2, 4, 6, *"I will not leave you!"*) Does Elijah really want to be alone at the moment of his ascension?[1] Does he want Elisha to leave him? If that is the case, then why does he permit Elisha to follow him? Why is Elisha rewarded with a double anointing of the Spirit (2 Kings 2:9-10) instead of being punished for his "disobedience"? Obviously Elijah did not expect Elisha to leave. The sons of the prophets had already indicated that the ascension would take place: *"the LORD will take away your master from over you"* (v. 3, 5), thus confirming the necessity of Elisha's presence at that particular moment. Does Elijah then wish to test Elisha to see the extent to which he is attached to him? Certain things in life have no value unless they are offered freely. Elisha is called to the ministry of a prophet, but this ministry is not easy. Will Elisha be ready to go as far as his master? Elijah wishes so but cannot demand it.

---

[1] "Did Elijah have such an urgent need for prayer that the presence of Elisha was undesirable at a time when the sacred and sovereign act was imminent?" John H. Alexander: *Elie, Elisée: messagers d'hier pour aujourd'hui,* p. 79.

Elisha is deeply attached to his master. His desire to follow him expresses his affection.[2] He knows that Elijah does not really wish him to leave, and he is deeply hurt by the departure of his master. He asks the son of the prophet who mentions the departure of Elijah to be silent so as not to push the knife further into the wound.

The triple reiteration of the ties between Elijah and Elisha draw the reader's attention to this relationship. This insistence also suggests the theme of "repetition". Elisha will succeed Elijah. He will continue the ministry begun, all the while giving it a new orientation. The relationship between the two men is significant because it illustrates the convergence of their ministries. The two vocations are different, but still display a profound unity. Elijah is primarily the prophet of judgment, but his ministry also reflects grace. The ministry of Elisha is essentially one of grace. Elisha does not contradict Elijah, but does develop the aspect which has been latent in the ministry of his predecessor.

The relationship between the two men also underscores their characters. Elijah is the prophet who aspires to solitude. On the other hand, Elisha is a more social man (see pp. 12-14). He regrets the departure of his master and wants to stay with him as long as possible. The sons of the prophets do not have any contact with Elijah, whom they perhaps fear. But they call Elisha twice, and he replies. Of course he asks them to be silent (v. 3, 5), but this is not to cut off all contact. Elisha knows that the sons of the prophets understand his pain in seeing Elijah leave, and he asks them not to speak of this event so as not to make him suffer more.

The identity of the "sons of the prophets" has been a popular subject.[3] One often speaks of schools of prophets or communities of prophets. Perhaps they were simply communities of the

---

[2] Elisha shows a loyalty towards his master which recalls Ruth's affection for Naomi: Rt 1:10, 16 (Nelson p. 159).

[3] H. L. Ellison (*The Prophets of Israel: From Ahijah to Hosea*, pp. 36-38), James G. Williams (*The Prophetic 'Father': A Brief Explanation of the Term 'Sons of the Prophets'* in *JBL* 85, pp. 344-348), Hobart E. Freeman (*An Introduction to the Old Testament Prophets*, pp. 28-34), *NDB* p. 492, *NBC* p. 318.

faithful. Today we would say "house groups" to describe those who are not satisfied with the official mainstream, who live and celebrate their faith outside of church structures. Let us not forget that in the northern kingdom the official religion centred in Bethel and Dan was, to a great extent, corrupted. These sons of the prophets perhaps did not exercise any particular prophetic activity, but faithfully followed the teachings of the prophets.[4] The sons of the prophets are informed of the departure of Elijah, but this could have been communicated to them previously by Elisha. These men thus remind the prophet of the imminent departure of Elijah.

The geographical route is described precisely. From Gilgal Elijah *"goes down"* (v. 2) to Bethel (located more than 800 m above sea level), from Bethel he goes to Jericho (300 m below sea level), then from Jericho he goes to the banks of the Jordan (about 400 m below sea level), and finally descends to the bed of the Jordan to cross the river without getting wet. The downward movement is obvious. It is followed by a double movement upwards: Elijah is raised to heaven and Elisha does a partially reverse movement from the bed of the Jordan to Jericho and then to Bethel.

---

[4] Certain groups of prophets already existed in the time of Samuel (1 Sam 10:10; 19:20). Were these true prophets or only faithful believers? The limited description of their prophetic activity prevents any dogmatic statement on this subject. Their "prophetic words" could have been simply words of encouragement and exhortation. The "prophetic" activity of Saul (1 Sam 10:10) creates confusion and gives rise to a proverb in the interrogative form: *"Is Saul also among the prophets?"* (1 Sam 10:12; 19:24). Saul perhaps simply expressed his amazement at the grandeur of God following the fulfilment of the divine signs announced by Samuel (cf. 1 Sam 10:2-9). Certain commentators think that Elijah consecrated much of his time to the sons of the prophets. "Elisha was very interested in education; he continued the schools of prophets founded by Samuel." (DeVries : "Elisha" in *The Zondervan Pictorial Encyclopedia of the Bible*, p. 287). "During the time which passed between his different appearances before the impious kings ... Elijah had trained disciples who were devoted to the practice and spreading of monotheism. He was the head of the schools of prophets which existed during his time." (Mangenot *Dictionnaire de la Bible* col. 1674). But this behaviour does not fit in with the solitary side of his personality. It was Elisha who lived with the sons of the prophets, and it was Elisha who served as an intermediary between Elijah and the sons of the prophets.

Gilgal is not the city located in the Jordan valley, near Jericho, because the two prophets *go down* to Bethel. It is more likely that this is the town situated 12 kilometres north of Bethel on the road to Shiloh (Jos 9:6).[5]

Apart from the geographical side of the question does the mention of the three cities indicate a symbolic dimension? If so, which? Gilgal, Bethel and Jericho were associated with the conquest of the land in the time of Joshua (Jos 2-8), but they were also cities marked by sin: Bethel was the place of an impure altar (1 Kings 12:28-29; 13:1-5), Jericho was cursed by Joshua (Jos 6:26; 1 Kings 16:34), and Gilgal was a den of prostitution (Hos 9:15; Amos 4:4).[6] Did Elijah pass through these impure cites one last time before ascending to his God, or did he choose this path to symbolise a new conquest of the Promised Land, a "country" situated in heaven? The sequel points to the second hypothesis, as Elijah crosses the Jordan without getting wet just as Joshua had done in the past.

Elijah Makes a Path for Himself toward the Promised Land (2:7-8)

[7]And fifty men of the sons of the prophets went and stood facing them at a distance, while the two of them stood by the Jordan. [8]Now Elijah took his mantle, rolled it up, and struck the water; and it was divided this way and that, so that the two of them crossed over on dry ground.

In Jewish tradition the crossing of the Jordan is associated with the conquest of the Promised Land. Elijah crosses the river, but in the opposite direction, thus indicating a different expectation from that of the past. Joshua had entered a "terrestrial" place, whereas Elijah ascends to the heavenly kingdom. Joshua had conquered the territory with his people; Elijah enters God's kingdom alone and without a battle.

---

[5] *BA* p. 121; *NBC* p. 318; *NCB* p. 361; Patterson: *The Expositor's Bible Commentary*, p. 174; Vos: *Bible Study Commentary*, p. 137; John C. Whitcomb: *Solomon to the Exile: Studies in Kings and Chronicles*, p. 401; Wiseman (195) tends toward Gilgal between Jericho and the Jordan.

[6] Hosea and Amos denounced the sins of Gilgal a century later, but the city could have already been impure during the time of Elijah and Elisha.

Elijah also reminds us of Moses, who himself had left a country of oppression (Egypt) by parting the waters of the Red Sea. Moses had raised his staff (Exod 14:16), whereas Elijah strikes the water with his mantle. The *rolled-up* mantle recalls the staffs of Moses and Aaron, which were so often used for miracles. At the end of their earthly existence the bodies of the two men mysteriously disappeared east of the Jordan (Deut 34:5-6; 2 Kings 2:12-18).

The fact that this miracle is confirmed by witnesses is important for the continuation of the story. The fifty sons of prophets could confirm that Elisha was the worthy successor of Elijah when he performed the same miracle.

Elijah Offers an Inheritance to Elisha (2:9-10)

[9]*And so it was, when they had crossed over, that Elijah said to Elisha, "Ask! What may I do for you, before I am taken away from you?" Elisha said, "Please let a double portion of your spirit be upon me."* [10]*So he said, "You have asked a hard thing. Nevertheless, if you see me when I am taken from you, it shall be so for you; but if not, it shall not be so."*

Elijah's offer is more than generous. It is proof of his satisfaction with Elisha. Never in the past had he offered the slightest thing and now he says *"What may I do for you?"* The proposition is unlimited.[7] This recalls the Lord's offer to Solomon at the beginning of his reign: *"and God said, 'Ask! What shall I give you?'"* (1 Kings 3:5). In Hebrew the two phrases are formed by four words, and only the verb changes. The Almighty proposes *to give* and Elijah *to do*. Solomon had made the right choice by asking for wisdom. What about Elisha?

"In this case it is not land that he has in mind, but *spirit*, for Elisha has already left behind normal life and normal rules of inheritance (cf. 1 Kings 19:19-21)".[8] He asks for a double portion of Elijah's spirit. Does he wish to surpass Elijah or simply receive the share of the inheritance of an oldest son,

---

[7] House (*The New American Commentary*, p. 258) attributes the words of Elijah to curiosity: "Elijah senses that Elisha has followed him for a reason and therefore asks what Elisha wants."

[8] Provan: *New International Biblical Commentary*, p. 173.

which was twice that of the other sons (cf. Deut 21:17)?[9] The union between the two men and the spirituality of Elisha exclude any notion of rivalry. Elisha wishes to walk in the footsteps of the one who has called him in the past (1 Kings 19:19-21). Does he seek power, sanctity or consecration? He is aware of the demands of the ministry and of his own limits. He knows he will not be able to carry out his task properly without the aid of the Almighty.

"You have asked a hard thing." At first sight it is not evident that he will be following the footsteps of Elijah. Elijah sets down a condition for the fulfilment of the wish: *"if you see me when I am taken from you, it shall be so for you; but if not, it shall not be so."* Why such a condition? The proposition of Elijah is unconditional (*"Ask! What may I do for you"*), because he wants him to have the best; but Elijah cannot himself grant what Elisha requests. God is sovereign in the area of prophetic calling, and only he can grant such a request.[10] Elijah knows that on Mount Horeb the Lord had designated Elisha to replace him, but would Elisha have a *double* portion of the Spirit? Would he be a prophet of Elijah's level or even superior to him? God alone knows. The Lord can nevertheless give a sign and that sign symbolises several things.

Firstly, on the human level, Elisha must follow Elijah to the end, up to the moment of ascension. This illustrates Elisha's *affection* for Elijah. Elisha must be ready to act like his predecessor. The ministry of Elijah must be taken up and further developed.

Secondly, Elisha must see Elijah *ascend into heaven*. This not only means that he will be physically present at the moment of the ascension, but that he will be able to discern *hidden* things. His ministry will touch the invisible world, the hopes of the

---

[9] The older son assumed certain responsibilities linked to the family patrimony and consequently received a larger share of the inheritance.

[10] The succession from Elijah to Elisha is the only example of a prophetic succession. The prophetic ministry was not transmissible, contrary to the political power of kings and the spiritual power of priests, which were passed from father to son. Kings passed their throne to their sons and the sovereign high priests were succeeded by their sons because the priesthood was restricted to and connected solely to the descendants of Aaron.

faithful, the inheritance that God reserves for them in the hereafter.

Thirdly, the ministry of Elisha will be marked by vision. He *will see* Elijah rise into heaven, but he will also see many other things. Elisha will know everything, even to the point of revealing all of the planned attacks of the Syrians. He will also be capable of giving or veiling sight. At Dothan his servant sees the heavenly armies, whereas the Syrian soldiers are blinded (2 Kings 6:8-23). Elisha will be the prophet of signs, as a large part of his ministry will be carried out in a visual manner.

The ministry of Elisha seems to be *superior* to that of Elijah (is it twice as great?)[11] because Elisha unveils the expectations of the saints, particularly the coming of the Messiah. Elisha's affection for Elijah heralds the ties which link the New Testament to the Old; it is a deep, complete affection, but also a renewal centred on grace.

Elijah's Ascension (2:11-14)

[11]Then it happened, as they continued on and talked, that suddenly a chariot of fire appeared with horses of fire, and separated the two of them; and Elijah went up by a whirlwind into heaven. [12]And Elisha saw it, and he cried out, "My father,

---

[11] Certain commentators assert that Elijah carried out seven miracles and Elisha fourteen. This type of calculation seems subjective, as it is difficult to set criteria for the miracles which should count and those which one should not. The following list mentions twenty-eight miracles or prophecies of Elisha: crossing the Jordan (2:14), purification of the well of Jericho (2:20-22), judgment of the adolescents of Bethel (2:24), prediction of the coming of water in the desert (3:17), prediction of a victory over the Moabites (3:18-19), oil multiplied (4:3-6), prediction of the birth of an infant (4:16), resurrection of a child (4:33-36), purification of soup (4:41), multiplication of loaves (4:43-44), healing of Naaman (5:14), judgment of Gehazi (5:27), floating axe head (6:6), Syrian plots revealed (6:9-10), army of God revealed to a servant (6:17), blinding of the Syrian army (6:18), restoration of sight to the Syrian (6:20), prediction of an imminent arrest (6:32), prediction of a swift change of mind by the king (6:32), prediction of the price of two items of food (7:1), prediction of the fate of an equerry (7:2), prediction of a famine (8:1), prediction of the healing of the Syrian king (8:10), prediction of the death of the Syrian king (8:10), prediction of Israel's suffering through Hazael (8:12), prediction of the identity of the next king of Israel (9:3), prediction of a victory over the Syrians (13:19), resurrection of a soldier (13:21).

my father, the chariot of Israel and its horsemen!" So he saw
him no more. And he took hold of his own clothes and tore them
into two pieces. [13]He also took up the mantle of Elijah that had
fallen from him, and went back and stood by the bank of the
Jordan. [14]Then he took the mantle of Elijah that had fallen from
him, and struck the water, and said, "Where is the LORD God
of Elijah?" And when he also had struck the water, it was
divided this way and that; and Elisha crossed over.

The man whose life was constantly threatened leaves this
world without dying. Elijah's experience is particular and
special, but also rich in general teaching. Elijah's ascension into
heaven shows that human life is not limited to the earth. There is
another life beyond, in the presence of God. The hopes of the
faithful should not be restricted to earthly matters. The taking up
of Elijah prefigures the taking up of all Christians at Christ's
return (cf. 1 Thess 4:15-17). This verse is at the core of 1–
2 Kings (see pp. 45, 46, 51).

A chariot of fire and horses intervene. They probably serve as
transportation for Elijah. The prophet who had refused to climb
into the royal chariot of Ahab so as not to associate himself with
a sinner (1 Kings 18:45-46) is now transported in a divinely
provided chariot. The man who refused compromises which
would have honoured him among men is honoured by God at the
end of his earthly existence. "The chariot was the mightiest
military instrument known to the ancient world and was
therefore symbolic of God's incomparable power."[12] The
whirlwind symbolises the forces of nature which are controlled
by God. The natural and supernatural worlds are involved in the
ascension of Elijah.

The tearing of garments is a gesture which is often mentioned
in Scripture. It generally symbolises mourning and dismay. In
the book of Kings, four kings and one queen do this: Ahab
(1 Kings 21:27), Joram twice (2 Kings 5:8; 6:30), Athaliah
(2 Kings 11:14), Hezekiah (2 Kings 19:1), Josiah (2 Kings
22:11). Here the gesture indicates rather the end of an era and the
beginning of a new one.[13] Elisha takes up the mantle left by

---

[12] Whitcomb p. 401
[13] At the time of his calling, Elisha had already destroyed all the links to his
past. He had sacrificed his oxen and burned the yoke (1 Kings 19:21).

Elijah to indicate that he will continue his ministry. This mantle had already been thrown on his shoulders at his first calling (1 Kings 19:19).[14]

Once he has gathered up the mantle Elisha crosses the Jordan in view of the sons of the prophets, who recognise that *"the spirit of Elijah rests on Elisha."* This first miracle recalls the act by which Joshua was elevated in the eyes of the people after the death of Moses (Jos 4:14). He also had crossed the Jordan to enter the Promised Land near Jericho. The names of the two men have the same meaning: Joshua means "Yahweh saves" and Elisha "God saves". The name of Jesus also has the same significance as it is derived from the name "Joshua". The three forerunners (Moses, Elijah and John the Baptist) precede three men whose names announce their ministry of redemption. The three redeemers are publicly acknowledged at the Jordan at the beginning of their ministry. Joshua and Elisha cross the Jordan, whereas at the baptism of Jesus at the Jordan a heavenly voice announces that he is the beloved Son (Matt 3:13-17; Mark 1:9-11; Luke 3:21-22; John 1:32-34). In summary we can say that *Elijah* recalls Moses and announces John the Baptist (see *Elijah between Judgment and Grace,* pp. 38-42 and pp. 50-55), just as *Elisha* recalls Joshua and announces Jesus Christ.

Elisha's first miracle is followed by many others. Elisha can begin his ministry once Elijah has left, just as later on Jesus begins his Galilean ministry from the moment of John the Baptist's arrest.[15]

---

[14] Patterson p. 176: "The young prophet had once had that mantle symbolically laid on his shoulders (1 Kings 19:19); now it would rest there permanently."

[15] According to the gospels of Matthew and Mark (Matt 4:12; Mark 1:14), Jesus began his ministry from the moment of the announcement of John the Baptist's arrest. On the other hand, the gospel of John lists the first miracles of Jesus one year earlier (John 2; cf. John 3:23-36). The gospel of John does not contradict the synoptic gospels, but rather completes them (cf. John 20:30-31). The main activity of Jesus before the passion took place in Galilee, shortly after John the Baptist's arrest. We also note that Elisha's calling takes place several years prior to Elijah's departure (1 Kings 19:19), but this ministry must have been discreet, as the author of Kings gives only one piece of information: *"Elisha the son of Shaphat is here, who poured water on the hands of Elijah."* (2 Kings 3:11).

Regarding the link which unites Elijah and Elisha we also note that the two men make the same gesture in sight of the faithful in order to cross the Jordan, but Elisha parts the Jordan in order to cross it in the opposite direction, thus indicating a ministry which is of the same order but at the same time different. Elijah is the characteristic prophet of the Old Testament—does he not represent the Old Testament on the Mount of Transfiguration? In contrast Elisha embodies the New Testament, particularly Jesus Christ, as his ministry is essentially one of grace. His miracles and his signs open a window on the glorious expectation of the Messiah.

Confirmation of Elijah's Ascension (2:15-18)

[15]Now when the sons of the prophets who were from Jericho saw him, they said, "The spirit of Elijah rests on Elisha." And they came to meet him, and bowed to the ground before him. [16]Then they said to him, "Look now, there are fifty strong men with your servants. Please let them go and search for your master, lest perhaps the Spirit of the LORD has taken him up and cast him upon some mountain or into some valley" And he said, "You shall not send anyone" [17]But when they urged him till he was ashamed, he said, "Send them!" Therefore they sent fifty men, and they searched for three days but did not find him. [18]And when they came back to him, for he had stayed in Jericho, he said to them, "Did I not say to you, 'Do not go'?"

The Jordan is crossed twice in the presence of witnesses. The sons of the prophets have proof that Elisha is Elijah's successor. Nevertheless, they remain confused about Elijah's ascension. Why do they want to look for his body? Do they doubt that the prophet has been raised to heaven, or do they think that he has departed only in spirit but that his body has remained on earth? In that case they would need to find the body and bury it quickly to prevent it from being desecrated.[16]

The dialogue between Elisha and the sons of the prophets at the end of this section recalls the dialogue between Elijah and Elisha at the beginning of the chapter. In both cases men argue

---

[16] The author of Kings frequently points out the disgrace of not having a burial place (1 Kings 14:11-13; 21:23-24; 2 Kings 9:33-37).

with their master, but there the resemblance ends. Elisha does not wish to be separated from his master, whereas the sons of the prophets ask permission to leave and search for the body of the one who has disappeared. Elisha disobeys Elijah in refusing to leave him but still does what is pleasing to him. On the other hand the sons of the prophets obey Elisha (they do not leave until they receive permission), but they still do what Elisha disapproves: *"Did I not say to you, 'Do not go'?"* (2 Kings 2:18). Elisha knows that Elijah has risen to heaven, not only in spirit but also in the flesh.

The attitude of Elisha towards the sons of the prophets shows his compassion. Because these men are sceptical Elisha allows them to verify the reality of the ascension. They discover by themselves that the word of the new prophet is entirely worthy of confidence, just like that of his predecessor.

THE WATERS OF JERICHO ARE PURIFIED AND THE CHILDREN OF BETHEL ARE CURSED (2 KINGS 2:19–25)

What a contrast between the miracle of Jericho and that of Bethel! Benediction on the one hand, malediction on the other. First we have a physical miracle based on a gesture, then a miracle of the animal world simply with words. The first is characteristic of Elisha, whereas the second seems to be far removed from the prophet of grace. The purification of the waters of Jericho inspires, encourages and gives back hope; the curse upon the youths of Bethel is frightening, shocking, and appalling to the point of casting doubt, in certain minds, on the ethics and inspiration of Scripture.

The discord between these two stories is obvious. But rather than hiding it the author unmistakably emphasises it, not only by placing the two texts side by side, but even putting them in the same literary frame for better comparison:

1. A succinct narration (four and three verses, whereas the preceding and following stories are much longer).
2. The same order of events: a group which addresses Elisha (the men of Jericho; the youths of Bethel), followed by a reply, then a miracle in the guise of a reply to the words of the prophet.
3. The mention of two well-known cities (Jericho and Bethel), which had been visited shortly beforehand by Elijah (2:2-4).

The Waters of Jericho (2:19-22)

[19]Then the men of the city said to Elisha, "Please notice, the situation of this city is pleasant, as my lord sees; but the water is bad, and the ground barren." [20]And he said, "Bring me a new bowl, and put salt in it." So they brought it to him. [21]Then he went out to the source of the water, and cast in the salt there, and said, "Thus says the LORD: 'I have healed this water; from

it there shall be no more death or barrenness.'" [22]So the water remains healed to this day, according to the word of Elisha which he spoke.

In order to comprehend the full ramifications of the blessing brought to Jericho, we must understand the particular situation of this city *before* the miracle. Since the conquest of the land five centuries earlier Jericho was under a curse issued by Joshua against anyone who would rebuild the city (Jos 6:26). The reason for this is not given, but it could be related to the sins of the Canaanites. In fact the conquest of the Promised Land represented not only a blessing for Israel, but also a judgment for the pagan nations who inhabited the land (Gen 15:16). By leaving Jericho in ruins Joshua probably wanted to leave a monument which would remind everyone of the divine condemnation of all iniquity. In king Ahab's time Hiel of Bethel reconstructed Jericho in violation of Joshua's prohibition and in contempt of the lives of his two sons, whom he sacrificed on that occasion (1 Kings 16:34).[1] The site of Jericho was once again occupied, but the curse remained on the land with the contamination of the spring.

These remarks show that Elisha not only purifies a source of water. By cleansing the waters of *Jericho*, the prophet lifts the curse of Joshua. Better still he replaces the curse with a blessing, as the city which should never have been rebuilt now has a source of water which will remain forever pure. Elisha is the man of reversals. In this story he accomplishes the opposite of Joshua. His ministry emphasises divine grace which heals and pardons rather than divine justice which condemns.[2]

A second peculiarity of this story is the use of salt and a new bowl to cleanse the spring. Elisha's action is characterised by symbolism. To understand the meaning of his gesture we must be aware of the inherent value of salt. Salt can be something

---

[1] The site of Jericho seems to have been inhabited before (cf. Judg 3:13; 2 Sam 10:5), but it is possible that the dwellings were situated near the location of ancient Jericho and not on the site of the city itself.

[2] Elisha also does the opposite of Elijah. The latter had begun by stopping the water from above (rain), whereas Elisha "opens" the waters below, letting the people benefit from a spring. Elijah had spoken a judgment over the land; Elisha lifts a curse.

good or bad. It gives flavour to food and keeps meat from decomposing quickly. Jesus uses the image of salt in a positive sense by exhorting Christians to be the salt of the earth (Matt 5:13). But salt can also mean a curse. The extraordinary saltiness of the Dead Sea prohibits all life there (it is truly a *dead* sea). A city covered with salt after a battle has no future (Judg 9:45). In the same way a salty spring is worth nothing.

At Jericho, ten kilometres from the Dead Sea, salt does not have a positive connotation. The same goes for salt in a spring. Therefore, contrary to all expectations, the salt thrown into the spring by Elisha has a positive effect.[3] Because the salt was first placed in a new bowl, we may conclude that the negative nature of the salt was *transformed* by the contact with the new bowl. Thus the curative element comes from the bowl and not the salt. In a certain fashion Elisha is like the *new* bowl. He is the *new* prophet who has just succeeded Elijah (2:7-15) and his coming transforms everything. His presence is the source of blessing. Elisha announces the ministry of the Messiah whose presence transforms the "nature" of individuals. Does not theology speak of the justice of Christ *imputed* to repentant sinners?[4]

---

[3] A Midrashic passage states: "R. Simeon b. Gamliel says: Come and see, how far different the ways of God are from the ways of human beings. Human beings use sweet to cure what is bitter. He by whose the word world came into being, however, is not so, but with bitter He cures what is bitter... But even good water, if you put salt into it, will taste bad, How so then? He puts a thing that spoils into a thing that has been spoiled, so as to perform a miracle therewith. In fact, then, we may distinguish two separate miracles, or, at least, two different elements in the one miracle: firstly, that the salt cured the waters of their harmful effects, and secondly, that the waters were themselves purified of the salt that Elisha threw into them. Or as Kimhi expresses it, in his comment to v. 20; there was 'a miracle within a miracle'" (quoted by Daniel Sperber, *Weak Waters* in *ZAW* 82, 1970, pp. 7-8)

[4] Despite these remarks, would it not be possible to give salt a positive connotation? In fact this substance generally carries a positive meaning. It is also a sign of alliance, because it should always be among the offerings made to the Almighty (Lev 2:13). But then why use a new bowl? For Jones (*New Century Bible Commentary,* p. 389 "The demand for a new bowl also indicates that a ritual was performed; there are many examples of using the new, in other words the uncontaminated or the unimpaired, in ritual (cf. 1 Kings 11:29; Judg 16:11; 1 Sam 6:7; 2 Sam 6:3)"); one had to avoid contaminating the salt with something impure (a used bowl might be

We also note that despite the recourse to material objects (a new bowl of salt), the miracle is attributed to the *word* of the prophet: *"So the water remains healed to this day, according to the word of Elisha which he spoke"* 2:22). Elisha is not a magician but a teacher. Material objects are used solely for their symbolic value.[5]

The Youths of Bethel (2:23-25)

[23]Then he went up from there to Bethel; and as he was going up the road, some youths came from the city and mocked him, and said to him, "Go up, you baldhead! Go up, you baldhead!" [24]So he turned around and looked at them, and pronounced a curse on them in the name of the LORD. And two female bears came out of the woods and mauled forty-two of the youths.

---

unclean). There are many examples where something new, i.e. something uncontaminated, is used in ritual acts (1 Kings 11:2; Judg 16:11; 1 Sam 6:7; 2 Sam 6:3). For J. Robinson (*The Cambridge Bible Commentary,* p. 28) "A new bowl: so that there would be no influence in the bowl left over from some previous use." These two hypotheses do not explain why Elisha did not throw the salt directly into the spring.

[5] "Elisha's act to purify the waters near Jericho recalls Moses' similar deed at Marah Exod 15.22-25" (Long *2 Kings* p. 35). "The Marah story of Exod 15:22-26 also furnishes a fascinating parallel to our passage. In that instance there was also a problem with the water (bitter, Exod 15:23), into which Moses, upon Yahweh's instruction, threw (*salak,* Exod 15:25, as here in v 23) a tree or piece of wood, and the water became sweet. Then follows a promise that in covenant fidelity Israel would continue to experience Yahweh as her 'healer' (*rapa'*, Exod 15:26; see vv 21, 22 of our passage)" (Dale Ralph Davis: *The Kingdom of God in Transition: Interpreting 2 Kings 2* in *WTJ* 46, 1984, p. 391). Thus the ministry of Elisha evokes the liberation from Egypt: the crossing of the Jordan corresponds to the crossing of the Red Sea, and the purification of the spring of Jericho is a counterpart of the purification of the waters of Mara. Ian M. Blake suggests that the well of Jericho was affected by radioactive contamination in the 14th century B.C. which had gradually worn off. Elisha had not "purified" the spring, but simply declared that this previously tainted spring was now fit for use: "Jericho (Ain Es-Sultan): Joshua's Curse and Elisha's Miracle - One Possible Explanation" in *Palestine Exploration Quarterly* (1967) pp. 86-97. Blake postulates that the radioactivity had mainly affected the new-born and was the origin of the stories about the deaths of infants (cf. Jos 6:26; 1 Kings 16:34). His theory rests on too many hypotheses to be convincing, all the more because it is coloured by a denial of miracles.

[25]Then he went from there to Mount Carmel, and from there he returned to Samaria.

As has already been pointed out the story of the youths of Bethel raises a number of questions. Why does Elisha curse these youths, and why is the judgment so severe? The prophet's behaviour does not at all appear to correspond to his character, and the sanction seems disproportionate to the offense.[6]

To begin with we would like to emphasise that Elisha does not kill anyone. He curses the youths, but his words in no way suggest that the mockers must die (contrary to Elijah, for example, who had twice announced that fire would descend from heaven to *consume* a troop of soldiers who were coming to arrest him: 2 Kings 1:10, 12). Elisha bows to the divine judgment. It is the Lord who chooses to punish the mockers with death!

Secondly, the Hebrew term *na'ar,* which is sometimes translated as *child,* can mean either a baby or a young adult. Moses at three months is called a *na'ar* (Exod 2:6), like Absalom, who had already raised an army against his father, King David (2 Sam 18:5). In our text these are *young* "na'ar", probably adolescents.

Thirdly, the city of origin of the mockers is a special city, like Jericho, and it is important to understand its history. During the time of schism between Israel and Judah Jeroboam I (the first monarch of the northern kingdom) had constructed two places of worship, one in the south of his kingdom at Bethel and one in the north at Dan. The king wanted to prevent his subjects from travelling to Jerusalem three times a year and coming under the influence of the priests of Judah. He feared that his people would end up recognising only a descendant of David as their sovereign (1 Kings 12:26-30). Jeroboam had also installed a new class of priests and modified the religious calendar (1 Kings 12:31-33).

---

[6] Bergen: "It has caused me to question the usefulness of Elisha's miraculous power, and thus to question the entire role of prophet as wonder worker" p. 72. "Even the Rabbis had difficulty with the brutality of this incident" p. 69. For Robinson (p. 29) "These stories fall far below the sensitive spirituality of the best of the deuteronomic tradition." Jones, (p. 389) quotes Montgomery, who (in *Critical and Exegetical Commentary on the Book of Kings, p.* 355) classifies it as a "story which is aimed, by frightening youngsters, to win reverence for the elders."

Even so, not the entire city of Bethel was devoted to a false cult, because certain sons of prophets lived there at the time of Elijah's ascension (2 Kings 2:2-3); yet the negative influence of the heretics must have been considerable, as proved by the large number of mockers.

The hurtful words directed at Elisha were certainly not limited to the physical appearance of the prophet. The severity of the divine judgment prevents us from thinking that we are faced with youths mocking the physical appearance of someone who is climbing and perspiring heavily: *"Go up, you baldhead! Go up, you baldhead!"* (Bethel and Jericho are separated by a distance of 25 kilometres and difference in altitude of 1000 metres). The *children* were most likely young adults, and the verb *climb* could possibly reflect the ascension of Elijah. The word *bald* could imply sterility beyond the simple absence of hair. The repetition of the words emphasises a particular insistence.

The entire region knew of Elijah's ascension. The sons of the prophets had openly spoken of it before it even happened (2:1-5). One can imagine the scepticism of the idol worshipers when the imminent departure of Elijah was announced: "The old fool is about to die and wants to make us believe that he will rise into heaven!" The news of the ascension does not seem to have convinced them: "His successor had to hide his body to make it look like a miraculous departure." In taunting Elisha to *go up* the new generation of Bethel ridicules the ascension of Elijah.[7] They tell Elisha to leave the area like Elijah had done: "Disappear from our presence forever. We don't want you here." The mention of baldness could be a reference a sterile ministry: "We don't need you here because you don't do anything good." If the mockers had already heard of the purification of the Jericho spring (this type of news spreads quickly), they would also be rejecting Elisha's ministry of blessing.

Elisha replies to their words of rejection with another rejection. Those who harden themselves against the miracles and

---

[7] Edersheim: *Practical Truths from Elisha*, p. 56. "The narrator draws attention to the theme of the ascension by using the verb 'go up' four times in verse 23: twice to describe Elisha's travel and twice in the words of the youths" (Long, *2 Kings* p. 33).

benedictions of the Lord cannot receive anything anymore.[8] Jesus condemned the Pharisees who accused him of performing miracles in the name of Beelzebub with the same severity (Matt 12:24), and it is in this context that the Son of Man speaks about the sin against the Holy Spirit, a sin which cannot be pardoned (Matt 12:31). The mocking young people of Bethel belong to the same category. They are proof of a complete rejection of the prophet of grace. The hard hearts of the Bethel mockers show once again that lack of faith is more difficult to heal than any physical lack. Elisha has no problem purifying the waters of Jericho. With a gesture and a word, he eliminates a 500-year-old curse. Lack of faith, on the other hand, is more tenacious. It clings to humans like the worst sickness. Jesus had also experienced it, he who was the greatest miracle-worker, and who was nonetheless abandoned by all and unjustly condemned. Even on the cross Jesus was scoffed at by his contemporaries, but instead of asking him to ascend into heaven, they asked him to descend from the cross (Matt 27:42). The humiliation did not take place at the beginning of his ministry, by adolescents who had never seen a miracle, but at the end of his ministry, after the people and their leaders had witnessed numerous miracles.[9]

These comments on the hardness of the human heart (Calvin spoke of complete corruption) should make us appreciate even more the grace which leads to salvation. Conversion is the greatest of miracles. Thus at Pentecost, when the Holy Spirit came with power, three thousand people were *converted*.

Finally we note that the Lord sent *two* bears to kill the mockers, as if one would not have sufficed! Bears normally do not attack in groups and tend to avoid humans. Only the maternal instinct[10] makes them ferocious and dangerous to man (cf. Prov 17:12). These two female bears leave the forest where

---

[8]   According to Rawlinson (p. 24), "The action cannot be defended from a Christian point of view – Christians have no right to curse any one." However, the New Testament is not that absolute about this point (cf. 1 Cor 5:5; 1 Tim 1:20).

[9]   Elisha has primarily announced the grace and power of the Messiah, but little of Christ's humiliation (see p. 152).

[10]   The feminine ending of the verb *come out* in the Hebrew text of verse 24 identifies the animals as females.

their offspring would be. Their strange behaviour reinforces the idea that they were sent by God to punish the mockers (outside of the forest the young people were no menace for the beasts). This is not a question of nature or coincidence. It is God who manifests his wrath by means of the two bears. Why two? Perhaps to symbolise a judgment without the possibility of an appeal (a sort of double witness of divine wrath), of a condemnation following the rejection of two prophets (Elijah and Elisha), or even the wages of the repeated rejection of the ministry of Elisha (*"Go up, you baldhead! Go up, you baldhead!"*).[11]

The purification of the waters of Jericho and the curse of the children of Bethel are two accounts which complement each other. Elisha is the prophet of grace (as shown by the purified waters of Jericho), but when this grace is rejected (as in the case of the mockers of Bethel), punishment is the only reply.

> *"For if the word spoken through angels proved steadfast, and every transgression and disobedience received a just reward, how shall we escape if we neglect so great a salvation, which at the first began to be spoken by the Lord, and was confirmed to us by those who heard Him" (Heb 2:1-3).[12]*

---

[11] Bethel is not only "marked" by Jeroboam, but also by Jacob, who had given his name to the city (Bethel means "the house of God"), following a vision which he had received (Gen 28:19). Jacob had seen angels climbing and descending a ladder between heaven and earth, and God had promised him that *"the land on which you lie I will give to you and your descendants."* The story of 1–2 Kings has many themes in common with the text of Genesis, but everything is reversed. Here there is also a geographical movement towards an elevated place, yet there are no angels rising and descending between heaven and earth, but rather a man of God who climbs from a blessed city (the spring of Jericho is purified) to a sinful one. Jacob had received God's vision favourably, whereas the adolescents of Bethel reject Elisha, who climbs bathed in sweat, and also mock the ascension of Elijah. Jacob receives the promise of an immense blessing for his descendants; the young mockers are cursed. Their entire future is wiped out immediately because they are torn to pieces by the two bears.

[12] Other New Testament texts go in the same direction: the cursing of the scribes and Pharisees by Jesus and the prediction of the destruction of Jerusalem (Mat 23); Peter's reproach of Ananias and Sapphira, who die shortly afterwards (Acts 5:1-11).

THE WAR AGAINST MOAB
(2 KINGS 3)

Chapter 3 of 2 Kings describes the military campaign of a tripartite coalition of Israel, Judah, and Edom against Moab. The story has three parts: (1) the initial catastrophic campaign of the coalition troops, (2) Elisha's intervention which saves them, (3) the thorough defeat of the Moabite army. Each section is subdivided into three parts and the entire chapter is organized in the form of a chiasm.

A.1	The sin of the king of Israel (3:1-3)	
B.1	Preparation for combat against Moab (3:4-8)	
C.1	On the verge of downfall (3:9)	
D.1	Calling the prophet (3:10-12)	
E	The reason for salvation (3:13-14)	
D.2	The vision of the prophet (3:15-19)	
C.2	Divine salvation (3:20)	
B.2	The battle against Moab (3:21-25)	
A.2	The sin of the king of Moab (3:26-27)	

The themes developed in this chapter are *discernment* and *short-sightedness*. Elisha discerns what no one else can see, whereas the heads of the four kingdoms involved make grave strategic errors.

Let us begin by examining in detail the failures of the kings.

1. The king of Israel reforms his country, but only partially: "*And he [Joram] did evil in the sight of the LORD, but not like his father and mother; for he put away the sacred pillar of Baal that his father had made. Nevertheless he persisted in the sins of Jeroboam the son of Nebat, who had made Israel sin; he did not depart from them.*" (3:2-3). Did he expect to receive the favour of the Lord? If that was his intention he went gravely astray, as the Lord is not satisfied with limited

reforms, and Elisha tells Joram: *And Elisha said, "As the LORD of hosts lives, before whom I stand, surely were it not that I regard the presence of Jehoshaphat king of Judah, I would not look at you, nor see you."* (3:14).

2. The kings of the coalition count on their political and military expertise to conquer Moab, but they fail when they try to take the enemy from behind, from the south (3:9).

3. The Moabites falsely interpret the reflection of the rising sun on puddles of water as being pools of blood, and imagine that the enemy kings have killed one other (3:22-23).

4. The Moabite king's sacrifice of his own firstborn would never have stopped the hostilities. The two camps lacked discernment (see Commentary pp. 84-86).

Elisha on the other hand shows exceptional discernment. He knows what will happen the next day in a different place: rain will fall abundantly on the hills of Judah and will fill the dry desert ravines of Judah with torrents of water (3:16-17). Elisha sees through time and space, and he knows what measures to take to best profit from a new situation. Elisha thus sees what no one else sees, whereas the four kings misinterpret the information which everyone knows.

The story of this military campaign has not been the subject of intense study. The pertinence of its message on blindness and discernment seems to be lost on many![1]

The narrator consecrates two thirds of the story to the unfolding of the military campaign, but Elisha remains the principal character, as his intervention, situated at the centre of the story, changes the course of events.[2] Certain elements of the

---

[1] Burke O. Long has analysed the structure of the story under a liberal perspective which postulates the existence of different sources: "2 Kings III and Genres of Prophetic Narrative" in *Vetus Testamentum* 23 (1973) pp. 337-348. As for Louis Gaussen (*Leçons données dans une école du dimanche sur les prophètes Elie et Elisée*), he frankly ignores Chapter 3 in a book of 420 pages. He ends his commentary at 2 Kings 6:7, prior to the sieges of Dothan and Samaria.

[2] Jones is astonished by the sudden appearance and disappearance of the prophet: "Elisha is introduced abruptly in v. 11, and no explanation for his presence with the kings is given, nor is it said whence he came on the scene. His disappearance after delivering his message in vv. 18ff. is even more abrupt" (p. 390). For Robinson, "Elisha does not play a prominent

account recall the story of the military action against Ramoth (1 Kings 22),[3] but the parallels to the siege of Samaria are more evident.[4]

Introduction to the Reign of Joram (3:1-3)

[1]Now Joram the son of Ahab became king over Israel at Samaria in the eighteenth year of Jehoshaphat king of Judah, and reigned twelve years. [2]And he did evil in the sight of the LORD, but not like his father and mother; for he put away the sacred pillar of Baal that his father had made. [3]Nevertheless he persisted in the sins of Jeroboam the son of Nebat, who had made Israel sin; he did not depart from them.

Joram[5] was the last king of the house of Ahab. He succeeded his brother Ahaziah who was childless (1:17). His behaviour is given a negative evaluation by the author because the king maintains the pagan cult next to the worship of Yahweh established by Jeroboam I, founder of the northern kingdom (1 Kings 12:26-33). Joram nevertheless partly reforms the country (*"for he put away the sacred pillar of Baal that his father had made"* 3:2). Was the new king unsettled by the exhortations and acts of Elijah (the demonstration at Mount Carmel and the death of two groups of fifty soldiers)? Did he want to placate the Lord or his worshipers? He reforms the country, but in limited measure, because the cult of Baal is still in full swing at his death. It is only the monarch who succeeds

---

part, and this is basically a story about the activities of the kings rather than a folk-tale about the exploits of a prophet" (p. 33).

[3]   "The similarities between 2 Kgs 3 and 1 Kgs 22 are noted by all commentators. In both chapters, a prophet of YHWH is sought out by Jehoshaphat, who has joined an Israelite king in battle. Validation of the prophet's position and his words come at the time of the prophecy's fulfilment. Identical phraseology lends support to these thematic similarities" (Mordechai Cogan & Hayim Tadmor: "2 Kings" in *The Anchor Bible*, p. 49.

[4]   (1) Elisha occupies a subsidiary place in the story. (2) The king or kings come to talk to Elisha when Israel's situation is desperate. (3) An army suddenly retreats when it is at the point of full conquest. One can also point out that the story of the campaign against Moab shares the theme of blindness and discernment with that of the siege of Dothan (see p. 141). For parallels which are antitheses to this story, see p. 142.

[5]   For the spelling of the name see footnote 7 p. 191

him (Jehu) that will eradicate Baal worship in the land (10:18-27). Joram, who thinks of himself as a cunning politician, seeks to reconcile diverging interests. He wants to gain the support both of the Lord and of the faithful without offending the followers of pagan practices.

Joram is thus an evil king, but not as evil as the others (*"And he did evil in the sight of the LORD, but not like his father and mother"* 3:2). In spite of the nuances, the negative behaviour of the king does not cancel God's judgment pronounced on the royal house of Ahab, to the effect that this house would disappear in the following generation (1 Kings 21:29; cf. 1 Kings 21:20-24). Chapters 9 and 10 relate the details of this judgment. The limited opening given by Joram to the worship of God benefits Elisha, who can thus travel freely within the kingdom.

"Now Joram the son of Ahab became king over Israel at Samaria in the eighteenth year of Jehoshaphat king of Judah." The synchronism with the kingdom of Judah is different from that indicated at the death of Ahaziah: *"So Ahaziah died according to the word of the LORD which Elijah had spoken. Because he had no son, Joram became king in his place, in the second year of Jehoram the son of Jehoshaphat, king of Judah."* (2 Kings 1:17). "The statements are not contradictory, since in Judah's involvement in Israelite politics Jehoram was probably co-regent with his father."[6] "The discrepancy arises from the fact that just prior to joining Ahab in the unsuccessful attempt to recapture Ramoth-Gilead from the Syrians, Jehoshaphat took the precaution to have his son Jehoram installed as coregent on the throne of Judah... It should be pointed out in this connection that this precedent for installing the crown prince as coregent in his father's lifetime was followed at least six times in the course of the Judean monarchy."[7]

---

[6]   John Gray: *1 & 2 Kings: A Commentary*, p. 430.
[7]   Archer: *Encyclopedia of Bible Difficulties*, p. 204.

First Phase of the Campaign against Moab (3:4-9)

⁴Now Mesha king of Moab was a sheepbreeder, and he regularly paid the king of Israel one hundred thousand lambs and the wool of one hundred thousand rams. ⁵But it happened, when Ahab died, that the king of Moab rebelled against the king of Israel. ⁶So King Joram went out of Samaria at that time and mustered all Israel. ⁷Then he went and sent to Jehoshaphat king of Judah, saying, "The king of Moab has rebelled against me. Will you go with me to fight against Moab?" And he said, "I will go up; I am as you are, my people as your people, my horses as your horses." ⁸Then he said, "Which way shall we go up?" And he answered, "By way of the Wilderness of Edom." ⁹So the king of Israel went with the king of Judah and the king of Edom, and they marched on that roundabout route seven days; and there was no water for the army, nor for the animals that followed them.

The revolt of Moab was motivated by the crisis in Israel. In less than two years king Ahab and his successor were dead and the Israelite army was defeated by the Syrians (1 Kings 22-2 Kings 1). The absence of a direct successor to Ahaziah also produced a wavering court. The Moabites profited from this temporary weakness and shook off the Israelite guardianship. [8]

---

[8]   The "Moabite stone", also known as the "stele of Mecha" reports the Moabite version of the revolt. This block of black basalt, originally 1.15m tall and 68cm wide, was found in 1868 in the ruins of Dibon, the city where the king of Moab was born. Alain Millard consecrates an entire chapter to this archaeological discovery, because "the stele of Mesha is the only monument of this type which is as well known for Israel and Judah as it is for Edom, Moab or Ammon", *Trésors des temps bibliques*, Sator, 1986, pp. 117-118. The inscription describes how "Mesha threw off the yoke of Israel, reconquered part of the territory which had previously belonged to Moab, and rebuilt several cities... The inscription is written in ancient Phoenecian characters which were also used to write Hebrew." The thirty-four lines of text on the stone are published in French in *NDB* pp. 863—864 and by J. A. Thompson in *La Bible à la lumière de l'archéologie*, pp. 135-136. For the English text see Prichard, *Ancient Near Eastern Texts Relating to the Old Testament* pp. 320-321).

Israel's reaction to this is also understandable. Weakened by the crisis the nation did not wish to lose an important source of revenue: *"one hundred thousand lambs and the wool of one hundred thousand rams"* is a heavy tribute. Rapid intervention against this vassal was required. With a shrunken army king Joram of Israel sought support from the two nations who also had an interest in limiting the power of Moab. Edom, south of Moab, and Judah in the west were the two nations who most feared a powerful kingdom at their borders.[9] Moreover king Jehoshaphat of Judah, principal ally of Joram, had already shown his goodwill towards Israel by fighting at Ahab's side (1 Kings 22). An ingenious plan of attack was worked out. Going *"by way of the wilderness of Edom"* (v. 8), the coalition sought to pass around Moab at the south end of the Dead Sea, in order to take action from behind (see map).[10]

The "wisdom" of Joram proved to be completely ineffective. From a military point of view the "ingenious" manoeuver of Moab turned into a catastrophe (3:9). Had they forgotten to take even the most elementary precautions, out of sheer pride? Did they underestimate the distance to be covered, the arid terrain to be crossed, the amount of water required for the large number of men and animals? Were the wells along the way dried out? Without water, and thus without strength, men and beasts became easy prey for the enemy.

---

[9] During the reign of Jehoshaphat the Moabites had joined forces with the Ammonites against the kingdom of Judah (2 Chron 20:1). The army formed *"a great multitude"* (2 Chron 20:2, 15) and seemed ready to devastate everything in its path (2 Chron 20:23). A disagreement between the Moabites and the Ammonites seems to have been exploited by God to save Judah, because after a first victory on the East Bank, the two armies *"helped to destroy one another"* (2 Chron 20:23).

[10] "The most direct line of attack would have been across the Jordan at Jericho and then southwards into Moabite territory to the east of the Dead Sea, but Mesha had regained and fortified the strong points north of the Arnon. An attack through Judah and the Arabah to the south of the Dead Sea with a thrust north was made impossible by the precipitous north bank of the Zared (Wadi 'l-Hesa). So the allies chose to make a long detour eastward around the Zared entering Moab from the east. This desert region was *the wilderness of Edom.*" (Robinson p. 34).

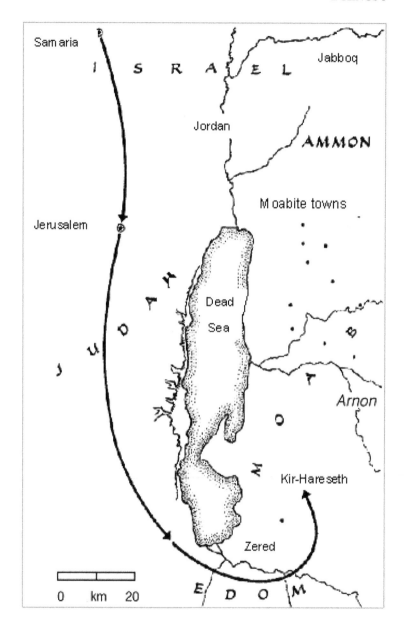

Can we assume that disagreements between the kings about the route to be followed were the reason for the time wasted in the desert? The author's reflections on the Moabites suggest that the coalition kings were rivals: *"the kings have surely struck swords and have killed one another"* 3:23). Joram may have forced an alliance with Judah and Edom to checkmate Moab, whereas sound judgment might have led him to wait. A military campaign undertaken with allies who are divided against each other is always risky. Joram, in his foolishness, may have favoured haste over patience.

Calling the Prophet (3:10-12)

> ¹⁰*And the king of Israel said, "Alas! For the LORD has called these three kings together to deliver them into the hand of Moab." ¹¹But Jehoshaphat said, "Is there no prophet of the LORD here, that we may inquire of the LORD by him?" So one of the servants of the king of Israel answered and said, "Elisha the son of Shaphat is here, who poured water on the hands of Elijah." ¹²And Jehoshaphat said, "The word of the LORD is with him " So the king of Israel and Jehoshaphat and the king of Edom went down to him.*

The king of Israel interprets the catastrophe as a judgment of God, but he forgets that hope is always possible for those who turn humbly towards the Lord. Jehoshaphat, on the other hand, seeks to consult God. He is a believer, and not fatalistic. Micah's prophecy before the siege of Ramoth could have meant their salvation if it had been received (1 Kings 22).

Jehoshaphat reacts favourably at the mention of Elisha. He knows the prophet, even though Elisha exercises his ministry in the north (3:12).

Elisha was known for his helpfulness: *"(he) who poured water on the hands of Elijah."* (3:11).[11] He was the prophet of

---

[11] "A reader might also notice here the irony of Elisha's being introduced as someone who pours water, in the context of water shortage. Or perhaps the introduction expresses within itself the reason why Elisha should be consulted, that is, his noted skill with water. While the phrase is likely a metaphor for a disciple/master relationship [this is also the opinion of Nelson, p. 166], the choice of metaphor shows the comic aspects of an otherwise serious narrative" (Bergen p. 75).

grace and not of judgment. Perhaps he might be able to rally the armies. His availability is surprising. The prophet can be found without difficulty, whereas the armies seem to have gone missing in the desert. Had he accompanied the troops as a chaplain, or was he staying there "by chance"? Had he accompanied the troops because he had known in advance that this trial awaited them and that he would aid them?[12] Once again Elisha is present where there are needs to be met. He is the prophet of grace and of the people (see pp. 9-14).

A Beneficial Association (3:13-14)

> [13]*Then Elisha said to the king of Israel, "What have I to do with you? Go to the prophets of your father and the prophets of your mother." But the king of Israel said to him, "No, for the LORD has called these three kings together to deliver them into the hand of Moab."* [14]*And Elisha said, "As the LORD of hosts lives, before whom I stand, surely were it not that I regard the presence of Jehoshaphat king of Judah, I would not look at you, nor see you."*

The words of Elisha to Joram are surprisingly harsh. Even though the king lives in compromise he confesses the sovereignty of the Lord and twice even seems to plead for divine aid (*"Alas! For the LORD has called these three kings together to deliver them into the hand of Moab."* 3:10, 13). Joram had also destroyed the statues of Baal (3:2); if Elisha were the prophet of grace we could expect a little more understanding. The words of Elisha are nevertheless clear: *"As the LORD of hosts lives, before whom I stand, surely were it not that I regard the presence of Jehoshaphat king of Judah, I would not look at you, nor see you."* (v. 14). Joram's attempts at reform are worth nothing in the eyes of God. He does not deserve to be saved, and if he is finally helped it is only due to the fact that he is associated with Jehoshaphat. Grace is closely attached to the ministry of Elisha, but it is neither formless nor vague. Salvation

---

[12] This hypothesis is congruent with the "omniscience" of the prophet (see p. 19). On the other hand, the lack of water could have been foreseen if someone had had some knowledge of the dryness of the wells in that region.

is possible only because of the *association* with Jehoshaphat the Just (who is also the descendant of David and an ancestor of the Messiah). This principle is fully expressed in the New Testament with the *imputation* of the justice of Christ on the sinner who believes in him.

Joram seems to comprehend this principle, in that his salvation depends on his association with other kings who are more righteous than he, because he draws attention to the *three* kings who will be lost (3:13). "I am not alone", he seems to say, "but there are three of us. If you do not care about me, then at least have mercy on them." Elisha gives him a favourable reply. On the other hand the prophet does not reproach Jehoshaphat for his association with Joram, as he is primarily the prophet of grace. Nonetheless the alliance between Jehoshaphat and the house of Ahab had been criticised by other prophets (2 Chron 19:2; 20:37).[13]

The Prophet's Vision (3:15-19)

> [15]*But now bring me a musician." Then it happened, when the musician played, that the hand of the LORD came upon him.* [16]*And he said, "Thus says the LORD: 'Make this valley full of ditches.'* [17]*For thus says the LORD: 'You shall not see wind, nor shall you see rain; yet that valley shall be filled with water, so that you, your cattle, and your animals may drink.'* [18]*And this is a simple matter in the sight of the LORD; He will also deliver the Moabites into your hand.* [19]*Also you shall attack every fortified city and every choice city, and shall cut down every good tree, and stop up every spring of water, and ruin every good piece of land with stones."*

Why does Elisha ask for a harp player? Music inspires and calms the spirit; the sound of the harp is particularly soothing and relaxing. Did Elisha need it personally in order to be calm or was he thinking of his listeners who needed to listen attentively to his astounding message?[14] As is often the case with Elisha the

---

[13] These reproaches can be found in the book of 1–2 Chronicles which deal exclusively with the kingdom of Judah. The author of Kings focuses on the kingdom of Israel at the centre of his book.

[14] Several commentators think that Elisha needed music in order to prophesy. "His spirit had been ruffled and troubled, and in a state of mind he was not

utilitarian aspect is secondary. Elisha uses objects to illustrate his messages. By asking for a harp player Elisha does the *contrary to* what one would expect of him. Swords, lances, iron chariots are required to help an army, but not a musical instrument. If necessary a trumpet can call men together and a drum can encourage a troop to march, but a harp has no military use. Its music weakens morale rather than stimulating combativeness and courage. By his use of a harp Elisha wants to show that the solution is out of the ordinary. Inner peace is essential for military victory, peace that is linked to communion with God. Basically it is peace with God which must be sought. Elisha has that peace. He can thus save his people.[15]

The instruction to dig holes in the desert is also surprising at first. Nevertheless those who are familiar with the region know that water can come unexpectedly to the dry wadies or ravines of the desert. Moisture-laden clouds coming from the Mediterranean are caught on the higher hills and release their water there. The resulting torrents flow rapidly towards the arid regions where the soil, hardened by drought, is almost impermeable. Elisha thus announces a phenomenon which is natural but not frequent. The water flushes through the wadies,

---

fitted either to receive the Divine light or to reflect it... The minstrel had ended, and the prophet's spirit was restored to calm." (Edersheim pp. 76, 78). "Jehoshaphat is not where he should be; that is why the Spirit of prophecy is concentrated in Elisha. It is a serious case. A musician must be brought so that the Spirit, in the prophet, can regain its free course and be full of grace." J.B. *Courtes méditations sur Elisée,* p. 15. "Elisha's spirit had been discomposed by this scene. He needed calmness. The Spirit of the Lord cannot speak till the soul has been brought into harmony" (Whitfield: *The Saviour Prophet or Incidents in the Life of Elisha,* p. 76). H.R. (*Méditations sur le second livre des Rois,* p. 53) is of the same opinion. This approach presupposes that Elisha had no idea of the kings' attitude before he met them, but one can reasonably imagine that the prophet of knowledge did not only just discover in the desert of Edom what his compatriots had already known for a long time.

[15] The liberal John Gray finds that this passage is not part of the Elisha cycle: "Indeed, in the prophet's use of music to induce ecstasy a certain limitation is implied which would never have been admitted by the hagiographers, whose aim was to magnify the power of the prophet" p. 419). Jones (p. 396) on the other hand, states "The reference to Elisha's dependence on such a stimulant is a ancient and genuine tradition, which places Elisha firmly in the category of ecstatic prophets."

some of which could then be collected in ditches. The prophet insists that this will not be visible. "You will be blessed, but you will not see the origin of the benediction." The sinful people who do not see God will not be able to see the rain. They will nevertheless be blessed, because God is merciful. For this to happen it is necessary to live by faith and believe the words of the prophet. This requirement of faith is often emphasised in the Elisha account.

Elisha announces the saving of the Israelites and also the defeat of the enemy. It will be a total victory. The country is to be devastated: *"you shall attack every fortified city and every choice city, and shall cut down every good tree, and stop up every spring of water, and ruin every good piece of land with stones."* (3:19).

The order to chop down good trees is surprising, as it seems to contradict Moses' injunctions: *"When you besiege a city for a long time, while making war against it to take it, you shall not destroy its trees by wielding an axe against them; if you can eat of them, do not cut them down to use in the siege, for the tree of the field is man's food. Only the trees which you know are not trees for food you may destroy and cut down"* Deut 20:19-20). A country should not be ravaged during a military campaign, but this order follows two other regulations concerning the siege of a city (Deut 20.10-20): a first part deals with the siege in a *foreign land* (Deut 20.10-15) and a second deals with the situation during a war in the *promised land* (Deut 20.16-18). Should it be understood that the instructions relating to the trees apply to two regions (foreign lands and the Promised Land) or only to the Promised Land, and if so that would resolve the dilemma? Elisha's order to devastate a *foreign* land would thus not be in opposition to Mosaic law.

For Israel the devastation of the land would appear to be counterproductive, because the goal of the campaign was be to control a country which would provide significant revenue. By ravaging a country over a long period (it takes time for trees to grow again, and great efforts are necessary to empty wells and remove stones from the fields), Israel would be punishing itself by destroying the land which would be bearing fruit for it. For Judah, on the other hand, the devastation would be positive, because the depletion of the Moabites' bounty would mean a general weakening of the country itself. This belligerent neighbour would be less of a threat. We also see that Elisha's order follows the prophesied meaning: God saves the coalition to help Judah and not to help Israel.

When we understand the acts and words of Elisha everything becomes logical. The prophet acts in full harmony with his ministry. He announces grace to those who have turned to the Lord (Judah), but rejects those who are indifferent to or try to use God (Israel).[16]

The Battle against Moab (3:20-25)

> [20]Now it happened in the morning, when the grain offering was offered, that suddenly water came by way of Edom, and the land was filled with water. [21]And when all the Moabites heard that the kings had come up to fight against them, all who were able to bear arms and older were gathered; and they stood at the border. [22]Then they rose up early in the morning, and the sun was shining on the water; and the Moabites saw the water on the other side as red as blood. [23]And they said, "This is blood; the kings have surely struck swords and have killed one another; now therefore, Moab, to the spoil!" [24]So when they came to the camp of Israel, Israel rose up and attacked the Moabites, so that they fled before them; and they entered their land, killing the Moabites. [25]Then they destroyed the cities, and each man threw a stone on every good piece of land and filled it; and they stopped up all the springs of water and cut down all the good trees. But they left the stones of Kir Haraseth intact. However the slingers surrounded and attacked it.

The Moabites were firmly entrenched and awaiting the enemy,[17] as their reconnaissance services had informed them of the coalition troops' movements. Joram's surprise attack from Edom in the south had evaporated into thin air after his troops had gotten lost in the desert. The *seven* days they were underway

---

[16] The judgment of Gehazi and that of the royal equerry bear the same lesson (5:27 pp. 131-134; 7:17-20 pp. 172-175).

[17] It is a general mobilisation because even older men are enrolled (3:21).

gave the Moabites plenty of time to regroup their forces and prepare their defences.[18]

An optical illusion was responsible for the Moabite confusion. The reddish reflection of the sun on the water collected by the coalition army made the Moabites believe that they saw blood spread over the enemy camp.[19] Rumours of dissent within the coalition may have substantiated the optical illusion. Furthermore the memory of the self-destruction of their own coalition army with Ammon shortly before the attack on Judah (*"they helped to destroy one another"* 2 Chron 20:23), may have nourished this particular interpretation.[20] "Our own troops destroyed themselves in the past and now the same misfortune befalls them also!"

The coalition forces throw themselves upon the Moabite enemy, whose troops have imprudently left their trenches. Encouraged by this apparently easy success and having skirted death, Israel, Judah and Edom attack the rest of the country, carry out the words of the prophet and lay waste to the land, Israel not realising that it is sabotaging its own project to subjugate Moab and to draw taxes from it (a ruined country has nothing left to offer).

The Sin of the King of Moab (3:26-27)

[26]And when the king of Moab saw that the battle was too fierce for him, he took with him seven hundred men who drew swords, to break through to the king of Edom, but they could not. [27]Then

---

[18] It should have taken three or four days at most to cover the 160 kilometres from Samaria.

[19] "The cause of this phenomenon was probably the red sand which is a notable feature of the Wadi 'l-Hesa. To this there may have been added a play on words. Edom means red (cp. Gen 25.30) and the Hebrew word for blood, *dam*, is almost identical" (Robinson p. 36).

[20] The conflict of Judah with Moab and Ammon described in the book of Chronicles (2 Chron 20) probably precedes the campaign undertaken against Moab with the help of Israel and Edom described in the book of Kings (2 Kings 3). Actually, the defeat of Moab described in 2 Kings 3 leaves the *country* ravaged, whereas the fight between the Moabites and Ammonites only concerns one army (2 Chron 20:23). After the annihilation of that army (2 Chron 20:29-30), the kingdom of Judah feels confident enough to attack Moab in order to further weaken it (2 Kings 3:7).

he took his eldest son who would have reigned in his place, and offered him as a burnt offering upon the wall; and there was great indignation against Israel. So they departed from him and returned to their own land.

In a last-ditch effort the king of Moab tries to attack the king of Edom (3:26). Does he wish to punish this king for having allied himself with Israel and Judah, or is he trying to make him change sides? Is he trying to kill the weakest of the three kings to give his troops courage? Whatever the reason he does not attain his goal, and ends up sacrificing his own son before his final defeat.[21] To everyone's surprise, when everything else has failed, the reader learns that this final abominable act ends the siege. Why do the Israelites leave after seeing the child sacrifice? Why depart when the enemy is on its knees?

Were the Moabites strengthened by the conviction that their God would help them? Were the Israelites afraid that the Moabites had regained their strength? Literally: "there was great *qasap* against Israel." *Qasap* means anger, fury, indignation, irritation, trouble, or even foam (for agitated water). It is probably less a case of anger than trouble which is emphasised here, the troubles of Israel who suddenly fear the wrath of Kemosh, the national deity of the Moabites.[22]

---

[21] According to Baruch Margalit ("Why King Mesha of Moab Sacrificed His Oldest Son" in *Biblical Archaeology Review*, Nov-Dec 1986, pp. 62-63), this type of sacrifice was carried out in situations of national calamity. The king either sacrificed his son as a burnt offering on the walls of the city in view of the enemy, or else put him on the top of the wall (the word *'ola* means *ascend* and does not always imply a burnt sacrifice) before throwing him down. Derchain (*VT* 10, 1970, pp. 351-355) defends this hypothesis and documents the "sacrifice by precipitation" with scenes carved on Egyptian temple walls of the XIXth and XXth dynasties. These reliefs illustrate the siege of Canaan and Phoenecian cities. One sees children being thrown from the walls while the besieged are praying, arms raised to heaven, and one man lifts a brazier with a gesture of benediction.

[22] John Barclay Burns makes an inventory of the interpretations of the Israelites' surprising behaviour in his article "Why Did the Besieging Army Withdraw? (2 Kings 3:27)" in *Zeitschrift für die alttestamentliche Wissenschaft* (1990) pp. 187-194. Four positions result: (1) The Israelites feared the reaction of the deity Kemosh after such an important sacrifice. The Israelites thus shared the faith of the Moabite king in the divinity's power. This opinion, also expressed in the notes of TOB, seems the most appropriate. (2) The Moabite king, aware of the idolatry of the Israelites,

The Israelites, who do not seem worried about the Lord, fear the anger of this pagan god, despite their military successes and the supernatural intervention of God, who has just shown his power and will to help Israel. Superstition is a form of madness. It clouds intelligence and suffocates common sense. Against all logic Israel retreats.

Joram is the king of the blind and Elisha the champion of discernment. That is why Elisha asks for a harp, a symbol of gentleness and peace, a symbol of communion with God at a time when the coalition must be saved from collapse. Neither armies nor force provide the victory (Israel had it at its fingertips), but rather the lucidity which comes from fellowship with God.

---

carried out this sacrifice more to impress the enemy than to compel the deity ("psychological" interpretation). According to this explanation, the Israelites' faith in Kemosh was even greater than that of the Moabites. (3) The author of Kings himself thought that the deity had power and that was what made the Israelites flee. This is the opinion of Burns, which is, in our opinion, very contestable. (4) The Israelites were disgusted with the behaviour of the Moabite king and simply went back home. But as Burns remarks, this interpretation ascribes a contemporary sentimentality to men hardened by war and by the rituals of human sacrifices.

THE WIDOW AND HER CHILDREN
(2 KINGS 4:1-7)

These seven verses appear to be out of context.[1] The husband is dead, his wife and children are not mentioned anywhere else. The story is condensed and information on the family is reduced to a minimum. No proper names are given. We know nothing of the tribe, the ancestors, the geographic location, the husband's profession, the reason for the family's poverty, the husband's cause of death. Elisha is known, but nothing about the relationship which he might have had with this family before or after the events related here.

This story appears lost between two highly developed accounts which are very different from it. It is in stark contrast to the preceding story, as it is difficult to see the connection between armed combat which opposes four armies (2 Kings 3) and the misery of a poor woman who is so defenceless that she is about to be separated from her children. The story of the Shunammite which follows (2 Kings 4:8-37) has certain analogies (the sorrow of another mother), but is also full of contrasts. The woman of Shunem comes from a specific town, she is rich, married and not widowed; on the other hand, she has no children. Elisha has frequent contacts with her, and the woman is also mentioned later (2 Kings 8:1-6).

The story of the widow and her children seems to be unrelated to anything, and therefore it ties in well with a woman who is apparently detached from everything. The solitude of the woman *and* the text are, however, only seemingly isolated. The widow receives exceptional help from the Lord and the story is strongly linked to the texts which precede and follow it, without counting the parallels to the story of the widow of Zarephath

---

[1]   Bergen (p. 83) speaks of "The abruptness of this transition" and further: "I am parachuted into an entirely different setting without any context, either geographical or chronological."

which have already been mentioned (1 Kings 17:8-16; see p. 33 point 3).

The account of the military combat of chapter 3 has some points in common with our story:

1. Both of the stories begin with debts. Mesha, the king of Moab, refuses to continue paying the annual tribute to the king of Israel, and the widow cannot repay her debts to her creditors. Specific punishments await "bad debtors": Joram, king of Israel, allies himself with two other kings and engages in a military expedition, and the widow's creditor threatens to take her two children and sell them into slavery.

2. Elisha is called to help in both stories, and gives surprising advice to the two faithful persons concerned (the king of Judah and the widow) so that they can resolve their dilemma: the coalition must dig holes in the desert and the widow must borrow empty jars. The digging of holes and the empty jars are needed in order to receive precious liquid: drinking water for the troops and oil for the widow.

3. In both cases faith is required for deliverance (the soldiers must dig holes and the widow must obtain jars), and the extent of the blessing depends on the earnestness of their commitment. The greater the number and depth of the holes, the greater the quantity of water that can be collected; the greater the number of jars obtained, the richer the widow will become.

4. The miracle is at the same time both private and public. The soldiers do not see the rain, but they notice the consequences: the torrents of water; the widow and her children are present for the multiplication of the oil, but their neighbours see only the results (the oil sold by the widow).

5. Elisha also gives advice on what is to follow these actions: the coalition must ravage Moab and the widow must sell the oil.

6. In both stories death strikes a family (but for different reasons): the king of Moab stupidly sacrifices his son, whereas the widow loses her husband, but can keep her children thanks to her faith.

The parallels to the story of the Shunammite, which follows this text, are further developed in the following chapter (see pp. 95-98). In a word, we can say that Elisha helps a faithful woman to keep, find or retrieve one or more children, in the total or partial absence of a husband.

In conclusion, the story of the widow and her children, which at first seemed to be without context, is surrounded by a rich one. The text integrates admirably into the context (see structure p. 42) and thus provides a smooth transition from the public domain (chapter 3) to the private (chapter 4).[2] These parallel stories, similarities and antitheses enrich the reading of the story. They cause the principal themes to stand out and emphasise the specific traits of each story.

A Dramatic Situation (4:1)

[1] *A certain woman of the wives of the sons of the prophets cried out to Elisha, saying, "Your servant my husband is dead, and you know that your servant feared the LORD. And the creditor is coming to take my two sons to be his slaves."*

Misfortune befalls an upright family: the father dies and leaves his wife and children in material poverty. A creditor tries to take the children away from their mother and sell them into slavery to recover the money owed him by their father. Poverty and mourning are difficult trials, but the loss of children, taken into slavery by an unscrupulous man, is unbearable.

Mosaic law authorised a certain type of slavery, but not the kind practised by this man. Temporary slavery was permitted to punish thieves who were unable to reimburse the sum stolen, and to pay damages (Exod 22:2 or 22:3). This form of slavery was equivalent to forced labour, and was subject to strict rules which guaranteed certain basic rights. The penalty could not exceed six years, and in the seventh year the criminal was freed regardless of the amount stolen. Sometimes poor people sold themselves into slavery as a voluntary act (Lev 25:39-41). The poor sought refuge in the house of a rich person, in whose service they placed

---

[2] Certain commentators primarily highlight the contrast between this story and the one in chapter 3 (Gaussen pp. 309-310). Edersheim (p. 81) feels that "Perhaps one of the sublimest lessons of all may be learned from this sudden transition", because it emphasises the universal love of Elisha. The prophet not only worries about national problems, but also about those of the weak and the poor who are left to fend for themselves.

themselves with their family. On the other hand, slave trade was an abomination on a level with murder and was penalised by Israel's most severe sanction: capital punishment (Exod 21:16).

Under Mosaic law the poor were to be treated with respect. The rich should lend money to those who were no longer able to live decently. Pledges or securities had to be returned each evening and the rich person had no right to violate the poor person's residence to take them back the next day (Deut 24:10-13). Loans were made without interest, and every seventh, sabbatical year debts were automatically cancelled. Furthermore the law exhorted mercy towards widows and orphans, and reminded people that the Lord watched over them and would punish anyone who oppressed them.[3] The rich were encouraged to give without expecting anything in return.

The creditor's desire to take two children from their mother by force was a flagrant breach of God's law. The man appears to have waited for the husband's death to put pressure on the wife, as he was probably frightened of the father's reaction towards such demands. The creditor abuses a helpless woman who is alone, without resources, disoriented and suffering from the loss of her husband.[4]

The widow has no one to defend her other than the Lord and Elisha, his representative. *"The woman cried out"*: her cry is not one of contention but of desperation. She demands nothing from Elisha. She asks neither for a miracle nor intervention with the political authorities to reprimand the creditor, but simply

---

[3] A century later, Amos denounces the rich peoples' abuse of the poor and condemns them: *"For three transgressions of Israel, and for four, I will not turn away its punishment, Because they sell the righteous for silver, And the poor for a pair of sandals. They pant after the dust of the earth which is on the head of the poor, And pervert the way of the humble. A man and his father go in to the same girl, To defile My holy name... "* (Amos 2:6-7).

[4] According to an Aramaic paraphrase of the biblical text (Targum of Jonathan), the widow was the wife of Abdias, the servant of Ahab who had hidden one hundred prophets (cf. 1 Kings 8:4, 13). Flavius Josephus adds that Abdias had borrowed money from Joram, son of Ahab, in order to feed the prophets, and that the widow herself had been sold into slavery (Flavius Josephus: *Antiquities* 9.4.2; *NCB* p. 363; Wiseman; *Tyndale Old Testament Commentaries*, p. 202; Patterson p. 183; Dilday: *The Communicator's Commentary*, p. 289).

describes her situation. We can also perceive spiritual distress in her outcry. "Why are these misfortunes happening to us, we who have always remained faithful, whereas the majority who worship Baal are doing well?"[5]

The Intervention of Elisha (4:2-4)

> [2]So Elisha said to her, "What shall I do for you? Tell me, what do you have in the house?" And she said, "Your maidservant has nothing in the house but a jar of oil." [3]Then he said, "Go, borrow vessels from everywhere, from all your neighbours—empty vessels; do not gather just a few. [4]And when you have come in, you shall shut the door behind you and your sons; then pour it into all those vessels, and set aside the full ones."

Elisha asks the woman two questions. The first is a difficult one, particularly for someone who has lost all her bearings. "What is to be done?" Even someone who had not suffered the same fate as the widow would find it difficult to answer. Should one call on the political authorities, exhort the creditor to have more compassion, organise a collection among the sons of the prophets? Why not bring the husband back to life? Elisha does not expect a reply, on the one hand because the woman is too weakened by the tragedy to think of a solution and on the other because it is not up to men to tell God what to do. The faithful are called simply to trust in the Lord, which is exactly what the woman has done and should continue to do.[6]

---

[5] Bergen (p. 84): "The woman's statement 'your servant my husband is dead; and you know that your servant feared YHWH' (v. 1) is a clever piece of rhetoric in other ways. Elisha, as man of God (v. 7), is further placed in a position of obligation both by the late husband's fear of YHWH and by his knowledge of this fact. Statements such as 'you know that' (v. 2), not only emphasize the factual nature of the statement, but heighten the possibility of the listener's consent to the statement, since the listener, who in this case is addressed as master/patron, is unlikely to confess ignorance of so important a claim."

[6] Arthur Pink (*Gleanings from Elisha: His Life and Miracles,* p. 64) finds that "Possibly the prophet was himself momentarily nonplussed, conscious of his own helplessness. Possibly his question was designed to emphasize the gravity of the situation. 'It is beyond my power to extricate you'. More likely it was to make her look above him. 'I too am only human'. Or again, it may have been to test her. 'Are you willing to follow my instructions?' "

The second question is much easier for someone who is penniless: "What do you have in the house?" "Practically nothing." Elisha asks the question, waits for the reply, and then gives a precise order: *"Go, borrow vessels from everywhere, from all your neighbours – empty vessels."* The order is concrete, easily carried out, and within the means of the widow. He demands only one thing: faith, great faith, faith which does not question the why or the how, obedient faith which carries out what is asked, faith which obeys all directives to the letter.[7]

The woman does not have the option to test the promise. She must look for jars, close the door and begin to pour oil. As soon as the miracle begins the woman cannot interrupt it to look for more jars. She will be blessed in direct proportion to her faith. Elisha encourages her to go to *all* of her neighbours and ask them for *many* jars. One great blessing is promised. The rest depends on her.[8]

The faith which is asked for is not blind faith. Of course, the woman cannot verify the promise before accepting it, but she knows its author. Elisha is the prophet of God who had revealed himself by miracles in favour of the faithful. Elisha had shown that he was the successor of Elijah, who had already multiplied oil and flour. Elisha had demonstrated his willingness to help others; his word had always been fulfilled. The widow can thus confidently commit herself.

---

[7] Elisha's questions to the widow also anticipate identical questions which Jesus asks certain people: "What do you want me to do for you?" (Mark 10:51), "How many loaves do you have?" (Mark 6:38; 8:5). The miracle of the multiplication of loaves is particularly close to our story: Jesus finds out what the crowd has, then multiplies the few loaves available, and the story ends with basketfuls of loaves which are left over. (Excell, *The Biblical Illustrator*, p. 44).

[8] We note that the help Elisha provides is similar to that given by Jesus (Bellett p. 18-20). Sometimes the Messiah blesses the penniless in direct proportion to their faith. He thus heals two blind men by saying *"'According to your faith will it be done to you'"* (Matt 9:29). The centurion who comes to him and asks him to heal his servant is sent away with the words *"'Go! It will be done just as you believed it would'"* (Matt 8:13).

The Miracle and Its Meaning (4:5-7)

> [5]*So she went from him and shut the door behind her and her sons, who brought the vessels to her; and she poured it out. [6]Now it came to pass, when the vessels were full, that she said to her son, "Bring me another vessel." And he said to her, "There is not another vessel." So the oil ceased. [7]Then she came and told the man of God. And he said, "Go, sell the oil and pay your debt; and you and your sons live on the rest"*

Every jar is full. Every effort has been rewarded. The author provides no indication of the quantity of oil obtained, as the importance lies not in measuring the woman's faith but in emphasising God's faithfulness. In addition, by not divulging the final result, the author leaves the reader with a question: how many jars did the woman assemble? According to the reply she could have found only enough to settle her debts, or, on the contrary, she and her children might have been able to live comfortably for the rest of their lives. The reader is also asked this question: How many jars would we have fetched? How much credit would we have given the prophet?

The last verse does not seem to add much, because the widow's behaviour is obvious: the oil must be sold in order to pay the creditor.[9] The remark on the miracle's usefulness leads to a deeper question. How is this miracle useful for *the faithful* in general? Why does Elisha choose to relieve this woman's troubles in this manner? Why didn't he organise a collection? Or if Elisha wanted to demonstrate God's power, why didn't he bring the husband back to life? (Elijah had already performed a resurrection before).

As always the answer is linked to Elisha's specific ministry. His miracles bear a message centred on Christ. The faithful live in a hostile world. Heartless men without mercy are legion. Illnesses and death strike the faithful and unfaithful alike. The hope of the faithful lies not within the short space of their existence but in the long term. On the promised day the Messiah

---

[9] For Bergen (p. 86) verse 7 serves "… to refocus attention on Elisha. The woman's voice is silent, and we hear only Elisha's command ('go, sell')."

will establish his kingdom.[10] In the meantime the faithful must remain confident and reject all discouragement. The widow loses her husband, but keeps her children. Life and family will continue. The future is assured.

Christ was victorious over death on the cross. Death, nevertheless, still rules the earth, but its term is fixed. When Christ returns he will re-establish everything. No good deed will be lost, no glass of water given with compassion will be forgotten (Matt 25:39-45). The promise is clear. Christ is worthy of trust. The last judgment will provide the final verification, when the door is closed. It will no longer be possible to add other good works. We must accomplish during this life *"...the good works, which God prepared beforehand that we should walk in them."* (Eph 2:10).

---

[10] One of the messianic signs is the cancellation of debts and the freeing of prisoners (Luke 4:18; Nelson p. 175). The sabbatical year and the jubilee are such types of liberation.

ELISHA AND THE SHUNAMMITE (2 KINGS 4:8-37)

This story is a second witness to the aid Elisha gives to a woman regarding her child or children. The story of the widow (4:1-7) and that of the Shunammite (4:8-37) follow one another and share one and the same theme.

1. In the first story Elisha helps a widow, who has just lost her husband, to avoid losing her two children. In the second story the prophet helps the Shunammite, deserted by a distant husband, to have a child, and then to get it back after its death.

2. In the first story Elisha saves two children, whereas in the second, he gives the same child to its mother twice (birth and resurrection).

The two stories, however, also contain several contrasts, although basically their messages complement each other.

1. The social context of the two women is very different. The first is poor, in debt, and her goods are limited to a bottle of oil, whereas the second is well-to-do, has no wants, and she declines Elisha's offer to speak to the king or the general on her behalf. She can be generous in her hospitality to Elisha on his travels, and offer him a furnished room which is permanently reserved for him. The background of the widow is unknown, but the Shunammite is a *"woman of high rank."*

2. Regarding the family, the widow has just lost her husband, but has two children; the Shunammite has an elderly husband, but suffers from her childlessness.

3. The two women's behaviour and their relationship to Elisha are basically quite different. Indeed both women turn to Elisha when confronted with a tragedy, but that is the only thing they have in common. The widow seems passive and dependent on the prophet. When the miracle takes place she approaches Elisha to find out what will happen afterwards, despite the fact that plain common sense should suffice to guide her (it was only necessary to sell the oil and pay the debt). On the other hand, the Shunammite is independent and

enterprising. She urges Elisha to accept a meal; she persuades her husband to build a permanent room for the prophet; she rushes to Elisha when her son dies, without informing her husband. She also neglects Gehazi: when Elisha sends his staff to be placed on the child's face, the woman urges him to come in person. The Shunammite appears to contradict Elisha several times: when he announces the birth of the child (*"No, my lord. Man of God, do not lie to your maidservant!"* 4:16); at the instant of its death (*"So she said, "Did I ask a son of my lord? Did I not say, 'Do not deceive me'?"*4.28); when Elisha entrusts his staff to his servant (*"And the mother of the child said, 'As the LORD lives, and as your soul lives, I will not leave you.' So he arose and followed her.* 4:30).[1]

4. On the spiritual level a great act of faith is required of the widow; whereas the general affection of the Shunammite for the prophet seems to suffice (she welcomes Elisha during his travels and goes to him when her child dies). Elisha offers what is needed (a child, the life of her son) without asking her for anything particular, in spite of her doubts.[2]

5. From the literary point of view, the first story is simple and short, whereas the second is long and complex.[3] The Shunammite's story contains two "miraculous" interventions by Elisha: the birth of a child (4:8-17), then its resurrection (4:18-37).

---

[1] Mary E. Shields emphasises the independence and authority of the Shunammite with numerous examples ("Subverting a Man of God, Elevating a Woman: Role and Power Reversals in 2 Kings 4" in: *Journal for the Study of the Old Testament* 58, 1993, pp. 59-69). Nevertheless, the story does not—as Shields does—allow for the confirmation that the Shunammite dominates Elisha.

[2] The manner in which the two women are blessed illustrates two aspects of the divine blessings. The "new birth" is a gift of Christ, for which the beneficiary does not do anything special, content to receive by faith the expiation of Jesus. On the other hand, the good works carried out by a Christian require a regular commitment and will be rewarded at the Last Judgment. The widow illustrates the final blessing and the Shunammite illustrates salvation from eternal perdition.

[3] "This story is also the first one in the Elisha corpus that presents a character other than Elisha who is portrayed with definite complexity" (Bergen p. 88).

The complexity of the Shunammite's story stems in part from the baffling conduct of the two principal persons. The behaviour of Elisha and of the Shunammite can be considered either as exemplary or as improper.

1. The Shunammite receives the prophet generously, then runs to him the moment her child dies, yet seems to doubt the prophet's word and acts.

2. Elisha performs one of the greatest miracles in the history of man, because death is the most tenacious enemy and the last to be destroyed (1 Cor 15:26). Only four people other than Jesus restored a person to life: Elijah, Elisha, Peter and Paul. The resurrection of the Shunammite's son is thus one of the most luminous pages of the revelation. In spite of this the prophet does not seem to act with the same ease here as in the other stories. For once Elisha faces defeat. The staff which he has his servant carry to the child has no effect (4:31). This setback is just the start, the tip of the iceberg. Behind the failure of the staff lies an entire set of difficulties which are linked mainly to a limited knowledge of the woman's needs. Particularly when the Shunammite comes to implore the prophet after the death of her child, Elisha confesses his ignorance: *"Let her alone; for her soul is in deep distress, and the LORD has hidden it from me, and has not told me"* (4:27). At the beginning of the story Elisha appears not to recognise the real and obvious need of the woman, because Gehazi informs him that *"Actually, she has no son, and her husband is old"* (4:14).

The behaviour of Elisha and the Shunammite is complex, but it becomes clear when we understand the woman's true need. The Shunammite is probably not suffering from sterility, but from a *genetic defect* which affects her children. The argument for this hypothesis is presented in the detailed analysis (see pp. 101-102). The behaviour of Elisha and the Shunammite, far from being complex or dubious, is instead quite remarkable.

The structure of the narration is linked to the geographical context. The story begins and ends in the dwelling of the

Shunammite. The centre of the text is marked by a rapid journey from Shunem to Carmel and back.[4]

A.1	The widow offers Elisha a place to stay (4:8-10)
B.1	Dialogue on Elisha's acts in favour of the widow. She is promised a son (4:11-17)
C.1	Rapid journey to Elisha (4:18-24)
D.1	Gehazi is sent ahead to the widow (4:25-26)
E	The widow expresses her distress and Elisha confesses his ignorance of its cause (4:27-28)
D.2	Gehazi is sent ahead of Elisha and the widow (4:29-30)
C.2	Rapid return to Shunem (4:31)
B.2	Elisha's intercession on behalf of the widow's son. He is restored to life (4:32-36)
A.2	The widow receives her living son from Elisha (4:37)

Reception of the prophet (4:8-10)

[8]Now it happened one day that Elisha went to Shunem, where there was a notable woman, and she persuaded him to eat some food. So it was, as often as he passed by, he would turn in there to eat some food. [9]And she said to her husband, "Look now, I know that this is a holy man of God, who passes by us regularly. [10]Please, let us make a small upper room on the wall; and let us put a bed for him there, and a table and a chair and a lampstand; so it will be, whenever he comes to us, he can turn in there."

These verses introduce the story. They allow the author to emphasize the *exceptional* hospitality shown to Elisha by the Shunammite and the entirely positive relationship between them. This point must be emphasised, as it orients the interpretation of the following story and prevents a negative sense of "debatable"

---

[4] This story also contains two other structures which have only three parts each. One places verses 18-28 in the centre (see p. 43); the other rests on the marker "one day" (4:8, 11, 18; Nelson p. 173).

behaviour of the woman or of a distant relationship between Elisha and the Shunammite.

The woman's affection for Elisha is instantaneous, permanent and deep. It is instantaneous, manifesting itself in the first journey to Shunem (*"one day"*). It is permanent, because from that day the woman welcomes him at every journey (*"So it was, as often as he passed by"*). It is deep, because the woman not only welcomes him for meals but also provides lodging. A room is specially constructed for him, and is permanently at his disposal.[5] No one else stays there. It is comfortably furnished (*"a bed for him there, and a table and a chair and a lampstand"*).[6]

The woman plans everything, and her enthusiasm convinces her husband. Elisha accepts the offer, because he recognises this woman's affection *for God* (the Shunammite takes him in because he is *a holy man of God*). Even though other families may have wished to invite the prophet, he goes every time to the Shunammite to honour her consecration.[7]

---

[5] Sometimes tents or temporary rooms made of wood were set up on flat roofs, but in this case a permanent habitation which was probably constructed by raising the protective walls.

[6] Nelson's eulogy (pp. 172-173) deserves to be quoted: "She is a powerful and admirable character. She is a woman of substance (v. 8) capable of building and furnishing a substantial guest lodge. She knows how to take advantage of circumstances (v. 10). She is an independent woman unwilling to take favours, relying on kinfolk rather than powerful strangers (v. 13), not subject to unrealistic hopes (v. 16). She knows how to behave properly (vv. 15, 27, 37) and speak properly (v. 16) towards prophets. She knows the value of silence at the right moment (vv. 23, 26), but can make a convincing and impassioned appeal when the time is ripe (v. 28). She is engagingly maternal (v. 20), but in a crisis acts decisively. Revealing by her actions in verse 21 that her plan is already formed, she hastens straight to Elisha, refusing to talk to subordinates, refusing to be turned aside from what she has planned for the prophet, and in the end is proved right by circumstances. She is one of the Old Testament's most attractive characters." Bergen (p. 90) compares the Shunammite to Queen Victoria. Thus, the respect which this wealthy and admirable woman shows Elisha (twice she kneels at his feet) serves to enhance and increase the prestige of the prophet.

[7] The interest of the narrator in these first verses is not centred on Elisha. Nevertheless a comparison of the attitude of Elisha to that of Christ is interesting: "Elisha, while manifesting such power towards others, has nothing himself during all of this time. He is poor, while at the same time he enriches many people. Although he seems to have all sorts of things, in

The Promise of a Birth (4:11-17)

> [11]*And it happened one day that he came there, and he turned in to the upper room and lay down there.* [12]*Then he said to Gehazi his servant, "Call this Shunammite woman." When he had called her, she stood before him.* [13]*And he said to him, "Say now to her, 'Look, you have been concerned for us with all this care. What can I do for you? Do you want me to speak on your behalf to the king or to the commander of the army?'" She answered, "I dwell among my own people."* [14]*So he said, "What then is to be done for her?" And Gehazi answered, "Actually, she has no son, and her husband is old."* [15]*So he said, "Call her." When he had called her, she stood in the doorway.* [16]*Then he said, "About this time next year you shall embrace a son." And she said, "No, my lord. Man of God, do not lie to your maidservant!"* [17]*But the woman conceived, and bore a son when the appointed time had come, of which Elisha had told her.*

There are three astounding things contained in these verses. The first is the apparent *ignorance* of Elisha regarding the woman's needs. In order to recompense the Shunammite for her hospitality, the prophet proposes to speak on her behalf to "*the king or to the commander of the army*" (4:13),[8] but this does not correspond to her needs because she is wealthy and well integrated ("*a notable woman*" 4.8; "*I dwell among my own people.*" 4:13).[9] When Elisha asks him about the woman's needs, Gehazi tells him what any traveller would have very quickly found out: "*Actually, she has no son, and her husband is old*" (4:14).[10] Elisha then announces the imminent birth of a

---

reality he has nothing at all. He receives free gifts and succour for all his daily needs, from people for whom he at the same time develops resources which are over and above the means of mortal men. ... Our prophet shows us the path of Jesus, like a reflection." (Bellett pp. 20-21).

8   "Since the events in the desert of Edom, Elisha probably had a certain influence at the Samarian court" (John H. Alexander p. 132)

9   According to Gray (p. 444): "The suggestion of Elisha... can only mean that there were certain state burdens on the community for fiscal and military purposes, imposed regionally by Solomon (e.g. 1 Kings 4) and retained after the disruption of the kingdom." For Robinson (p. 43): "She was unwilling to receive special treatment. Her security lay in the close-knit loyalty of the local community."

10   "Barrenness was the greatest reproach to a wife, and the promise of a child correspondingly the greatest blessing." (Robinson p. 43).

child to his hostess. Was he unaware of or did he forget such an obvious need? This seems unusual coming from a man who normally not only knows everything but also regularly eats at the family table and has a permanent lodging especially for him.

The second surprise is the woman's reply: *"No, my lord. Man of God, do not lie to your maidservant!"* Does the woman doubt the prophet's words? Yet the narrator has just emphasised her affection and the admiration for him.

The attitudes of these persons can be better understood if we assume that the woman's problem was not sterility but rather a genetic malady which prevented the normal development of the child. The woman might have had children previously, but lost them because of a congenital illness that afflicted them. The announcement of a new birth does not please the Shunammite, because she does not wish to grieve yet again. She says "Do not deceive me" in anticipation of another disappointment. Her reaction at the child's death confirms this approach: *"Did I ask a son of my lord? Did I not say, 'Do not deceive me'"* 4:28.[11]

The hypothesis of a congenital disease also explains Elisha's behaviour. He does not immediately speak of another birth, because he knows of the woman's past suffering. His frequent contacts with the family have informed him about the problems of the past, apart from the fact that Elisha is the prophet of knowledge. On the other hand, Gehazi does not know the family well. In other accounts he has confessed his limited knowledge and made mistakes in his reasoning. When Elisha asks him about the woman's needs Gehazi blurts out the first thing he sees: the woman does not have any children and her husband is old. A man with limited discernment stops at appearances. Because the woman does not have children and her husband is old, a child will solve the problem. This is obviously not the Shunammite's opinion.[12]

---

[11] Among the different genetic deficiencies which can cause death, it is possible that the child could have suffered from *Cystic fibrosis*, an illness characterised by chronic respiratory trouble. Actually, *"the child sneezed seven times"* (4:35) the moment it came back to life, which might indicate the permanent healing of the condition.

[12] Those who prefer the hypothesis of the woman's sterility are confronted with difficulties. The three main persons in the story would be behaving

If this interpretation is correct, then Elisha has probably already envisaged not only the birth but subsequent problems. This is perhaps why he proposes to speak to *"the king or to the commander of the army"* on behalf of the woman, not in the sense that he was going to speak to Joram and to his general, because the two could do nothing, but to *the King of kings,* the Messiah, who is the commander of the *heavenly* army (cf. Jos 5:15). In other words, Elisha is proposing to intercede in this woman's favour for her basic need.[13]

The third surprising element of this story is the communication between Elisha and the woman, and the role of Gehazi in it. When Elisha wants to reward the woman, he asks Gehazi to call her and when she appears before him, the prophet asks his servant to transmit his message to the woman: *"Then he said to Gehazi his servant, 'Call this Shunammite woman.' When he had called her, ... he said to him, 'Say now to her'"* 4:12-13). The prophet uses his servant as one uses an interpreter. Doesn't Elisha speak the same language as she? On the other hand, on two occasions the prophet also uses his servant as an intermediary to call the woman and speak to her (4:15, 36). If it were a linguistic problem, Elisha could have spared himself an interpreter and rendered her resurrected son to her directly (4:36).

The topography and the cultural context clarify the relationship between the woman and the prophet. Elisha calls for the Shunammite from his room on the second floor, and she comes to the foot of the stairs. It was improper for a woman to enter a man's dwelling. Rather than raising his voice the prophet

---

differently than recounted elsewhere in the narrative. The Shunammite would be doubting the words of the prophet, despite having demonstrated her deep and lasting affection (an affection which is again confirmed afterwards, cf. 8:1-2). Elisha does not know the need any passing traveller could discover, despite knowing the most intimate secrets of others (see "The Prophet of Knowledge" p. 19). Gehazi would thus be more discerning than his master, although he is off track afterwards. On the other hand, the hypothesis of a congenital disease allows us to understand the three persons' behaviour in the light of the previously outlined characteristics, as well as other details of this story.

[13] At the chiasm of the narration, these verses correspond to Elisha's intercession for the deceased son (points B.1 and B.2; see p. 100).

asks his servant to transmit his message to the woman (*"What can I do for you?"*). Then Elisha asks Gehazi privately, as he is at his side, what she wants (*"What then is to be done for her?"*). He replies discreetly to his master that she has no children. Elisha calls the woman to him, she climbs the stairs and stops in front of his door. There he announces directly, without going through Gehazi that she will soon give birth to a child.[14]

Why does the narrator transmit this conversation in so much detail? Could he not have gone directly from the calling of v. 12 to the announcement of the birth in v. 16?[15] At least three reasons justify the presence of these verses. First, they underscore the characters of the persons and their reciprocal relationships. The woman shows great respect for the prophet, and Gehazi, limited as he is in his discernment, stops at appearances in the context of the close relationship.[16] Next, the presence of another man (Gehazi) between a married woman and the voyager whom she receives, and who announces the birth of a child to her, "was important... to inhibit mockers, jesters, and infidels of later generations from abusing this story of Elisha and the Shunammite, and from casting doubt on the prophet's purity and the lady's chastity" (Yannai p. 131). Lastly, the presence of a third person between the prophet and the believing woman illustrates a spiritual lesson which we shall examine at the end of this study, where we shall develop the theme of intermediaries (see p. 111).

---

[14] It is not necessary to reverse the indications of location (first "at the doorway" v. 15, then "before him" v. 12), as Y. Yannai proposes, in an otherwise stimulating article: "Elisha and the Shunammite (2 Kings 4 :8-37): A Case of Homoeoteleuton, or a Text Emendation by Ancient Masoretes?" in *Estudios masoreticos*, 1983, pp. 123-135. Certain commentators suggest that the woman has withdrawn between v. 13 and v. 15 (Montgomery, quoted by Yannai p. 126).

[15] Montgomery (p. 374) names several commentators who omit verses 13 to 15 of the original story: Klostermann, Benzen, Stade, Haupt, Baumgarner, Gunkel, Gressmann.

[16] "The narrator insistently enforces a respectful distance between Elisha and the Shunammite" (Long "A Figure at the Gate: Readers, Reading, and Biblical Theologians" p. 169). Regarding Gehazi, Yannai (p. 127) finds that "The servant's eye is earthly, covetous, and materialistic (as evident from Naaman's story, detailed in the following chapter)."

"About this time next year you shall embrace a son." This promise echoes the one made to Abraham and Sarah regarding Isaac (Gen 18:10).[17] In both cases (1) the father is old, (2) the woman reacts strangely (Sarah laughs, the Shunammite protests), (3) great hospitality is shown to the divine messengers (Abraham feeds the three angels; the Shunammite has constructed a permanent lodging for Elisha), (4) the birth is announced for the *following year,* a precision one does not find in the other announcements (Jacob, Samson, Samuel, John the Baptist and Jesus). Furthermore the child is taken away and returned as if by resurrection (sacrifice of Isaac: Gen 22; Heb 11:19).[18] Amongst the differences we note that in Genesis, the emphasis is on the miraculous birth (Sarah was sterile, which was not the case with the Shunammite) and in Kings the son of the Shunammite is truly brought back to life, whereas Isaac did not have to die on Mount Moriah. The proper names in Genesis are those of family members (Abraham, Sarah and Isaac), and not of angels, whereas in Kings God's messenger and his servant are mentioned by name (Elisha and Gehazi), but the members of the family are not. Thus the birth of the Shunammite's son announces a new step in the divine plan, a plan which is not limited to a family (Abraham) or a line (Isaac), but is open to all families who exercise faith. The accent is no longer on physical birth but the resurrection and victory over original sin. The fundamental role is not played by the human actors, but by God's messenger.

---

[17] "This chapter, 2 Kings 4, is traditionally bound with Genesis 18:22... In Judaism, the former constitutes the *Haftarah* of the latter, namely, it is the portion of the prophets which is read in the synagogue (on the Sabbath and holy days) immediately after the reading of the *Parashah* (i.e., the *Torah* portion) of *Wa-Yera,* comprising Genesis 18:22" (Yannai p. 130).

[18] "Isaac, first brought to life in Sarah's womb by the power of God, was returned to Abraham as if by resurrection. The same happens here. The sentence of death is passed on the promised child, but he is resurrected by the same power of God, through Elisha." (Bellett p. 24). H.R. (pp. 66-67), Nelson (p. 171), Smith (*Elie et Elisée,* p. 137) also mention the link to Genesis 18.

Death and the Call for Help (4:18-28)

> [18]*And the child grew. Now it happened one day that he went out to his father, to the reapers.* [19]*And he said to his father, "My head, my head!" So he said to a servant, "Carry him to his mother."* [20]*When he had taken him and brought him to his mother, he sat on her knees till noon, and then died.*
>
> [21]*And she went up and laid him on the bed of the man of God, shut the door upon him, and went out.* [22]*Then she called to her husband, and said, "Please send me one of the young men and one of the donkeys, that I may run to the man of God and come back.* [23]*So he said, "Why are you going to him today? It is neither the New Moon nor the Sabbath." And she said, "It is well."* [24]*Then she saddled a donkey, and said to her servant, "Drive, and go forward; do not slacken the pace for me unless I tell you."* [25]*And so she departed, and went to the man of God at Mount Carmel.*
>
> *So it was, when the man of God saw her afar off, that he said to his servant Gehazi, "Look, the Shunammite woman!* [26]*Please run now to meet her, and say to her, 'Is it well with you? Is it well with your husband? Is it well with the child?'" And she answered, "It is well."* [27]*Now when she came to the man of God at the hill, she caught him by the feet, but Gehazi came near to push her away. But the man of God said, "Let her alone; for her soul is in deep distress, and the LORD has hidden it from me, and has not told me."* [28]*So she said, "Did I ask a son of my lord? Did I not say, 'Do not deceive me?'"*

"The narrative seems to close with the boy's birth, but a third 'one day' in verse 18 drives the plot further" (Nelson p. 173). "*And the child grew.*": The child's entire life is summarised in these few words. The narrator does not even indicate the child's age when he dies. His interest obviously lies elsewhere.[19] The reactions of the father and mother regarding the illness and death of their child are described in much greater detail.

The father is passive. When the child complains about his head, he sends him to his mother. He himself does not move, and

---

[19] "The narrator transports us through tremendous space and time: from birth to death without a significant childhood" (Long: *2 Kings*, p. 57). When the child is suffering the father shows no interest in this being with which he does not seem to have forged any bond.

asks a servant to bring the child.[20] When the mother informs him of her intention to go see the man of God, the father seems to have forgotten the child's pain and is surprised by his wife's journey (*"So he said, 'Why are you going to him today? It is neither the New Moon nor the Sabbath'"* 4:23). How is the father's attitude to be understood? Were the symptoms of the illness insignificant when the child complained about its head?[21] Nevertheless the father sends the child to his mother, and the repetition of the child's complaint (*"my head, my head"*) is emphatic. Is the father completely insensitive to his son? If the couple had already lost several children and perhaps even all of their children because of a similar ailment, one could comprehend a certain paternal detachment. "The illness strikes once again", he might be saying, with resignation. When he addresses his wife he does not mention the health of the child, a forbidden topic for the couple.

The mother's attitude is the opposite of the father's.[22] She watches over the child until it dies (*"he sat on her knees till noon, and then died"* 4:20). She then places the body of her child on the bed of the man of God, indicating that she is not retreating from the face of death, but expecting something from the prophet as she runs quickly to him.[23] The woman does not delay and orders her servant not to stop anywhere (4:24). When the child's father asks about the reason for her journey,[24] she does not even tell him of the child's death so as not to lose time in useless lamentations which in any case the father would not wish to hear. *"It is well"*, she says, without giving any reasons for the journey of her last hope. At any rate, no explanation

---

[20] Nelson (p. 173) thinks that he might have been too old to carry the infant himself.

[21] Cogan (p. 57) and Robinson (p. 44) suggest an insolation.

[22] For Nelson (p. 172), "Her husband is described as a sort of 'hollow man' whose character defects serve to highlight her virtues."

[23] The distance between Shunem and Carmel is estimated at between 24 km (Robinson p. 45) and 50 km (Nelson p. 174), the difference being due to the uncertainty about the exact location of the prophet's residence.

[24] *"It is neither the New Moon nor the Sabbath"* (4:23). Robinson p. 44: "These were the rest days when no work was done and so visits to consult a prophet were usually made on them." For Bergen (p. 99) "The husband is of the opinion that Elisha's role is limited to new moon or Sabbath").

would have convinced someone like him, who apparently had long since given up.

When the Shunammite meets Gehazi, sent by Elisha to get the latest news, she repeats that all is well, not wanting to explain to the servant what she wishes to communicate directly to Elisha. The woman wants to go as quickly as possible to the only person who can still save her son. Her faith and behaviour are remarkable. Her "lies" are not meant to deceive, but to prevent any delays. On the other hand, are her words truly lies, because hope remains as long as the prophet has not yet said anything which would exclude resurrection?[25]

The Shunammite throws herself at the prophet's feet in supplication. Her words appear to imply a certain challenge (*"Did I ask a son of my lord? Did I not say, 'Do not deceive me'?"* v. 28), but they could also be an expression of her confidence: "I did not ask for a son in the past", she tells the prophet; "You gave me a gift. Now act consequently."[26]

In the central section of the narration (4:18-28; see structure p. 42), Elisha is passive. He acts before v. 18 and after v. 28, but here he is only a spectator.[27] The narrator does not use his name, but identifies him simply as *"the man of God"*.

This is the only instance in his ministry when Elisha expresses limitation of knowledge. He does not know the reason for the Shunammite's visit: *"for her soul is in deep distress, and*

---

[25] Several commentators interpret the *"it is well"* as an expression of the woman's faith (Alexander p. 134; Fereday: *Elisha the Prophet,* p. 47; H. R. p. 67). The same goes for Bellett (p. 25): "The words 'it is well' are the language of faith and the expression of a sure and certain hope for the resurrection of the dead." Nevertheless, Elisha speaks of the "bitterness" of his soul (4:27), a word which expresses profound sadness.

[26] The Shunammite characterises the attitude of a committed believer. She shows profound respect for God, for example with her welcome of Elisha and her position at prophet's feet. She nevertheless dares to express her doubts and fears. She does not challenge the prophet as Shields ("Subverting a Man of God, Elevating a Woman: Role and Power Reversals in 2 Kings 4") and Long ("A Figure at the Gate...") think: "The transformed Shunammite, who now challenges Elisha's dominance" (p. 170).

[27] Elisha contents himself with sending Gehazi to get information, but does not receive any.

the LORD has hidden it from me, and has not told me" (4:27).[28]
This, however, does not mean that Elisha does not discern
anything at all. He sees the woman's trouble from afar, because
he sends Gehazi towards her in order to find out news about her:
*"Is it well with you? Is it well with your husband? Is it well with
the child?"* (4:26). The woman's hurried approach is unusual.[29]
When she throws herself at his feet, Elisha discerns signs of
suffering, contrary to Gehazi who, insensitive as he is, wants to
push her back. Finally, when the Shunammite says a few words,
Elisha understands the reason for her bitterness.

This limitation of his "omniscience" is not a handicap to his
ministry. Elisha knows that the Lord is with him, and on the
announcement of the child's death he knows what he must do.
Once again, Elisha announces Christ, even within this limitation,
because Jesus also knew everything, except the date of his return
(Matt 24:36).

The "Failure" of the Staff (4:29-31)

> [29]*Then he said to Gehazi, "Get yourself ready, and take my
> staff in your hand, and be on your way. If you meet anyone, do
> not greet him; and if anyone greets you, do not answer him; but
> lay my staff on the face of the child."* [30]*And the mother of the
> child said, "As the LORD lives, and as your soul lives, I will not
> leave you." So he arose and followed her.* [31]*Now Gehazi went
> on ahead of them, and laid the staff on the face of the child; but
> there was neither voice nor hearing. Therefore he went back to
> meet him, and told him, saying, "The child has not awakened."*

Elisha orders his staff to be placed on the face of the child
and that it be done quickly (*"If you meet anyone, do not greet
him; and if anyone greets you, do not answer him; but lay my
staff on the face of the child."* 4:29). Obviously utmost urgency

---

[28] *"The Lord has hidden it from me, and has not told me."* This remark is
particularly meaningful when one recalls that the story of Elisha does not
contain any of God's words to Elisha. Thus the author, who is unable to
mention the innumerable words of God to Elisha, limits himself to
mentioning the only exception. This remark is at the heart of the chiasm
(see p. 100).

[29] High-ranking persons try to move with dignity, without hurry, thus
showing their mastery over men and circumstances.

is required. However, the staff does not bring the child back to life. (*"...there was neither voice nor hearing. Therefore he went back to meet him, and told him, saying, 'The child has not awakened.'"* 4:31). Why this failure? Was Elisha mistaken about the "influence" of his staff?[30] Did Gehazi neglect a detail in the execution of his orders?[31] These are probably the wrong questions to ask. Why speak of failure? Gehazi sees it that way, but the servant is often mistaken in his interpretations. Elisha never announced that the staff would bring the child back to life. He merely wished to signal to the father and those close to him that things were not over yet, and that one should not yet bury the child; in that country, burials were carried out rapidly after death. The mother had probably placed the child's body in the prophet's room, which no one else entered, for the same reason. This prevented the body from being buried immediately. Elisha promptly sends Gehazi with his staff to prevent the husband, who might be alerted by the odour of the cadaver, from prematurely burying the child.

How should we understand the words of the Shunammite when she affirms *"As the Lord lives, and as your soul lives, I will not leave you."* (4:30)? The woman realises that the staff will not return her child to life, and that the prophet will have to come in person. Is she trying to put pressure on Elisha to make him leave quickly (she would not leave the prophet's dwelling until his departure)? It is more likely that she is expressing her confidence in the prophet's procedure. As Gehazi has left to prevent the burial, she can relax and return at ease together with the prophet. She can keep him company, and see to his needs in Gehazi's absence, for example by preparing his meals.

---

[30] Shields: "Subverting a Man of God, Elevating a Woman: Role and Power Reversals in 2 Kings 4" in *JSOT* 58 (1993) p. 65.

[31] According to Jewish tradition, Gehazi failed due to lack of faith (Slotki; *Kings*, p. 187, quoted by Bergen, note 160 p. 102). John H. Alexander feels the same way (pp. 135-137): "If Gehazi had dared, he could have told all passers-by to accompany him and witness the miracle for which he would be the instrument by placing the staff on the child's face! Elisha had probably forbidden him to speak to anyone because he knew his servant's predilections very well."

The Resurrection of the Child (4:32-37)

> [32]*When Elisha came into the house, there was the child, lying dead on his bed. [33]He went in therefore, shut the door behind the two of them, and prayed to the LORD. [34]And he went up and lay on the child, and put his mouth on his mouth, his eyes on his eyes, and his hands on his hands; and he stretched himself out on the child, and the flesh of the child became warm. [35]He returned and walked back and forth in the house, and again went up and stretched himself out on him; then the child sneezed seven times, and the child opened his eyes. [36]And he called Gehazi and said, "Call this Shunammite woman." So he called her. And when she came in to him, he said, "Pick up your son." [37]So she went in, fell at his feet, and bowed to the ground; then she picked up her son and went out.*

Elisha must intervene twice to bring the child to life. This double intervention is not the sign of difficulty or partial failure.[32] In fact, from the first contact, life is restored because the body becomes warm. Elisha must intervene twice because the child has a twofold problem: death and the genetic illness. To revive the child without healing its illness would have only kept death at bay for a few months. Elisha fills the body with warmth and also with the breath of life. He revives the body and at the same time removes its hereditary ailment.

The comparison between the resurrection accomplished by Elisha and the one by Elijah is interesting. The two men proceed in almost the same way: they lie upon the body of the child in their entire length, Elisha twice and Elijah three times.[33] Yet with Elijah there is no sign during the first two interventions, because Elijah is the prophet of perseverance. With him everything takes time. On the other hand, with Elisha, there is immediate improvement. His interventions are testimonies of perfection. This explains why the healing is not only temporal (with the

---

[32] John H. Alexander (p. 137) thinks that the story teaches perseverance in prayer. Gray (p. 447) feels it was "An act of relaxation after intense physical and spiritual concentration which had temporarily exhausted him". As for T. R. Hobbs (*Word Biblical Commentary* p. 53) "the walking back and forth reflects a sense of agitation on the part of the prophet at the failure to wake up the dead boy."

[33] For more details on parallels, see point 4 p. 36.

restoration of life), but also permanent (healing of the genetic disease).

Elisha's intervention announces the Messiah who comes to heal people, not only of their physical ills but also of their sinful nature inherited from Adam. With his death Christ saves men from eternal perdition. Jesus, like Elisha, heals people of *hereditary* illnesses. Elisha's body stretched over the child's body (mouth on mouth, eye to eye, hands on hands) gives life fully, just as the body of Jesus, offered completely on the cross for mankind, gives eternal life.

Every gesture of Elisha has its reason, which is also true for Jesus. The latter healed a blind man at Bethesda in two stages (Mark 8:22-26) to *illustrate* the two fundamental steps of his ministry. During a first stage Jesus multiplies the miracles in order to witness to his divinity. Then when Peter recognises his lordship (Mark 8.29), he begins a new stage and announces the Passion (*"And He began to teach them that the Son of Man must suffer many things, and be rejected by the elders and chief priests and scribes, and be killed, and after three days rise again."* Mark 8:31). The miracle in two steps immediately precedes Peter's confession and a new direction to Jesus' ministry. The miracle illustrates on the physical level that which takes place on the spiritual level. A double intervention by Christ is necessary to give the disciples a complete view of his ministry.[34]

The resurrection of the Shunammite's son also recalls the resurrection, carried out by Jesus, of the son of a widow in Nain, a location which may be identical with Shunem. Jesus merely *touches* the coffin (Luke 7:11-17; see p. 25).

In conclusion let us return to the theme of the intermediaries. Throughout the story the Shunammite rejects all persons and objects coming between herself and Elisha. She continually puts aside her husband, Elisha's servant and his staff. She is interested only in the prophet. Her attachment is complete from start to finish: first the welcome of the prophet into her home (4:8-10), then the hasty voyage after her child's death (4:22-26),

---

[34]   D. Arnold: "Une guérison en deux étapes" in *Ichthus* 135 (1986) pp. 21-24.

and finally her refusal to leave him (4:30). The woman's attachment to Elisha is remarkable and should stimulate our attachment to the Messiah. We cannot escape from eternal damnation without attaching ourselves completely to Jesus Christ. He is the alpha and omega, the first and the last, the beginning and end of all things (Rev 22:13).

Let us also note that the indirect communication between Elisha and the Shunammite at the beginning of the story, in that the prophet often addresses the woman through Gehazi (see p. 102), possibly illustrates the communication between God and men *before* the coming of the Messiah, when the Lord spoke to men through his representatives the prophets. Perhaps it illustrates even better the relationship between God and men *after* the coming of the Messiah, when the Holy Spirit is the intermediary through whom Christ reveals himself to mankind.

TWO MIRACLES WITH FOOD
(2 KINGS 4:38–44)

The narrator moves on to two short accounts (four and three verses) which describe the miraculous interventions of Elisha concerning food. Elisha once again helps human beings: not two isolated individuals, but now two communities.

These two stories form a parenthesis, or transition, because the two which follow once again deal with individuals (the story of Naaman and that of the labourer who loses his axe: 2 Kings 5:1-6:7). The brevity of the two miracles with food could tempt us to neglect them, inasmuch as they are bracketed by two long stories (that of the Shunammite and that of Naaman).[1] Nevertheless, these two "food" miracles have a crucial structural position, situated as they are in the centre of the Elisha account (see chiasm p. 42). These two miracles dealing with food carry important messages.

Purification of Soup and Multiplication of Loaves (4:38–44)

38 And Elisha returned to Gilgal, and there was a famine in the land. Now the sons of the prophets were sitting before him; and he said to his servant, "Put on the large pot, and boil stew for the sons of the prophets." 39 So one went out into the field to gather herbs, and found a wild vine, and gathered from it a lapful of wild gourds, and came and sliced them into the pot of stew, though they did not know what they were. 40 Then they served it to the men to eat. Now it happened, as they were eating

---

[1]   Furthermore, these "food" miracles only fill a temporary need (hunger), whereas the long stories deal with permanent aid. Bergen (p. 107) sees a link between the first food miracle and the story of the Shunammite: "The movement of the plot is in this way very similar to the previous story. Elisha provided food in time of famine, as he provided a son in time of barrenness. Something goes wrong, which is not directly Elisha's fault. Nevertheless blame is (correctly) placed at his feet. He then is obligated to do another miracle (again depicted in rather non-miraculous terms) in order to make his original offering not turn into disaster."

the stew, that they cried out and said, "Man of God, there is death in the pot!" And they could not eat it. ⁴¹So he said, "Then bring some flour." And he put it into the pot, and said, "Serve it to the people, that they may eat." And there was nothing harmful in the pot.

⁴² Then a man came from Baal-Shalishah, and brought the man of God bread of the firstfruits, twenty loaves of barley bread, and newly ripened grain in his knapsack. And he said, "Give it to the people, that they may eat." ⁴³But his servant said, "What? Shall I set this before one hundred men?" He said again, "Give it to the people, that they may eat; for thus says the Lord: 'They shall eat and have some left over.'" ⁴⁴So he set it before them; and they ate and had some left over, according to the word of the Lord.

The two stories develop the same theme: Elisha intervenes miraculously to feed two groups of men. There are many points in common, but also obvious contrasts.

1. The two stories start with the arrival of one person to a place (Elisha in the first story; a man in the second). The first place is identified (Gilgal), but not the second. Nevertheless, each story contains the name of a place: Gilgal (destination of the first traveller) and Baal-Shalishah (place of departure of the second traveller). *Gilgal* has a positive connotation, because the name recalls the conquest of the Promised Land under Joshua, whereas *Baal-Shalishah* is a reminder of infidelity and alliances with the pagan deity Baal.

2. The first community which benefits from the miracle is identified (the sons of the prophets), but not the second, which remains anonymous.

3. Elisha begins by asking one of his servants[2] to provide food. In both cases, he merely orders the distribution but does not bring anything himself. This is a constant characteristic of prophets: their calling consists in transmitting God's words and not in providing material goods. Jesus and his apostles did the same.

4. The first order involves an *initiative* to accomplish the impossible (the man adds wild gourds to the soup, but ends

---

[2] Gehazi is not mentioned in the two accounts, whereas he plays an important role in the stories of the Shunammite (4:8-37) and Naaman (Chpt. 5).

up ruining what was still good), whereas the second order provokes a *question* on how to accomplish the apparently impossible.

5. The first miracle consists in neutralising something bad and the second in multiplying what is good. The first miracle is necessary because of pollution and the second due to lack. Yet the presence of famine is only mentioned in the first story. Each story involves a small but insufficient quantity of good food at the beginning: flour and loaves. In the first story the bit which is good is purified and in the second the bit which is good is multiplied.

The Meaning of the Two Miracles

The Purification of the Stew

At the heart of Elisha's ministry the reader can discern a message which emphasises the ministry of Jesus Christ. The purification of the stew echoes the purification of the waters of Jericho (2:19-22): two fine, white foodstuffs (salt and flour) are thrown into a liquid (the spring and the soup) to eliminate pollution (sterility and death). The evil disappears when the good touches the bad. The new bowl touches the salt, which then touches the spring; the flour is thrown into the stew. The purification of the waters of Jericho announces the "mastery" over the inherited curse of original sin (see pp. 64-66). The case is the same here. The *wild* vine and the *wild* gourds[3] evoke the forbidden fruit of the garden of Eden. Because of one person's initiative, the entire community is contaminated.[4] The man and the community do not *know* these plants, just as Adam and Eve did not *know* evil, and did not have access to the tree of *knowledge* of good and evil. The flour (symbol of salvation) is

---

[3] Certain commentators (Jones p. 410-411; Robinson p. 47) identify these "gourds" as a plant called "citrullus colocynthus" which grows in the Jordan valley and produces yellow-green fruit the size of a large orange or a small melon. This fruit is known for its laxative effect. Eaten in large quantities, it can be fatal. This identification remains hypothetical (Bergen pp. 105-106).

[4] Bergen p. 106: "The man is clearly a fool, and should have known better... Renteria's suggestion that famine leads to the eating of unfamiliar food is possible."

different from the wild vine and gourds in the fact that it is produced by the work of man and not by nature. Flour is ground wheat, perhaps a symbol of Christ who was bruised for us. The white colour could symbolise Christ's pure and spotless work. Moreover, Christ is the bread of life. Flour also results from sowing and reaping, images of the long preparation necessary for Christ's coming. The prophets prophesied by their words and gestures, just as Elisha does. The flour is brought by people (the "*sons of prophets*"), but thrown into the stew by Elisha to illustrate the role both of God's people and of the Messiah for salvation.

The Multiplication of the Loaves

The multiplication of loaves accomplished by Elisha is without a doubt the most obvious christological miracle. Elisha fed one hundred men with only twenty loaves. Jesus performed a similar miracle, but in an even more extraordinary manner. He did so twice, by feeding larger crowds (five thousand and four thousand families), with less loaves (five and seven, as well as a few fish). Both with Jesus and Elisha there was so much that some food was left over (see p. 24).

Multiplication of food was carried out only by Elisha and Jesus. Other miracles dealt with food, but never in the form of a multiplication. There were several miracles of this type: (1) During the time of the Exodus, God saw to the nourishment of his people by sending manna and quail; (2) Elijah was fed by crows at the brook of Kerith; (3) The oil and flour of the widow in Zarephath never ran out (but did not increase); (4) The widow about to lose her children saw oil multiplied, not as food for her but rather as a commodity to be sold.

What meaning should be given to the *multiplication* of food performed by Elisha, then by Jesus? The loaves multiplied by Elisha are first fruits or offerings. They are special loaves, made from the first ears of wheat and reserved for the sacrificing priesthood (Lev 23:10, 17-20; Nm 18:13; Deut 18:4). These loaves are given to Elisha, a man of God, not a high priest but a prophet. However, it is possible that certain social laws concerning the support of priests also applied to prophets. Astonishingly, Elisha has these loaves distributed amongst the entire community. All of the men seemingly are suddenly consecrated and apt for ministry. By this gesture Elisha anticipates the new covenant in which all Christians are high priests (*"But you are a chosen generation, a royal priesthood, a holy nation, His own special people, that you may proclaim the praises of Him who called you out of darkness into His marvellous light"* 1 Peter 2:9). The whole people of God is sanctified and set apart by Christ and for him.

We also note that the first multiplication of loaves performed by Jesus takes place when he emphasises the commitment of his disciples. In the Gospels of Mark and Luke the miracle takes places just after the twelve have been sent *into mission* (Mark 6:7-13, 30-44; Luke 9:1-6, 10-17). This is the only miracle in which the disciples are actively associated with Jesus. The multiplication of the loaves thus illustrates the ministry of the apostles after Jesus' departure: that of preaching. They are charged with transmitting Christ's word, multiplying and distributing it to all who wish to receive it. It will be so abundant that there will always be some left over.

Conclusion

These two incidents involving food illustrate two aspects of Christ's work: the salvation performed by Christ and the salvation spread by the disciples through the action of the Holy Spirit. The stories may be short, but their message is fundamental.

THE HEALING OF NAAMAN
(2 KINGS 5)

The Naaman's account is familiar. A leper is healed after washing in the Jordan. The story is well known, but is it well understood? The author of 1–2 Kings, not content with summarising the event in one sentence, devotes an entire chapter to it. A number of details are given: ten persons or groups intervene; seven express themselves; poignant portraits are developed.[1]

The narration is alert, passionate, often surprising. Why heal the general of the enemy army? Why ask him to wash in the waters of the Jordan seven times? Why accept Naaman's compromise when he asks the prophet for permission to prostrate himself in the temple of a pagan deity, after having revealed his intention to worship the Lord (5:18-19)? Why punish Gehazi so severely for an offense which appears to be minor (5:27)? Naaman, the general who has ravaged the Promised Land, is healed of his leprosy, whereas Elisha's closest collaborator (and all his descendants) are punished forever. It is a world turned upside down![2] Naaman not only remains unpunished for his previous misdeeds (war against Israel), but is freely healed of his leprosy, and obtains acquittal in advance for future compromises. On the other hand Gehazi, who has received little recompense for past services (he feels his salary is modest), is punished severely for having coveted a legitimate

---

[1] Among the persons, Hobbs (p. 59) mentions the following: "There are Naaman, his wife, her maid, the king of Syria, the king of Israel, Elisha, Gehazi, Naaman's servants, Elisha's unnamed messenger, and the additional unidentified servants who carry Gehazi's loot for him." For Bergen (*Elisha and the End of Prophetism*, p. 113), "It is not one simple plot line, but a complex of vignettes. The narrator adopts various terms for and attitudes towards the characters, and the characters themselves move beyond the boundaries of mere types."

[2] According to Robert L. Cohn: "As a unified narrative 2 Kings V is a study in reversals." ("Form and Perspective in 2 Kings V" in *VT* 33, 1983, p. 182).

benefit (in his view) which harms no one, as Naaman is happy to offer money and clothing, and Elisha refuses any gifts.

The plot of the story is also complex because it ends three times before the story itself ends. In fact the story could have finished when Naaman was healed in v. 5:14, or when Elisha refused to be paid for the healing in v. 5:17, or even just before the episode of Gehazi, when Elisha approved the future behaviour of Naaman in v. 5:19.

Furthermore the first part of the story could have been shortened by leaving out two sections: (1) The dialogues between Naaman, the king of Syria, the king of Israel and Elisha could have been omitted (5:4-8); one would then pass directly from the girl's testimony (5:3) to Naaman's arrival at Elisha's dwelling (5:9). (2) In the same fashion, Naaman's first reaction to Elisha's message could have been omitted (5:11-13); one would then move directly to Naaman's obedience and healing.

The story could therefore have been shorter and simpler, but the author has chosen to transmit an elaborated version. Every element has its own importance: "By imagining how a narrative might have been, we gain a firmer grip on how it is" (Cohn p. 172). Naaman's physical healing is important (the first part of the story), but the recognition and the submission of the Syrian general are just as important (the second part), as is the judgment inflicted upon Gehazi for his sinful behaviour (the third part).

The text is structured. We can discern a simple three-part structure (see general structure p. 42) or a more elaborate one in seven parts, organised as a chiasm.

A.1	The exemplary testimony of a little Israelite slave (5:1-3)
B.1	The support provided by the king of Syria to Naaman (5:4-8). Elisha approves the procedure.
C.1	Naaman's anger when Elisha sends him to the Jordan (5:9-12)
D	Naaman's healing at the Jordan (5:13-14)
C.2	Naaman's recognition when he returns from the Jordan (5:15-16)
B.2	Naaman's submission to the king of Syria (5:17-19). Elisha approves the procedure.
A.2	The deplorable testimony of Elisha's servant (5:20-27)

The story of Naaman's healing echoes the story of the Shunammite (2 Kings 4:8-37).

1. An important person (the Shunammite; Naaman) is helped by Elisha.
2. Each one offers or wants to offer her/his worldly goods to the prophet (the woman feeds and lodges Elisha; Naaman offers him a fortune). The two insist (4:8; 5:15-16). Elisha accepts the woman's offer, but refuses the man's.
3. For both persons communication with Elisha passes through an intermediary (particularly at the beginning of the story): Elisha delegates Gehazi to speak to the Shunammite (see p. 103, 111), and he sends a messenger to inform Naaman on the steps to be taken for his healing (5:10-11).
4. Elisha blesses both the Jewess and the Syrian with healing (resurrection of the Shunammite's son; purification of Naaman's leprosy).
5. In both accounts, Gehazi has an important role but shows limited discernment.
6. A king and his general are mentioned. Elisha proposes to the Shunammite to seek aid from the Israelite king and general, and in the second story the Syrian king and the general ask Elisha for help.
7. Both stories are long and contain several parts. The Shunammite account could have ended at the birth of the child (4:17), and the possible endings of Naaman's story have been indicated above.
8. The two stories are separated by two brief episodes relating to Elisha's miracles dealing with food.
9. In both stories healing is related to the number seven: the child sneezes seven times before opening his eyes (4:35) and Naaman immerses himself seven times in the Jordan before being healed of his leprosy (5:14).[3]

The Testimony of an Israelite Girl (5:1-3)

[1]Now Naaman, commander of the army of the king of Syria, was a great and honourable man in the eyes of his master, because by him the LORD had given victory to Syria. He was

---

[3] See also note 10 p. 127.

also a mighty man of valour, but a leper. ²And the Syrians had gone out on raids, and had brought back captive a young girl from the land of Israel. She waited on Naaman's wife. ³Then she said to her mistress, "If only my master were with the prophet who is in Samaria! For he would heal him of his leprosy."

Naaman is a powerful man who leads the army of the region's dominant nation. He has gained the respect of his countrymen by a decisive victory for his country. Was it a war against Israel or against the Assyrians? The text does not clarify this point, but it is probable that the victory was over Israel. In fact, although the author never mentions the Assyrian menace during that period, he does report the military conflicts between Israel and Syria (1 Kings 20; 22) and adds that the young Jewess had been taken prisoner during a Syrian raid (5:2). Furthermore, the entire account centres on the exceptional grace shown to Naaman; the reaction of Gehazi would be better understood if Naaman had defeated Israel.[4]

"He was also a mighty man of valour, but a leper." All of Naaman's mightiness is negated by his leprosy. The term used here, *tsara'at,* designated different skin diseases, but "rarely Hansen's disease, which is more commonly called 'leprosy'."[5]

The behaviour of the young Jewish slave girl is exemplary. Despite the gravity of the situation she witnesses remarkable faith. Where others would doubt the power of the Lord she manifests amazing assurance. The Lord, through his prophet Elisha, can save those who trust in him. But more than her faith it is her spiritual discernment and her love of her fellow human beings that amazes us. She believes that God can do good to foreigners, even to those who oppress Israel: *"Then she said to her mistress, "If only my master were with the prophet who is in*

---

[4] Flavius Josephus (*Antiquities* 8.15.5) writes that Naaman is the man who shot the arrow which killed Ahab (1 Kings 22:34), but there is no basis of proof for this assertion.

[5] *NCB* p. 363. "Hanson's bacillus disease (leprosy - *Elephantiasis graecorum*) is as yet first identified in Egypt in the second century BC." (Wiseman p. 207). Chapters 13 and 14 of Leviticus describe the disease of "leprosy" (*tsara'at*) in different ways, none of which, however, correspond to Hansen's disease. The term describes different skin diseases for people as well as moulds on clothing and walls of houses.

Samaria! For he would heal him of his leprosy." (5:3). The young girl shares her hope with her mistress concerning Naaman's possible healing. The slave girl seeks the good of her fellow men, even of those who hold her prisoner. Her selfless love contrasts sharply with Gehazi's selfishness.[6] The witness of the young Jewess is exemplary, and Christians would do well to be inspired by it and witness to divine grace, even to their enemies.

The Reactions of Naaman and of the King of Syria (5:4-6)

[4]And Naaman went in and told his master, saying, "Thus and thus said the girl who is from the land of Israel." [5]Then the king of Syria said, "Go now, and I will send a letter to the king of Israel." So he departed and took with him ten talents of silver, six thousand shekels of gold, and ten changes of clothing. [6]Then he brought the letter to the king of Israel, which said, "Now be advised, when this letter comes to you, that I have sent Naaman my servant to you, that you may heal him of his leprosy."

The words of the young slave are transmitted with lightning speed. The author omits the exchange between the woman and her husband in order to express better the speed with which the message is accepted and believed.[7] The king of Syria writes a diplomatic note and Naaman organises a convoy to transport a fortune.[8]

The general is a man of honour who is ready to pay what he owes. The quantity of gifts transported indicates that the Syrian is not going to Israel as a conqueror but as a man in need, ready to recompense his benefactor generously. The ten talents of

---

[6] Naaman certainly rewarded the young girl upon his return—perhaps he set her free—but the narrator says nothing about this, because he does not want to return to the subject of the young girl at the end of his story. The omission of any recompense also serves as a stronger emphasis on the selfless ("free") love of the young Israelite.

[7] Cohn p. 174. The incredulity of the King of Israel is all the more obvious.

[8] The goods designated for the prophet could have been transported on one camel (see footnote 3, p. 188), but the general needed to be accompanied by guards and servants.

silver alone were worth five times the amount that Ahab had paid for the founding of Samaria (1 Kings 16:24).

The impact of the weakest (a young slave girl) on the most powerful (the king of Syria and his general) foreshadows the testimony and witness of unlearned, lowly people that would transform the ancient world. The apostle Paul said to the Corinthian Christians: *"For you see your calling, brethren, that not many wise according to the flesh, not many mighty, not many noble, are called. But God has chosen the foolish things of the world to put to shame the wise, and God has chosen the weak things of the world to put to shame the things which are mighty; and the base things of the world and the things which are despised God has chosen, and the things which are not, to bring to nothing the things that are, that no flesh should glory in His presence."* (1 Cor 1:26-29).

The Reaction of the King of Israel (5:7-8)

> [7]*And it happened, when the king of Israel read the letter, that he tore his clothes and said, "Am I God, to kill and make alive, that this man sends a man to me to heal him of his leprosy? Therefore please consider, and see how he seeks a quarrel with me."* [8]*So it was, when Elisha the man of God heard that the king of Israel had torn his clothes, that he sent to the king, saying, "Why have you torn your clothes? Please let him come to me, and he shall know that there is a prophet in Israel."*

The king of Syria does not mention Elisha in his letter, perhaps to avoid offending the king of Israel by telling him how and to whom he should turn. It goes without saying for the king of Syria that a man who has the power to heal leprosy is known to all.

The king of Israel completely lacks discernment. Had he forgotten Elisha, or did he not believe in his power? He therefore interprets the Syrian monarch's initiative as a pretext to start war. The Syrians first demand something impossible in order to then react violently to a refusal of humanitarian aid. The king of Israel's blindness endangers the fragile peace between two rival nations. The contrast between the king of Israel and the young girl is striking: on the one hand we see an adolescent captive full of discernment and living faith (she has not forgotten Elisha); on the other hand a forgetful monarch who is devoid of basic common sense.

"Let him come to me": Naaman has gone to the wrong person. Elisha therefore advises the king to send the sick man to him. Elisha behaves like a king. "The prophet issues orders to the king, not the reverse."[9] Note the lack of power of the king who confesses *"Am I God...?"* and the mightiness of the *"the man of God"* who promises to heal the sick man in order to foster the nascent faith of a stranger. The narrator emphasises this forcefully by omitting the message of the king to Naaman, suggesting thereby that the king's authorisation is secondary. Elisha's order is the final word. The king of Israel, powerless and useless, leaves the stage through the side exit.

Naaman's Healing (5:9-14)

> [9]*Then Naaman went with his horses and chariot, and he stood at the door of Elisha's house.* [10]*And Elisha sent a messenger to him, saying, "Go and wash in the Jordan seven times, and your flesh shall be restored to you, and you shall be clean."* [11]*But Naaman became furious, and went away and said, "Indeed, I said to myself, 'He will surely come out to me, and stand and call on the name of the LORD his God, and wave his hand over the place, and heal the leprosy.'* [12]*Are not the Abanah and the Pharpar, the rivers of Damascus, better than all the waters of Israel? Could I not wash in them and be clean?" So he turned and went away in a rage.*

Although the dignitary has undertaken a long voyage to see him, the prophet responds through a simple servant.[10] And yet

---

[9]   Cohn p. 176.

[10] In this story, Elisha does not move (he does not meet the general at his door nor does he accompany him to the Jordan), contrary to the story of the Shunammite where he seems to be constantly on the move. The contrast between Elisha's immobility and Naaman's mobility is mentioned in the analysis of Cécile Turiot: "La guérison de Naaman" in *Sémiotique et Bible* 16 (1979) pp. 8-32.
"Then Naaman went with his horses and chariot": "The fact that Naaman was able to drive up in his chariot to the house of Elisha indicates either that Samaria under Omri and Ahab had been more spaciously laid out than the normal eastern city, or, more probably, that Elisha lived either in an isolated house, or in the proximity of the official quarters, and not in the normally congested quarters of the populace." (Gray p. 454).

even the severest hygienic precautions did not forbid a person from speaking to a leper. Apparently without regard neither for this noble traveller nor for the sacred laws of hospitality, Elisha sends him away. The stranger must go to the Jordan, more than a day's march from the capital. If Elisha had not wanted to see Naaman again he would not have acted differently.

This is the crucial point. Elisha discourages Naaman from coming back to him once he has been healed, not wishing to receive anything for this miraculous intervention. The Jordan is chosen as the place of healing because the river is on the road that Naaman will take for his return, more than 50 kilometres from Samaria. Once healed the Syrian would merely continue in the same direction to return home. The expeditious manner in which the sick man is treated provokes bitterness which would discourage him from returning to the prophet. Elisha wants to offer the healing entirely as a gift.

The way the healing is to be carried out announces a *unique* salvation. Naaman must wash in the Jordan seven times. The instruction is simple and precise. Nothing else is required: neither the hand of the prophet, nor other rivers, nor a different number of immersions. For Naaman the rivers of Damascus appear to be more appropriate for purification. Their water is clear, descending straight from the snow-covered mountains, whereas the Jordan, limpid when it leaves the lake of Galilee, becomes murky and takes on a dirty brown colour because of its bed. The general's logic almost makes him risk losing his chance, because he forgets or is unaware of the fact that God's ways often seem like folly to men. The Jordan was the only way to Naaman's purification, just as Jesus is the only way to God (*"I am the way, the truth and the life. None comes to the Father except through me."* John 14:6). Like the Jordan, Christ did not attract any looks (cf. Is 53:4-5: *Yet we esteemed Him stricken, smitten by God, and afflicted. But He was wounded for our transgressions, He was bruised for our iniquities; The chastisement for our peace was upon Him, And by His stripes we are healed."*). Salvation is simple, but it is not without content. It is not faith which saves, but faith in Christ. Jesus died on the cross for our sins. As Paul says, *"For the message of the cross is foolishness to those who are perishing, but to us who are being saved it is the power of God.*" (1 Cor 1.18).

> [13]*And his servants came near and spoke to him, and said, "My father, if the prophet had told you to do something great, would you not have done it? How much more then, when he says to you, 'Wash, and be clean?'" *[14]*So he went down and dipped seven times in the Jordan, according to the saying of the man of God; and his flesh was restored like the flesh of a little child, and he was clean.*

The servants, more accustomed to executing orders than receiving honours, are not perturbed by Elisha's form of welcome. What the prophet orders is easy to do, so why not carry it out?

Naaman is a competent general (cf. 5:1). He knows how to command, but he also knows how to listen, because a good general always appreciates wise counsel. In the past he paid attention to the testimony of the young Israelite, and now he listens to his servants' exhortations. Naaman, chilled by the prophet's frosty reception, does not dwell on his disillusionment. His preconceptions concerning the manner in which the healing should be carried out (5:11) are not irrevocable. The man has an open mind. He is humble enough to put himself in question.

The healing is described concisely to better emphasise how "easy" it is. When a man obeys God the greatest problems can be solved.

The Inner Transformation of Naaman (5:15-19)

> [15]*And he returned to the man of God, he and all his aides, and came and stood before him; and he said, "Indeed, now I know that there is no God in all the earth, except in Israel; now therefore, please take a gift from your servant." *[16]*But Elisha said, "As the LORD lives, before whom I stand, I will receive nothing." And Naaman urged him to take it, but he refused.*

Naaman is a grateful man. The distance to the prophet's home does not keep him from turning back to thank his saviour. His return to Syria and the announcement of the good news to his family and friends can wait. Naaman is like the leprous Samaritan whom Jesus healed who also returns to thank him (Luke 17:11-19; see p. 25 for more details).

Naaman's offer of a gift to Elisha is categorically refused: *"As the LORD lives, before whom I stand, I will receive nothing."* (5:16). The words are so solemn that there is no doubt about his true intentions. In spite of the general's insistence Elisha does not yield to persuasion. There is no hint of a mercantile attitude in the prophet. Elisha does not exploit the general's healing to improve relations with Syria or to negotiate the release of a few prisoners of war.

The healing offered by Elisha is disinterested from start to finish. It announces the gratuitous salvation granted by Jesus Christ: *"For by grace you have been saved through faith, and that not of yourselves; it is the gift of God, not of works, lest anyone should boast."* (Eph 2:8-9). Naaman's healing also announces the extension of the ministry of grace to pagans, as emphasised by Jesus: *"And many lepers were in Israel in the time of Elisha the prophet, and none of them was cleansed except Naaman the Syrian"* (Luke 4:27). This grace granted to a foreign individual, not to a group requires faith to be accomplished.

> [17]*So Naaman said, "Then, if not, please let your servant be given two mule-loads of earth; for your servant will no longer offer either burnt offering or sacrifice to other gods, but to the LORD.* [18]*Yet in this thing may the LORD pardon your servant: when my master goes into the temple of Rimmon to worship there, and he leans on my hand, and I bow down in the temple of Rimmon – when I bow down in the temple of Rimmon, may the LORD please pardon your servant in this thing."* [19]*Then he said to him, "Go in peace."*

Having thanked Elisha, Naaman now wishes to honour *the Lord* (*"Your servant will no longer offer either burnt offering or sacrifice to other gods, but to the LORD."*) He understands that the prophet is only an intermediary. He also knows how to use symbols. If the Jordan represents the Lord, the earth of Israel can also do so. No magic is meant here, but rather the idea of God revealed in Israel. Naaman desires a part of the earth of Israel, probably so he can kneel on it to worship the Lord.[11]

---

[11]   There is a reversal: Cohn p. 178 "Naaman reverses his earlier attitude toward the territory of Israel. Whereas before his 'conversion', he

His request concerning prayer to the Lord in the temple of Rimmon does not reflect spiritual compromise. Elisha had not asked anything of him nor had he passed on any instruction on how to live his faith in pagan territory, far from the community of the faithful. This reasoning is from Naaman's, who sincerely wishes to serve the Lord, but does not know where to go to do so. He realises that his new-found faith could cost him his life, but he is ready for that. In asking Elisha his question, he risks refusal. If the Lord tells him to burn all bridges to his culture he will do so.

Elisha's surprising answer is: *"Go in peace."* Faith in a pagan land will be lived differently from that in Jewish territory. Even the way to salvation is unique (Naaman must wash seven times in the Jordan): daily worship will find different means of expression, with a common denominator of complete commitment. The manner in which to live this faith in varied situations is not given. The text opens a door which some would prefer to keep closed; but in the domain of faith not everything is set down by law. Certain things are and must be respected to the letter, while others are left to our individual judgment. Jesus said to the Samaritan woman that it is not the geographical location which counts when worshiping, but the spirit in which it is done (John 4:19-24).

Naaman will live his faith in a unique way: he will kneel in the temple of Rimmon, probably on the soil of Israel which he will have placed there.[12] The permission given by Elisha is not an encouragement to compromise as some might understand it, but an indication that pagans saved by the Lord will not express their faith like the Jews. Non-Jews will not be subject to any of the laws on food, holy days, purification rituals and innumerable animal sacrifices. A believer of Jewish origin might view the liberties accorded to the pagan believer as a compromise to God's laws. No, says Elisha to Naaman: *"Go in peace"* (5:19).

---

denigrates the 'waters of Israel' (v. 12), now he wants the soil of Israel, presumably to build an altar, in order to worship Yahweh in Syria." His request might be linked to the idea that each country is consecrated to one deity.

[12] The request to take earth is linked to the desire to adore the Lord alone, excluding all other gods.

Paul will say to believers of the new covenant: *"Eat whatever is sold in the meat market, asking no questions for conscience's sake"* (1 Cor 10:25). The Christian is in the world without being of the world.

It is appropriate here to emphasise the gratuitousness of salvation. Nothing is imposed on Naaman, but he who is touched by grace can only give himself to the Lord. In the new covenant the believer is saved by faith, but true faith is confirmed by works.

The Sin and the Judgment of Gehazi (5:20-27)

[20]But Gehazi, the servant of Elisha the man of God, said, "Look, my master has spared Naaman this Syrian, while not receiving from his hands what he brought; but as the LORD lives, I will run after him and take something from him." [21]So Gehazi pursued Naaman. When Naaman saw him running after him, he got down from the chariot to meet him, and said, "Is all well?" [22]And he said, "All is well. My master has sent me, saying, 'Indeed, just now two young men of the sons of the prophets have come to me from the mountains of Ephraim. Please give them a talent of silver and two changes of garments.'" [23]So Naaman said, "Please, take two talents." And he urged him, and bound two talents of silver in two bags, with two changes of garments, and handed them to two of his servants; and they carried them on ahead of him. [24]When he came to the citadel, he took them from their hand, and stored them away in the house; then he let the men go, and they departed. [25]Now he went in and stood before his master.

When Gehazi appears on the scene in verse 20 the readers are still under the shock of Elisha's reply to Naaman (*"Go in peace"* 5:19). Gehazi criticises his master for having *"spared Naaman"* (5:20), not for the freedom given to Naaman, but for not having accepted Syrian's silver. While the reader may be questioning Naaman's spiritual commitment and his respect for the divine honour given to him, Gehazi is preoccupied with himself and his material well-being.[13]

---

[13] Gray (p. 444): "The tentative suggestion of BDB (*Brown-Driver-Briggs*) that the name Gehazi means 'valley of vision' is extremely unlikely. We think that it is more probably derived from a cognate of the Arabic *jahida*

Gehazi is the opposite of Naaman. Comparing the two we have a Jew and a Syrian; a subaltern and a general; a man instructed in the ways of God and a pagan deprived of any special revelations; a greedy pauper and a generous rich man: "Naaman had asked pardon in advance for showing loyalty to his lord, while Gehazi criticizes his lord for sparing Naaman and excuses himself in advance for his treachery."[14]

From a human point of view Gehazi's reasoning holds true. Why care for this rich foreigner and enemy of the nation? Everything pushes him to fleece the Syrian: greed, xenophobia, rancour. But God's ways are not men's ways.

Gehazi, blinded by worldly thoughts, believes that the prophet is losing his power of foresight. He thinks that, unbeknown to Elisha, he can catch up with Naaman. Did he recall the confession of Elisha when the Shunammite had visited them after the death of her child? Elisha had confirmed not knowing the reason for her visit (2 Kings 4:27). But Gehazi is mistaken, because he confuses the exception with the rule. Elisha is gifted with exceptional discernment. Not only does he quickly spot the lie, he announces future failings (5:26). Having placed Mammon at the top of his list, Gehazi will always defraud his fellow man.

Gehazi plans his deed well. He lets Naaman leave and does not pursue him until a *"certain distance"* separates him from Elisha. He expects to extract a significant sum from Naaman.[15] With complete disregard for the truth and for his master, Gehazi not only lies but places lies in Elisha's mouth.[16] Gehazi communicates a double message: he lets Naaman believe that Elisha remains disinterested because he asks for the silver on behalf of other persons (5:22), yet at the same time the quantity of silver requested suggests that Elisha has changed his mind and

---

('to be avaricious'). This might, as the termination of Gehazi suggest, be a nickname, perhaps a reflection of the incident in 5:20 ff, where Gehazi extorts the reward which Elisha had waived."

[14] Cohn p. 180.

[15] "Although Naaman did not specify to Elisha the *beraka* ('gift') which he offered, cunningly Gehazi has discovered it and now requests precisely what he apparently knows that Naaman has with him." (Cohn p. 181).

[16] Cohn p. 181.

wishes to receive a compensation. Fifty kilogrammes of silver are the equivalent of 6000 New Testament drachmas, or a labourer's salary for twenty years of work.[17] Naaman interprets the message in the manner that Gehazi hopes for, and offers double the amount, which Gehazi is careful not to refuse. Naaman is generous. He does not give everything because he believes that Elisha has refused the full amount. The number of visitors announced (*"two young men"* v. 22) are an indication of the amount expected.

> *Elisha said to him, "Where did you go, Gehazi?" And he said, "Your servant did not go anywhere."* [26]*Then he said to him, "Did not my heart go with you when the man turned back from his chariot to meet you? Is it time to receive money and to receive clothing, olive groves and vineyards, sheep and oxen, male and female servants?* [27]*Therefore the leprosy of Naaman shall cling to you and your descendants forever." And he went out from his presence leprous, as white as snow.*

While Naaman progresses (he is healed, he becomes a believer, then makes a commitment of faith), Gehazi slips back step by step. He silently criticises his master (5:20), deceives Naaman and tarnishes the reputation of the prophet (5:22), then lies straight-faced to Elisha (5:26), who foresees the next offences and their progression: *"Is it time to receive money and to receive clothing, olive groves and vineyards, sheep and oxen, male and female servants?"* (5:26). The lie to Naaman is followed by a lie to Elisha. The first is planned and the second cannot be avoided (*"Your servant did not go anywhere"* 5:25).

Gehazi is judged severely, because under a pious appearance he scoffs at true faith. Having coveted Naaman's possessions, Gehazi becomes like the pagan and is stricken with leprosy.[18]

Gehazi's judgment prefigures the terrible consequences which await those who reject salvation by grace. Salvation is basically not a question of nationality or education but of faith.

---

[17] This is the amount given to the bad servant in the parable of the talents (Mat 25:24-30).

[18] Gehazi had criticised his master for having been too gentle with Naaman, because he did not comprehend the depth of grace. The reader who now criticises Elisha of being too harsh with Gehazi belittles God's justice.

Gehazi is an Israelite who has benefitted from Elisha's instruction whereas Naaman is a pagan with only a vague knowledge of God. Nevertheless it is Naaman who accepts the divine gift, and Gehazi who refuses it to others. Gehazi's descendants are also punished (*"Therefore the leprosy of Naaman shall cling to you and your descendants forever."* 5:27) in order to announce a similar judgment to those who belong *spiritually* to Gehazi's family.[19]

This judgment completes our text on the story of the Shunammite, because in 2 Kings 4 the woman's faith leads to the healing of her son's congenital disease, whereas in 2 Kings 5 Gehazi's hardening of heart produces a hereditary link which leads to misery. In theological terms we are either the heirs of Christ or of Adam.

---

[19] Leprosy *"white as snow"* is mentioned twice in Scripture: for Moses (Exod 4:6) and for Miriam (Num 12:10). Does the sanction indicate that Elisha has the same power as Moses (Gray p. 456) or that this type of leprosy punishes unbelief and contention as in the times of the Exodus?

THE IRON AXE HEAD
(2 KINGS 6:1-7)

The account of the floating axe head is different from the preceding story.

1. Naaman's story is long and complex, whereas the account of a labourer who loses his tool is short and simple. One thing stands out: an iron axe head floats.
2. The main character is not a rich, powerful foreign general, enemy of Israel, but a poor workman, member of the community of the faithful.
3. Elisha is much closer to the main character. Naaman had been treated coldly and dealt with swiftly (the prophet used a messenger to communicate with the Syrian, and then had sent Naaman faraway). In this new account Elisha lives in the same area as the Jewish workman, and accompanies him to another place for the period needed to build housing.
4. The miracle no longer concerns a sick man's body, but a mislaid object.
5. Money plays an important role in both stories, but each in a different way. In the first story an enormous amount (ten talents of silver, one thousand pieces of gold, as well as sumptuous garments) is involved, whereas in the second material goods are limited to a piece of forged iron (the axe head); this object is worth more to the labourer than the extent to which Naaman values his own fortune, because the workman has no other possession.[1]
6. Naaman tries to separate himself from his money, but is confronted with Elisha's refusal. When Gehazi takes hold of it he is severely punished by the prophet. On the other hand the Jewish labourer borrows the axe, then loses it before

---

[1] Nelson p. 184: "The story of the floating axe head is something of an embarrassment for modern readers. The miracle seems both trivial and pointless. In part this is caused by our inability to empathize with a poor man's consternation over an expensive borrowed tool. Iron was not cheap in those days."

being able to return it. All of the movements are reversed from one story to the other.

7. The most astonishing and interesting contrast concerns the Jordan. The two miracles occur on the banks of this river. Naaman's leprosy disappears when Naaman plunges into the Jordan's waters, whereas the workman suffers misfortune when the axe head disappears in the waters. The contact with the water is prolonged in both cases. Naaman must immerse himself seven times, and the axe head remains submerged at the bottom of the river. Finally salvation occurs when Naaman emerges from the water for the seventh time, and when the axe head floats.

The account of the floating axe head echoes another story: that of the widow and her two children (2 Kings 4:1-7), but this time the parallels are synonymic, not antithetical.

1. The two stories are brief and deal with individuals, members of the community of the "sons of prophets".

2. The two stories are elements which balance each other in the general chiasm (see structure p. 42).

3. The two faithful are poor who are confronted with a new, severe loss. The widow lives in debt, has just lost her husband, and here comes a creditor who wants to take her two children and sell them into slavery. The workman is deprived of everything because he had to borrow an axe to build a shelter, then suddenly loses this precious tool.

4. The miracle lets the two believers "keep" their possessions. The woman does not need to lose her children, and the workman finds the borrowed object which he had lost and can return it to its owner. For the miracle to be accomplished the woman must exercise great faith, which is not the case for the workman who needs only to reach out his hand to grasp the object. The woman's wealth depends directly on the measure of her faith, whereas the workman is brought back to his previous state by a simple gesture.

An Axe Head Lost and Found (6:1-7)

¹And the sons of the prophets said to Elisha, "See now, the place where we dwell with you is too small for us. ²Please, let us go to the Jordan, and let every man take a beam from there, and

136

let us make there a place where we may dwell." So he answered, "Go." ³Then one said, "Please consent to go with your servants." And he answered, "I will go." ⁴So he went with them. And when they came to the Jordan, they cut down trees. ⁵But as one was cutting down a tree, the iron ax head fell into the water; and he cried out and said, "Alas, master! For it was borrowed." ⁶So the man of God said, "Where did it fall?" And he showed him the place. So he cut off a stick, and threw it in there; and he made the iron float. ⁷Therefore he said, "Pick it up for yourself." So he reached out his hand and took it.

The community of believers is growing. The ministry of Elisha and the absence of harsh religious persecution doubtless explain the growing popularity of the Mosaic faith. To resolve housing problems the decision is made to start a new colony. The banks of the Jordan are chosen, perhaps because there are plenty of trees there and the river guarantees an abundant supply of fresh water.[2]

More than ever Elisha reveals himself here as the *social* prophet (see pp. 12-14). He lives with the community, shares their preoccupations, counsels, then give his blessing to worthwhile projects. He accompanies the workers in their travels, even if lodgings are scarce at the construction site.

The crucial moment comes when a workman loses his tool in the Jordan. The man laments (*"he cried out"*), apparently not having the means to reimburse the borrowed item. Before we examine Elisha's intervention three things must be emphasised:

1. Elisha's approval of the construction project does not mean that the workers will be spared any difficulties.

2. In the same manner, the prophet's presence does not prevent risk. Accidents can still happen.

3. The waters of the Jordan are not magical, as some might believe after the story of Naaman. The Syrian had found healing there, yet the same waters are disastrous for the workman. The lesson should be clear. Blessings and curses

---

[2] The banks of the Jordan "are covered with high and low copses of trees" (*BA* p. 136). According to certain commentators (Nelson p. 185): "Permanent residence by the Jordan would be historically unlikely because of malaria", but there can be no certainty regarding this subject. The dwellings could have been constructed at some distance from the river.

are not linked to objects or to geographical locations. The material world can serve only as *an illustration* for spiritual lessons, but objects and places have no spiritual virtue in themselves. This holds true for the most "sacred" objects, like the temple of the Lord.[3]

Elisha begins by gathering information at the scene of the accident (6:6). Why does the narrator indicate his request? The author could have passed directly from the announcement of the accident to the miracle. Thus, the author returns to this detail three times, indicating Elisha's question (*"Where did it fall?"*), the information provided by the servant (*"he showed him the place"*) and the place where Elisha throws the stick (*"So he ... threw it in there"*). Elisha's question and the narrator's insistence draw attention to the place of the accident. To have redemption intervention must take place at the site of the accident. We must discern here a spiritual dimension and not a physical one.

The most interesting detail concerns to the nature of the miracle. Elisha makes the axe head float by means of a stick he throws onto the surface of the water. The prophet could have chosen other methods to solve the problem, such as organising an underwater search or, failing that, taking a collection amongst the sons of the prophets to remedy the problem.[4]

The miracle consists of a transfer of property. The floating stick transfers its capability to the axe head. The miracle illustrates salvation in Jesus Christ. Adam's sin is the origin of

---

[3] The value of the temple was linked with the covenant which the Lord had sealed with his people. In view of their repeated contempt of this alliance, God finally destroyed the temple (2 Kings 25:9). On the occasion of its dedication, the author of Kings expounds at great length on the "symbolic" value of the temple as opposed to its intrinsic value (1 Kings 8:12-61). Even when they are far away from the temple, the people can turn towards it, i.e. cast their glance towards the place which embodies the divine covenant (1 Kings 8:44-48). They must turn toward the God of the covenant.

[4] The liberals Gray (p. 460) and Jones (p. 422) state that Elisha fished the axe head out with the stick. "The water was probably deep, but he managed either to raise the axe-head by inserting the tip of his stick into it, or else by moving it along the river bed into a shallower part from which it could be lifted out by hand." (Jones p. 422).

human corruption. For redemption to take place Christ, the second Adam, had to come to the place where sin was committed. He took on human nature to become a man, a true man. He then had to live a perfect life in order to offer it in expiatory sacrifice on the cross, to *impute* his justice to mankind. Even as the properties of the stick are transferred to the iron axe head, so the justice of Christ is imputed to men.[5] Finally Elisha tells the poor man to grasp the object (6:7), because each man must *grasp* by faith Christ's atonement for our sins.[6]

We also observe that the *wooden* stick can "symbolise the fact that it is by the way of the cross that God brings us to himself"[7]: the apostle Peter expresses this in 1 Peter 2:24, where he uses the word *tree* to speak of the cross: *"Christ who Himself bore our sins in His own body on the tree (or wood), that we, having died to sins, might live for righteousness – by whose stripes you were healed."*[8]

The miracle of the floating axe head illustrates the imputation of Christ's justice for the repentant sinner, just as the miracle of the multiplied oil illustrates the heavenly recompense attending the good works of the saints. These two aspects of salvation are represented by these parallel texts (see p. 42 and p. 136).

---

[5] Nelson p. 185: "Iron floats like wood; wood attracts magnetically like iron. ... God's power invades the world of the ordinary to effect strange reversals. The lowly are raised to places of honour (Luke 1:51-53). The unrighteous are justified (Luke 18:9-14). The lost are found (Luke 15:3-10). The dead are raised. These are as much incredible reversals as an iron that floats."

[6] The transfer of properties illustrating the imputation of Christ's justice upon the repenting sinner has already been suggested in other stories, but with less clarity. The spring of Jericho was purified upon contact with salt, an element which had previously touched a new bowl (2 Kings 2:20-22). The body of Elisha brought back to life the son of the Shunammite (2 Kings 4:34-35). The flour thrown into a stew neutralised the pollution of the wild gourds (2 Kings 4:41).

[7] Francis Dixon: *Notes sur la vie du prophète Elisée: 12 études bibliques*, p. 46.

[8] Other passages use the word *tree* or *wood* to designate the cross (Acts 10:39; 13:29; Gal 3:13, cf. Dt 21:23).

THE SIEGE OF DOTHAN
(2 KINGS 6:8–23)

In this story Elisha emerges as the prophet of *salvation* more clearly than in all of the other accounts. He helps five groups of individuals or groups.

1. Several times he informs the Israelite king of Syrian ambushes (6:9-10).
2. He encourages his servant by revealing to him the existence of the heavenly army (6:15-17).
3. He saves the city of Dothan from a murderous siege by drawing away the enemy army (6:18-19).
4. He frees the Syrian soldiers from the hands of the king of Israel (6:21-23).
5. He temporarily[1] protects the nation of Israel from enemy attacks, as Syria does not attack the country anymore (*"So the bands of Syrian raiders came no more into the land of Israel."* 6:23).

The theme of salvation is omnipresent, but the theme of *sight* marks this story even more. The prophet sees everything and knows everything. Moreover he gives to and takes away sight from whomever he pleases.

1. Elisha knows the secret strategies of the enemy (6:8-12).
2. He can show the presence of the heavenly armies to his servant (6:15-17).
3. He can blind the Syrian soldiers enough to prevent them from doing harm. The soldiers can follow him for several hours without recognizing him (6:18-20).
4. At the right moment, when the soldiers arrive at the capital, Elisha returns their sight (6:20).

Although Elisha is the undisputed champion of vision, his actions are surrounded by mystery. Why unveil the existence of heavenly armies to his servant, when these armies will never

---

[1] See p. 159.

intervene in the battle? Why drag the enemy soldiers to Samaria and then release them? The Israelite soldiers of Dothan could have easily massacred the Syrians while they were blinded by Elisha. Why save these men who wished to harm the prophet? And why save them in this manner?

To understand Elisha one must remember that his ministry is not limited to the 8th century B.C. He is a witness to greater realities, and these realities are what we must discover. The teachings of the champion of vision are not restricted to his own times.

The structure of the account of the siege of Dothan is organised as a chiasm, with several antithetical elements.

A.1	Message of Elisha to the king of Israel (6:8-10). Elisha protects the king.
B.1	The king of Syria feels that Elisha is guilty (6:11-14). The Syrians want to capture Elisha. Syrian troops on the march.
C	Conversation with the assistant of Elisha who sees the heavenly host (6:15-17)
B.2	Elisha blinds the Syrian army (6:18-20) and captures it. Syrian troops on the march.
A.2	Question of the king of Israel to Elisha (6:21-23). Elisha protects the Syrian soldiers.

On a higher structural level the text corresponds to the story of the first armed conflict in which Elisha is engaged (2 Kings 3: see structure p. 42).

1. In the first conflict Israel leads the initiative against Moab (2 Kings 3:4-7), whereas in the second Syria invades Israel.
2. The Israelite army was reinforced by two other armies (Judah and Edom) against Moab; faced with the impressive Syrian army (*"Therefore he sent horses and chariots and a great army there"* 6.14), Dothan must defend itself alone.
3. During the first period Elisha had refused to help the king of Israel (3:13-14), but now he helps him without having been asked (the king does not even know that he is in danger). In the first instance Joram had wanted to surprise the adversary

by moving around the country to the south, and now the king of Syria wants to surprise the king of Israel by different ambushes. In both cases the kings' attempts to surprise the enemy fail.

4. Regarding the subject of vision, the Moabites had confused water with blood, whereas the Syrians also have a problem with vision, not recognising that it is Elisha who is speaking to them and leading them to Samaria.

5. In the first story Israel is saved without knowing of the storm which sends the water; in the second the servant knows of the heavenly armies, yet they never intervene in the conflict.

Elisha Protects the King of Israel (6:8-10)

[8]Now the king of Syria was making war against Israel; and he consulted with his servants, saying, "My camp will be in such and such a place." [9]And the man of God sent to the king of Israel, saying, "Beware that you do not pass this place, for the Syrians are coming down there." [10]Then the king of Israel sent someone to the place of which the man of God had told him. Thus he warned him, and he was watchful there, not just once or twice.

The king of Syria tries to capture the king of Israel. The period is not clearly defined because the names of the kings are not even mentioned.[2] Elisha rescues the king of Israel by divulging the locations of the planned Syrian ambushes.[3]

The prophet is capable of knowing the best-kept secrets on the human level. The enemy's confidential military secrets are known to him. He hears all of the king of Syria's words, even

---

[2] "They appear almost as background for the main character." (Hobbs p. 74). This story could have taken place prior to that of Naaman. Thus, Naaman's slave could have been captured during one of his raids (Vos p. 154; *BA* p. 138). But chronological information relating to the stories of Elisha is sparse. Due to the fact that Elisha lived for a long time after the ascension of Elijah, several different political situations may have evolved (see "The Timeless Prophet" pp. 16-19 and item 3, p. 208).

[3] Elisha saved Naaman, but he is clearly not pro-Syrian, because he now saves the king of Israel. Later on, he saves the Israelite city of Dothan, then the soldiers of the Syrian army. Elisha is not a nationalistic prophet, but rather the forerunner of the saviour of humanity. He saves people, no matter what their nationality may be.

"the words that you speak in your bedroom." (6:12), the best protected part of the enemy camp.[4] His knowledge is complete, instantaneous and apparently not limited by time (*"Thus he warned him, and he was watchful there, not just once or twice. "* 6:10).

The king of Israel's knowledge is also good, as he receives information to protect him against the enemy ambushes. He even takes the trouble to verify the information transmitted to him by the prophet (*"Then the king of Israel sent someone to the place of which the man of God had told him."* 6:10).

Yet the king of Israel's knowledge is not on the level of Elisha's. On one hand the king of Israel is not informed of all of the king of Syria's words spoken in his room, but only those which are relevant to his security. Elisha does not reveal to the king of Israel where the Syrian troops are stationed, which would have enabled him to lead an offensive. Elisha is the prophet of life, not of death. He protects people (Jews and pagans), but never encourages aggression. On the other hand the king of Israel is sceptical, because he takes the trouble to verify the Elisha's words (6:10). Such a man would be of limited knowledge, because much information revealed by God can never be verified on this earth.[5]

The King of Syria Discovers the Author of the Leaks (6:11-14)

> [11]*Therefore the heart of the king of Syria was greatly troubled by this thing; and he called his servants and said to them, "Will you not show me which of us is for the king of Israel?"* [12]*And one of his servants said, "None, my lord, O king; but Elisha, the prophet who is in Israel, tells the king of Israel the words that you speak in your bedroom."* [13]*So he said, "Go and see where*

---

[4] Kings always feared coups and assassinations, particularly during their sleep. Only the most trustworthy soldiers were entrusted with the guarding of the bedroom.

[5] Gray (p. 464) and Jones (p. 426) display a more pronounced scepticism, because they divest Elisha of any supernatural knowledge, and state that the information was passed on to the prophet by Israelite slaves who had become concubines of the king and of his officers. As Elisha travelled around frequently, he would consequently have been well informed.

he is, that I may send and get him." And it was told him, saying, "Surely he is in Dothan." ¹⁴Therefore he sent horses and chariots and a great army there, and they came by night and surrounded the city.

The king of Syria appears to be well-informed. When he realises that his strategy is ineffective he soon thinks that there are information leaks and is immediately informed of their origin (*"but Elisha, the prophet who is in Israel, tells the king of Israel the words that you speak in your bedroom."* 6:12). The text is brief. Nothing is said about the manner in which the Syrians arrive at this conclusion. The narrator simply emphasises the fact that they know. The Syrians also know where to find Elisha: *"So he said, 'Go and see where he is, that I may send and get him.' And it was told him, saying, 'Surely he is in Dothan.'"* (6:13). Once again the story is brief. The difficulties involved in conducting such a search are ignored. The only important thing is that the Syrians know.

However, the king of Syria's knowledge is not as good as it seems. He errs grievously for a while, attributing the indiscretions to a traitor (*"The king of Syria... called his servants and said to them, "Will you not show me which of us is for the king of Israel?"* 6:11). The king is then naïve enough to think he has the power to capture Elisha. How does he imagine that he can simply capture the prophet who has already thwarted all of his plans? He does, of course, manage to identify the source of the indiscretions, and then discover the location of the prophet's residence. He even succeeds in surrounding the city of Dothan at night, prior to the prophet's departure. But this does not mean that he will succeed. The sequel of the story shows the contrary. It is not the Syrians who capture Elisha, but rather Elisha who takes the Syrians prisoner. The prophet masters the whole event. He shows no intention of fleeing, either before or after the Syrians' arrival. Logic might lead us to think that Elisha would know all about the king's plans of revenge against him, and that he simply waits in Dothan for the troops to arrive in order to deal with them in his own fashion. It would not be surprising if he had even helped them to locate him.

Would then his place of retreat have any specific significance? The city is mentioned only twice in Scripture: in our story and in Genesis 37:16-17. During the time of the Patriarchs Jacob had sent Joseph to find his other sons in order to bring him news of them. After several futile searches Joseph eventually found his brothers in Dothan, where they were plotting against him. They seized him and threw him into a dry well, then sold him as a slave to Midianite merchants who took him to Egypt. The texts of Genesis and Kings contain some interesting *antithetical* parallels. These parallels become even more interesting when one knows that Dothan means "double wells" (the city has two wellsprings)[6] and when we realise that Elisha and Joseph are the two persons in the Ancient Testament whose lives best foreshadow the ministry of the Messiah typologically. The following table assembles the main points of comparison:

Joseph	Elisha
Jacob does not know how his sons are faring. Joseph must travel to get news of them (37:12-14).	Elisha knows everything without having to travel. He recommends to the king of Israel to avoid passing through certain areas in order to avoid the Syrians' traps.
Joseph leaves Hebron, in the far south, to look for his brothers. He finds out that they are in Dothan, probably outside of the city, as they are grazing their herds (37:15-17).	Elisha is sought by the Syrians, the enemies to the north of Israel, who rapidly find out that he is at Dothan
Joseph is stopped by his brothers from the moment they see him. They want to kill him, but end up sparing his life because of Reuben's advice (37:18-22).	Elisha masters the entire situation. He goes out to meet the Syrians, captures their army and takes it to Samaria. The king of Israel wants to kill the soldiers, but Elisha spares their lives.
Joseph is mistreated, as he is thrown into an empty well, then sold into slavery. While Joseph is suffering in the well, his brothers eat a meal (37:23-28).	Elisha treats the Syrians well, and he gives them something to eat before he frees them.

---

[6] *Zondervan Pictorial Encyclopedia of the Bible*, vol. 2, p. 157 (the article on Dothan is written by the archaeologist J.P. Free who, in 1953, first excavated the site of Dothan).

The parallels are obvious antitheses. Why? Joseph and Elisha foreshadow the redemption of the Messiah throughout their lives, but do not prefigure the same character traits.

Joseph personifies the *two* parts of Jesus' ministry: His first coming in pain (seized by his brothers, enslaved in Egypt, imprisoned), then the second coming in glory (promotion to prime minister, which enables him to save both his brothers and the world). Elisha personifies only the first coming of the Messiah, not in humiliation but in the glory, particularly the Lord's miraculous ministry. Could it be that Elisha withdraws to Dothan to underscore the contrast to Joseph? At the "well" in Dothan, where Joseph *began* his typological pilgrimage of the Messiah's humiliation, Elisha *completes* the glorious culmination of the Messiah's ministry.[7] We may add that Joseph embodies the life of the Messiah *unknowingly* (he would have done everything to prevent himself from being taken to Egypt into slavery), whereas Elisha seems to master the course of events. We may imagine that the prophet of knowledge knew that by all of his acts he embodied the ministry of the Messiah.[8]

Elisha Unveils the Existence of the Heavenly Army to His Assistant (6:15-17)

> [15]*And when the servant of the man of God arose early and went out, there was an army, surrounding the city with horses and chariots. And his servant said to him, "Alas, my master! What shall we do?"* [16]*So he answered, "Do not fear, for those who are with us are more than those who are with them."* [17]*And Elisha prayed, and said, "LORD, I pray, open his eyes that he may see." Then the LORD opened the eyes of the young man, and he saw. And behold, the mountain was full of horses and chariots of fire all around Elisha.*

---

[7] In the story of the siege of Dothan, Elisha exercises the greatest sovereignty of his ministry. Afterwards, during the siege of Samaria, the events take place while the prophet remains in the background. He is locked in a room and does not change the course of events, but merely predicts the imminent liberation of the city (see pp. 154-155).

[8] At Jericho and Bethel Elisha's behaviour is also opposite to that of Joshua and Jacob (see p. 66 and footnote 11 p. 71).

At the heart of the story Elisha shows his close collaborator the fundamental realities hidden to most mortals. Surrounded by the Syrian enemy Elisha displays no fear, because he knows that the army of the Lord is guarding him. He first encourages his servant by means of his faith (*"So he answered, 'Do not fear, for those who are with us are more than those who are with them.'"* 6:16), then by prayer (*"And Elisha prayed, and said, 'LORD, I pray, open his eyes that he may see.' Then the LORD opened the eyes of the young man, and he saw. And behold, the mountain was full of horses and chariots of fire all around Elisha".* 6:17). The servant can see with his eyes a shining army distinctly and in full daylight (6:15). This is not an optical illusion (as in the case of the Moabites who had mistaken a reflection of the sun for blood, 3:22-23). The army *surrounds* Elisha, and thus the city of Dothan. It does not matter whether the sun is shining in one's face, or from behind: the result is the same. Nor is it simply a dream, because the servant sees what is actually there.[9]

Elisha Blinds the Syrian Army (6:18-20)

[18]So when the Syrians came down to him, Elisha prayed to the LORD, and said, "Strike this people, I pray, with blindness." And He struck them with blindness according to the word of Elisha. [19]Now Elisha said to them, "This is not the way, nor is this the city. Follow me, and I will bring you to the man whom you seek" But he led them to Samaria. [20]So it was, when they had come to Samaria, that Elisha said, "LORD, open the eyes of these men, that they may see" And the LORD opened their eyes, and they saw; and there they were, inside Samaria!

Elisha clouds the vision of an entire army. What is clear to everyone else becomes opaque for the soldiers. Elisha prays to the Lord to affect their vision (*"'Strike this people, I pray, with blindness.' And He struck them with blindness according to the word of Elisha."* 6:18), then promises the attackers that he will lead them to the man they seek, and takes them to Samaria. Thus between two prayers, one for his servant (6:17) and one for the

---

[9] Jones (p. 427) rejects the miracle and thinks that "The boy, who was under an emotional stress, had a psychological experience in which he saw the Israelite chariotry as horses and chariots of fire."

Syrians (6:18), one goes from light to darkness, from an exceptional revelation to total confusion.[10] The soldiers become Elisha's plaything as he leads them to the Israelite capital, located 14 kilometres to the south of Dothan.

We note that the soldiers are not completely blind, because they can walk behind and follow Elisha. They see the prophet but cannot identify him. They are naive enough to believe the words of the first person they meet: *"Now Elisha said to them, 'This is not the way, nor is this the city. Follow me, and I will bring you to the man whom you seek' But he led them to Samaria."* (6:19). Yet their investigations had revealed that the prophet was to be found in Dothan (6:13). Upon entering Samaria the Syrians do not see the Israelite troops around them. Not until Elisha prays again is their sight restored: *"So it was, when they had come to Samaria, that Elisha said, 'LORD, open the eyes of these men, that they may see' And the LORD opened their eyes, and they saw; and there they were, inside Samaria!"* (6:20). Thus from the time they leave Dothan to their entry into Samaria the Syrians are troubled and confused, without actually being blind.

The blindness of the Syrians recalls that of the Sodomites in Genesis 19:11. The same rare word for *blindness* is used, and the attackers are stricken with a similar lack of sight, because although they cannot find the door they still keep their mobility.[11]

Regarding Elisha's invitation to the soldiers to follow him, some authors are embarrassed by the prophet's "lie" when he says to the Syrians: *"'This is not the way, nor is this the city.*

---

[10] This story contains the only three prayers of Elisha. The narrator thus emphasises the dependency of this prophet, who up to now had been sovereign. This digest of prayers is characteristic of the intensive prayer life of the prophet (see "the prophet of perfection" pp. 14-16).

[11] The word *sanwerîm* (blindness) only appears in these two texts (Gen 19:11 and 2 R 6:18). Robert LaBarbera mentions the irony of the situation: "In Genesis the men of Sodom were struck with confused vision (*sanwerîm*) because they intended to violate the ancient law of hospitality. Here, in what may be an intentional irony, the Arameans have been struck in the same way so that hospitality might now be given to them" ("The Man of War and the Man of God: Social Satire in 2 Kings 6:8-7:20" in *The Catholic Biblical Quarterly*, 1984, pp. 644).

Follow me, and I will bring you to the man whom you seek' But he led them to Samaria." (6:19). But is it really a lie? Elisha keeps his promise. He leads them to Samaria where he has his residence (5:3, 8-9).[12] We cannot therefore claim that Elisha lied. He did, however, lead his attackers astray with an ambiguous statement. Nevertheless let us remember that Elisha was in a situation of legitimate defence. Furthermore he did not deceive his fellow men in order to harm them, but to prevent them from doing harm. God obviously approves of Elisha, because he instantly grants Elisha's three prayers.

Elisha Protects the Syrian Soldiers (6:21-23)

[21]Now when the king of Israel saw them, he said to Elisha, "My father, shall I kill them? Shall I kill them?" [22]But he answered, "You shall not kill them. Would you kill those whom you have taken captive with your sword and your bow? Set food and water before them, that they may eat and drink and go to their master." [23]Then he prepared a great feast for them; and after they ate and drank, he sent them away and they went to their master. So the bands of Syrian raiders came no more into the land of Israel.

The king of Israel once again displays limited discernment. He wants to kill the captured Syrians, which contradicts all common sense, as the prophet demonstrates to him: *"You shall not kill them. Would you kill those whom you have taken captive with your sword and your bow?"* (6:22). In military strategy prisoners of war were often more useful alive than dead. If alive they could be used for difficult labour or exchanged for Israelite captives (Naaman's young slave girl was certainly not the Syrians' only Jewish prisoner: 5:2). Elisha opposes the king with a firm "no". The prisoners shall not be killed. It would not only be contrary to military logic; Elisha is simply not the prophet of death, but far better, the prophet of life. He will release the captives, after having restored them (*"Set food and water before*

---

[12] "What the original hearers of our saga probably liked about it was not only the irony of Elisha capturing the soldiers sent to capture him, but the irony of Elisha actually enabling the Aramean troops to fulfil the command of their king and his ruling elite. The king of Aram had said, Go and see... where he is' (v. 13)." (LaBarbera p. 643)

them, that they may eat and drink and go to their master." 6:22).
Elisha wants no compensation for his generous gesture. The
prophet's selfless love is evident.

Grace together with justice, guide all of his acts. Elisha
applies the *law of retaliation*, a law which punishes the crime in
proportion to the offense committed.

1. The Syrians had come to capture Elisha. He captures them.
2. They wished to surprise him by a night-time attack (*"the king
   of Syria ... therefore ... sent horses and chariots and a great
   army there, and they came by night and surrounded the city."*
   6:14). Elisha throws the attackers into darkness through
   partial blindness. It is difficult to recognise people in the
   dark, but one can still move about with the help of a guide.
3. The Syrians probably did not intend to kill Elisha, but rather
   wished to exploit his talents. A reconnaissance agent who
   was as gifted as he would be very useful if he accepted to
   collaborate with them. Naaman's healing showed that Elisha
   did not harbour hatred against Syria, but even showed certain
   sympathy. In addition Gehazi had shown Naaman that Elisha
   accepted money. It was therefore possible that the prophet
   could be bought by the Syrians.[13] Because the Syrians
   probably intended to treat Elisha well, he treats them well in
   return.
4. The Syrians doubtless wanted to use Elisha's powers for
   military purposes. The prophet does something similar to the
   Syrians. He sends them back home so they can testify to his
   power and to discourage the Syrians from engaging in any
   new military offensive. In this way he checkmates Syrian
   aggression (*"So the bands of Syrian raiders came no more
   into the land of Israel"* 6:23).

Above all, Elisha's acts are marked by grace. We have
already mentioned how Elisha saves both Jews and Syrians. We
would also draw attention to the *Messianic dimension* of his acts.

1. The good dispensed to the weak angers the strong. The king
   of Syria (the dominant country of the region at that time)

---

[13] The Syrians hoped to bribe Elisha and make him their magician (Whitcomb
p. 78).

attacks Elisha because of the salvation he has brought to the king of Israel (victim of the Syrian incursions). In the same way the Jewish religious authorities could not tolerate the popularity of Jesus and attacked him for his healing the sick (cf. Mark 3:1-6).

2. Faced with massive attacks by their enemies Elisha and Jesus could both have drawn on a heavenly army to defend themselves, but did not make use of them (*"Or do you think that I cannot now pray to My Father, and He will provide Me with more than twelve legions of angels?"* Matt 26:53).

3. Both went out to face the enemy. Elisha went to the Syrian troops, and Jesus surrendered himself to the forces who had come to arrest him (*"Jesus therefore, knowing all things that would come upon Him, went forward and said to them, 'Whom are you seeking?'"* John 18:4; *"Jesus answered, 'I have told you that I am He. Therefore, if you seek Me, let these go their way,'"* John 18:8). Both also saved the friends around them.

4. The enemies are blinded and do not know what they do. The Syrians' blindness is physical, that of the Jewish and Roman authorities is spiritual (*"Then Jesus said, 'Father, forgive them, for they do not know what they do.' And they divided His garments and cast lots."* Luke 23:34).

5. The enemy is vanquished: the Syrian soldiers are prisoners in Samaria, and Satan is defeated on the cross.

6. The blinded troops are pardoned and their sight is restored. The Syrian soldiers can see again and the king of Syria understands that he must leave Israel alone. The Jews who crucified the Lord recognise their mistake (Acts 2:36-37), and receive the Holy Spirit, as do the pagans (Acts 11:16-18). It is possible that Elisha took the Syrians to Samaria to open their eyes, not only physically but also spiritually. He reveals to them his power, his hospitality to strangers and his pardon for sinners. This revelation takes place *in the capital*: perhaps as a foreshadowing of the revelation at Pentecost, when the Holy Spirit descended on Jerusalem and into men from all over the civilised world (Acts 2). The speaking in tongues which accompanied this event emphasises the universal extent of redemption.

Elisha illustrates the *victorious* dimension of Christ's passion. Jesus also dominated the scene of the passion, but in a different way. For him, the passion is related to a disgraceful death, but a death which is voluntary. Jesus remains the master of events. He accepted giving his life to ransom many. No one took his life. He decided the hour of his arrest himself. He let himself be arrested. He refused to defend himself and on the cross he could finally say that he had finished his work (*"It is done"*). On the other hand, Elisha only testifies to the victorious aspect of the Messiah, because other prophets testified to Christ's suffering, beginning with Elijah. This shows the limit of Elisha's witness. He is not the Messiah, but simply a type of the Messiah.

THE SIEGE OF SAMARIA
(2 KINGS 6:24–7:20)

This is the most detailed story in the Elisha account, but, paradoxically, the prophet himself plays only a minor role. The narrator deals with other persons besides the prophet. He reports the crazed demands of a famished woman who has just eaten her own child, he emphasises the hasty, senseless reactions of the king of Israel, he describes in detail the hesitant, surprising visit of four lepers to the Syrian camp, he lingers on the death of the unbelieving officer.[1]

These individuals appear to lead the reader away from Elisha, but if we look more closely, they give him merit, for the contrast between the prophet's perfect knowledge and the limited wisdom of the other men is enhances Elisha's qualities. As a black velvet jewel box brings out the brilliance of a small diamond, so the blindness or short-sightedness of these persons demonstrates the prophet's perspicacity.

Elisha sees (1) the murderous intention of the king, (2) the sending and the coming of the messenger, (3) the king's rapid change of heart (6:32b), (4) the liberation of the country, (5) the astonishing prices of two items of food, (6) the death of the officer, (7) the circumstances of that death.

On the other hand the other people are either completely or partially blind. One "cannibal" *woman* is deceived by another woman, then expects to receive a favourable judgment from the king for her abomination. The *king of Israel,* instead of

---

[1] "The story integrates character and plot tension in a way that creates suspense, sympathy, and anger" (House p. 277). "This story is the longest and most complex in the Elisha corpus. It contains six interconnected subplots, which will be read together in order to fashion a coherent picture of narrative movement and narrative motivation. Each subplot contributes to the overall picture, and each is even allowed to briefly dominate the story" (Bergen p. 136). For Nelson (p. 188), "The report of the siege of Samaria (6:24-7:20) seems to have been moulded together from three distinct stories (the lifting of the siege, the case of cannibalism, the captain's fate) into a single, artistic whole."

punishing the woman, takes it out on Elisha. *The officer* mocks the message of hope which Elisha brings, but then plans to reap a commercial profit from God's grace (7:17-20; see pp. 175-178). The *lepers* selfishly pounce on the enemy booty before realising the madness of their behaviour.

Elisha manifests exceptional discernment, and yet his role remains secondary. He does not change the course of events by provoking the liberation (contrary to his preceding interventions), but simply foretells it.[2] This story marks the beginning of the prophet's retreat to the background. His role is more discreet in the following stories.[3]

Elisha's ministry is to announce the Messiah, whose ministry is marked by different steps: first the miracles, then the humiliation. The demonstration of power is characteristic of much of Jesus' ministry (particularly the first years), but the last hours of his life are marked by lowliness. Some expected him to defend himself physically at the moment of his arrest (John 18:3-11), to reply to his accusers at his trial (Matt 27:12-14) or to perform a mighty sign on the cross (*"If You are the Son of God, come down from the cross."* Matt 27:40). In this way, like the ministry of Jesus which ends in humiliation, Elisha comes to the end of his ministry by holding back. Elisha does not embody Christ's sufferings; other prophets have taken care of that. He restricts his role to foretelling the power of the Messiah during his first coming, but even as the demonstration of this power is put on hold during Jesus' passion, Elisha performs no miracle

---

[2] "The stories concerning Elisha in this chapter are unusual. The miraculous element is minimal. No miracles are performed of the type seen thus far" (Hobbs p. 81). "Yet unlike the instances in which he performed some wondrous act in providing food for the hungry (cf. 4:38-44), in Samaria Elisha merely delivers a prophetic prediction in classic fashion: 'Thus said YHWH' (7:1)" (Cogan p. 83).

[3] In chapter 8, Elisha is simply mentioned in the first story (8:1-6). In the second story (8.7-15), Hazael is the principal character; Elisha contents himself with announcing his ministry. In the two stories which follow (8:16-24 and 8:25-29), Elisha is not even mentioned. At the beginning of chapter nine, he is supposed to anoint Jehu, but instead confides this task to one of his servants (9:1-10). From this moment on, the narrator continues the stories of Kings without the slightest reference to Elisha, except for the moment of his death (2 Kings 13:14-21).

during the last phase of his ministry. He is satisfied with predicting imminent liberation (7:1), just as Jesus reminded his disciples several times that he would be resurrected after three days. During this final phase God acts directly. He expels the seemingly all-powerful Syrians, before anybody realizes it, just as he conquers death, man's greatest enemy, by resurrecting Christ on a quiet Sunday morning. The soldiers guarding the tomb of Jesus flee before the angels, just like the Syrian army flees before the army of the Lord. Once the miracle is accomplished, the marginalised lepers in Elisha's time intervene to confirm the miracle and spread the news of it. In Jesus' time Mary Magdalene, formerly demon-possessed, and other women do the same on Easter Sunday. In this way, from the siege of Dothan to the siege of Samaria, we pass from the most spectacular manifestation of Elisha's power to the prophet's withdrawal, in the same way that Jesus gave the greatest sign of his power through his resurrection of Lazarus, who had been dead for four days, shortly before dying on the cross (John 11:4, 14). Elisha's triumphant entry into the capital city of Samaria foreshadows Jesus' triumphant entry into Jerusalem on Palm Sunday.

In the story of the siege of Samaria the narrator also develops the theme of desperation. What can one do when no hope is left? He gives several examples: the women who decide to eat their child (6:28-29); the lepers who decide to surrender to the enemy (7:3-4), the king who vents his anger on a scapegoat (6:31); the royal counsellor who encourages taking the only chance left (7:13).

Parallels and Contrasts to the Siege of Dothan

The story of the siege of Samaria follows the account of the siege of Dothan (6:8-23). The two have several elements in common, while presenting obvious contrasts.

1. Both stories start off with an aggression by the king of Syria: sporadic raids followed by a massive attack. The name of the enemy king is mentioned only in the second story (Ben-Hadad, 6:24).
2. The Syrian army besieges two Israelite cities: a less important one (Dothan) and the capital (Samaria).

3. Food plays an important role: at the end of the first story (6:22-23) and throughout the second. During the first siege the king of Israel feeds the Syrians generously (*"Then he prepared a great feast for them"*), but he does so reluctantly (he would have preferred to kill them), and during the second siege, the starving Israelites can eat all they want from the supplies the Syrians have involuntarily abandoned. The Syrians are fed at Israel's expense, then Israel is fed at the Syrians'.

4. Elisha is threatened by a king. First the king of Syria wants to capture him because of the services he has rendered to the king of Israel; then the king of Israel want to kill Elisha, who in his opinion is responsible for Israel's disaster. Each time the menace is easily averted. These signs of hostility towards the prophet are the only ones reported in the stories of Elisha.[4]

5. Elisha is attacked while surrounded by friends (the Jews of Dothan; the elders of Samaria). The first time Elisha leaves the city to meet the enemy, whereas the second time he locks himself in a room with his companions to prevent the royal messenger from arresting him.

6. The Syrian troops lift the siege each time. The first time Elisha leads them away from Dothan; the second time the Lord causes them to flee.

7. The army of the Lord is present both times. At Dothan it is visible, but passive, whereas in Samaria it makes itself heard and puts the enemy to flight.

8. The Syrian troops' senses are deceived by sight at Dothan, and by hearing in Samaria.

9. The siege of Dothan is described briefly, but that of Samaria is reported in great detail.

10. Both conflicts extend over a long period. The author mentions different attacks during the first conflict (6:8-10) and the severity of the famine during the second (6:25).

11. "In both, servants convince their king of the proper course (6:12; 7:13) and scouts are sent to 'go and see' (6:13; 7:14)"[5]

---

[4] The youths of Bethel only mocked the prophet (2:23).

[5] Nelson p. 188.

12. Elisha is the central and almost only person in the first story, whereas other persons compete with him for attention in the second.
13. Elisha's intervention is essential for Dothan, as he is the one who draws the attackers away; on the other hand his role in the liberation of Samaria is negligible.[6]

The Structures within the Story

The story of the siege of Samaria is built around a triple structure. The first arrangement is organised around the four prophetic interventions of Elisha.[7]

A.1	Introduction: severe famine (6:24-25)
B.1	The story of two women and the king's short-sightedness (6:26-31)
C.1	Two prophecies of Elisha regarding the king (6:32-33)
C.2	Two prophecies of Elisha on the fate of the city and of the officer (7:1-2)
B.2	The story of four lepers and the king's short-sightedness (7:3-15)
A.2	Conclusion: abundance of food (7:16-20)

Secondly, Rick Dale Moore[8] distinguishes two movements (6:24-33 and 7:1-20) which reinforce the preceding structure,[9] the first of which introduces and describes the problem in detail and the second of which does the same for the solution. The first part takes place in the city and the second outside. In each section the king retracts a hasty decision. He first calls back the servant he has just sent out (6:32-33), then sends out the servants

---

[6] For parallels to the military campaign against Moab, see footnote 4, page 75.

[7] The antithetical parallels of points B.1 and B.2 are described in detail on page 166.

[8] *God saves: lessons from the Elisha stories*, JSOT Supplement Series 95, Sheffield, 1990, pp. 95-98.

[9] The dividing line between the two structures is at the beginning of chapter 7.

whom he had wanted to keep in the city (7:12-14). The two sections begin and end with corresponding elements. They start by mentioning the prices of food, which are first exorbitant and then derisory (6:25; 7:1). The two movements end with the story of a door: Elisha locks himself into a room to protect himself against the passing rage of the king (6:32), whereas the king's officer, who wants to prevent the populace from breaching the city gate, is trampled by the enthusiastic crowd (7:17, 20).[10]

A third structure centres on the discernment of the lepers.[11]

A.1	The people are suffering from a famine; Elisha is contested; a child is killed by its mother and the king lacks discernment; the narrator presents several aspects (the mothers and the king; the king, Elisha and the servant; 6:24-7:2).
B.1	The Syrian camp is visited by blind persons who are deprived of resources (7:3-5)
C.1	The Lord brings liberation and sows confusion among the Syrians (7:6-7)
D.1	First reaction of the lepers: they want to take everything for themselves (7:8)
E	Reflection and discernment of the lepers (7:9)
D.2	Second reaction of the lepers: they decide to share with the others (7:10)
C.2	The king of Israel interprets the Syrians' departure (the liberation), but lacks discernment (7:11-12)
B.2	The Syrian camp is explored by two Israelite chariots, the only ones available to the besieged (7:13-15)
A.2	The people have abundance; Elisha's word is vindicated; a servant without discernment dies; the narrator repeats himself (7:16-20).

We again note that the mathematical "centre" of the story coincides with the God's action (see p. 170). Thus the three

---

[10] Moore's comparison of the behaviour of the king in the first section and that of the lepers in the second is less convincing, particularly because the king is also mentioned in the second section.

[11] Points A.1 and A.2 are not equally long, but mention analogous elements.

principal "persons" Elisha, God, and the lepers are all in a sense "at the centre" of the story in a certain manner.

The Context of the Siege (6:24-25)

[24]And it happened after this that Ben-Hadad king of Syria gathered all his army, and went up and besieged Samaria. [25]And there was a great famine in Samaria; and indeed they besieged it until a donkey's head was sold for eighty shekels of silver, and one-fourth of a kab of dove droppings for five shekels of silver.

The story of the siege of Dothan concludes with a sumptuous meal and the permanent departure of the Syrians, yet the story begins with the Syrian invasion and a severe famine. The contrast is obvious. Two questions arise; the first concerns the chronological link between the two stories. Has the author respected the chronological order or has he reversed it in favour of his thematic arrangement? This question is not easy to answer.[12] The thematic arrangement is evident, but it does not exclude a simultaneous chronological arrangement. Political situations change rapidly and it is possible that the peace obtained after the capture of the Syrian troops at Dothan and their ensuing liberation lasted only a few years. The king of Syria is mentioned by name, but he is difficult to identify because "Ben-Hadad" was a general term like "Pharaoh" or "Darius".[13]

A second difficulty arises from the apparent conflict between the last verse of the preceding story (*"So the bands of Syrian raiders came no more into the land of Israel."* v. 23) and the first verse of this account (*"And it happened after this that Ben-Hadad king of Syria gathered all his army, and went up and*

---

[12] For the *NCB* (p. 364), the question is settled: "One fact is certain, there is no unity of time between v. 23 and 24." On the other hand, Hobbs (p. 78, quoted by Dilday p. 320) suggests that the Syrians bands no longer made raids (6:23) because they want to launch a general attack to wipe out the preceding insult. See also commentary pp. 16-19, "The Timeless Prophet" and point 3, p. 208.

[13] A Ben-Hadad had already intervened in 1 Kings 15:18 (Ben-Hadad I); here it is Ben-Hadad II. Regarding the king of Israel, several commentators think that he is Joram (*BA* p. 140, *NCB* p. 364, Patterson p. 197, Whitcomb p. 80). Others suggest Joash (Dilday p. 321, Slotki p. 200).

besieged Samaria" v. 24). The expression *"came no more"* (6:23) does not mean a total expulsion or a final end, but only a temporary pause. Other examples can be found in Scripture.[14]

The author obviously wants to compare two scenarios. A very good situation turns into a very bad one. The political situation is often unstable. Peace between nations is never attained. "One day follows the next, and they do not resemble each other." Only God stays the same. He intervenes in the history of mankind in various ways. During the siege of Samaria he waits for the situation to become intolerable before making his move.

Why does Ben-Hadad oppose Israel again? Has he not witnessed the Lord's power several times already: the healing of Naaman, the failed ambush plots of the Syrians, the capture of his army during the siege of Dothan? Several reasons could explain his behaviour. The defeat at Dothan had taught Ben-Hadad that *Elisha* could not be captured; therefore the Syrian king does not now attack the prophet, but rather the king of Israel in his capital city. The Syrians may not have known that Elisha was in Samaria. Did he think the prophet and the king of Israel were at odds? During that last armed conflict Elisha had not shared the king's opinion on the treatment of the Syrian army. The prophet had also shown sympathy towards the Syrians by healing Naaman. Did the Syrians know of Elisha's harsh words to the king of Israel during the campaign against Moab (3:13-14)? Perhaps Ben-Hadad doubted some of the miraculous events. The failed ambushes could have been due to information leaks and the capture of the Syrian army at Dothan could be attributed to the incompetence of the generals. Ben-Hadad might have taken measures to correct certain weaknesses: replacement of the royal guard and the generals, modification of military strategy (instead of penetrating a city he sets up a blockade to prevent anyone from getting out). Whatever the reasons, Ben-Hadad errs once again.[15] The defeat is moderate because no

---

[14] Haley (*Alleged Discrepancies* p. 344) quotes the case of the Philistines (1 Sam 7:13; cf. 9:16; 10:5; 13:5, 17) and of Pharaoh (2 Kings 24:7; Jer 37:5).

[15] Edersheim (pp. 219-220) and Whitfield (pp. 205-206) remark on the madness of the Syrian king.

Syrian dies, yet it is nevertheless more severe, because all supplies are lost.

Samaria was a well-fortified city, located high on a hill and surrounded by thick walls. This advantageous strategic location doubtlessly explains the long duration of the siege. The Syrians refrain from a frontal attack, the issue of which would be uncertain. Perhaps they wished to avoid weakening their army. An economic blockade would make the city eventually surrender.

The narrator enters into the heart of the subject when the famine is at its peak.[16] The most wretched food is sold at exorbitant prices. Two examples are given: a donkey's head and pigeon excrement. Both were impure and not fit for proper consumption. The heads of animals were not eaten; moreover, donkeys were considered impure by the Jews. Excrement is defiling, and no-one would even think of eating it.[17] The price is set at twenty-four pieces of silver for the former, and five pieces for the latter.[18]

The Testimony of a Desperate Woman (6:26-31)

> [26]*Then, as the king of Israel was passing by on the wall, a woman cried out to him, saying, "Help, my lord, O king!"* [27]*And he said, "If the LORD does not help you, where can I find help for you? From the threshing floor or from the winepress?"* [28]*Then the king said to her, "What is troubling you?" And she answered, "This woman said to me, 'Give your son, that we may*

---

[16] "All of these many scenes are further united by the narrative device of unity of time; the action takes place within a single day." (Cogan p. 84). Several commentators identify this famine with the one predicted in 8:1, but the situation is quite different. Here we have a city under siege, whereas in chapter 8, it is a drought.

[17] Animal excrement can be used as fuel (Whitcomb p. 79). During Shalmanasar's siege of Jerusalem, the Assyrian spokesman mentions the consummation of human excrement (2 Kings 18:27). "Cow's dung was eaten during Titus's siege of Jerusalem" (Flavius Josephus: *Guerre* 5.13.7 quoted by Vos p. 156). Some think that pigeon droppings was "the common name for some sort of grass" (*NCB* p. 364) Translations: NIV: seed pods, JB: wild onions. Perhaps the expression was used to designate abominable food (Keil p. 328).

[18] According to Wiseman (p. 210), the price given for the pigeon droppings was the equivalent of more than a month's salary.

eat him today, and we will eat my son tomorrow.' [29]So we boiled my son, and ate him. And I said to her on the next day, 'Give your son, that we may eat him'; but she has hidden her son." [30]Now it happened, when the king heard the words of the woman, that he tore his clothes; and as he passed by on the wall, the people looked, and there underneath he had sackcloth on his body. [31]Then he said, "God do so to me and more also, if the head of Elisha the son of Shaphat remains on him today!"

The attentive reader of the entire book of Kings will not fail to compare this episode with that of the two women who asked king Solomon for justice (1 Kings 3:16-28). In both cases, after the death of a child, the king is called on to settle a dispute between two mothers on the subject of a living child; the king condemns an innocent to death (*"Divide the living child in two,"* 1 Kings 3:25; "Cut off the head of Elisha" cf. 2 Kings 6:31), but then quickly suspends the sentence.

If the points the stories have in common are obvious, the differences are equally so. In the first story the two women are orientated towards life. The first death is accidental and causes the mother intense pain, to the point that she steals another baby so she can raise another child in her grief. On the other hand the woman who has been wronged is prepared to give away her son in order to save his life. When Solomon proposes to divide the child in two, she cries out *"O my lord, give her the living child, and by no means kill him!"* (1 Kings 3:26). In the second story, the two women are orientated towards death. They mutually agree to murder the first child and eat it. The woman whose child has been eaten then makes a claim to the king for the other child so that it, too, can be eaten. The reason why the mother of the living child hides it is not given. Is it to save it from death or so she can have it all to herself to eat? The attitude of these two women leads us to assume the worst.[19]

---

[19] The woman who goes to Joram is so unconcerned with her sin that she demands justice without the slightest shame. "Retaining an absurdly narrow focus on a relatively trivial issue while ignoring a colossal problem is typical of characters in comedy. Could this account of atrocities committed during a siege actually contain elements of grotesque humour?" (Stuart Lasine: "Jehoram and the Cannibal Mothers (2 Kings 6:24-33): Solomon's Judgment in an Inverted World" in *JSOT* 50, 1991, p. 28). But the misery is too great to see anything but a tragedy. "Cannibalism serves

The desperate, abominable act of the two women had been prophesied by Moses (Lev 26:29; Deut 28:53-57), and then by the prophets (Ezek 5:10). It is repeated during the fall of Jerusalem in the VIst century B.C. (Lam 2:20; 4:10), then during the second fall of Jerusalem in the Ist century A.D. (Flavius Josephus: *Jewish War*, 5.13.7; 6.3.4).

The contrast between the two stories is also apparent in the attitude of the two kings. Solomon, in a proverbial act of wisdom, feigns the worst possible injustice in order to identify the true mother (*"And the king said, 'Divide the living child in two, and give half to one, and half to the other.'"* 1 Kings 3:25) whereas a century later the king of Israel decides on the worst injustice without solving the dispute between the two women. Instead of sentencing the two mothers for murder and saving the living child from them, he decides to arrest Elisha, an incomparably just man. Justice is mocked. The guilty go scot-free and the innocent are condemned: the child is left in the hands of the two murderesses and Elisha is threatened with death (*"Then* [the king] *said, 'God do so to me and more also, if the head of Elisha the son of Shaphat remains on him today!'"* 6:31).

Solomon had reacted with a great deal of sang-froid (while at the same time letting the women believe he was reacting emotionally), whereas the king of Israel in Elisha's time reacts emotionally by punishing an innocent and ignoring the guilty. The comparison of this episode with that from the life of Solomon, facilitated by the author, shows how much Israel is removed from the blessed era of Solomon, when the Lord was honoured. When the Creator of life is rejected, life and human justice are violated.

Why does the king accuse Elisha? Was he "angry at Elisha for having given advice which had led to such dire consequences

---

as the most violent symbol of a society characterized by lack of trust, disruption of family ties, and advancement at others' expense" (Lasine p. 29 "The narrator abstains from making any emotional response or making any judgment concerning the atrocities he or she is reporting" (Lasine p. 39). He thus conveys the icy coldness of a world where all other emotions have been banished.

and for having falsely promised deliverance?"[20] Had Elisha warned the king in the past that such a judgment would come upon the nation if there was no repentance?[21] Did the king bear a grudge against Elisha for not having punished the Syrians more severely in the previous episode?[22] Perhaps he reproached Elisha for having done nothing, because the prophet is much more passive in this story than in the previous ones. Perhaps he was merely using Elisha as a scapegoat.[23] In his desperation he vents his rage on an innocent.

Elisha's Behaviour (6:32-7:2)

[32]*But Elisha was sitting in his house, and the elders were sitting with him. And the king sent a man ahead of him, but before the messenger came to him, he said to the elders, "Do you see how this son of a murderer has sent someone to take away my head? Look, when the messenger comes, shut the door, and hold him fast at the door. Is not the sound of his master's feet behind him?"* [33]*And while he was still talking with them, there was the messenger, coming down to him; and then the king said, "Surely this calamity is from the LORD; why should I wait for the LORD any longer?"*

[1]*Then Elisha said, "Hear the word of the LORD. Thus says the LORD: 'Tomorrow about this time a seah of fine flour shall be sold for a shekel, and two seahs of barley for a shekel, at the gate of Samaria.'"* [2]*So an officer on whose hand the king leaned answered the man of God and said, "Look, if the LORD would make windows in heaven, could this thing be?" And Elisha said, "In fact, you shall see it with your eyes, but you shall not eat of it."*

The senseless judgment of the king of Israel is not only at odds with Solomon's justice, but also with Elisha's discernment. The prophet predicts four things. The first two prophesies concern the life of the prophet, and are immediately fulfilled; the other two are related to the people and the king's officer and are fulfilled the following day.

---

[20] *BA* p. 139. Keil p. 329; Marshall: *Scripture Union Bible Study Books*, p. 33; *NCB* p. 365.

[21] Whitcomb p. 80.

[22] Dilday p. 322.

[23] Gray p. 471, quoted by Bergen p. 139.

166

Elisha begins by predicting the king's decision to arrest and kill him (6:32) followed by the king's about-face (*"Look, when the messenger comes, shut the door, and hold him fast at the door. Is not the sound of his master's feet behind him?'"* 6:32). Elisha knows that the king is unjust – he calls him *"son of a murderer"*[24] – but he also knows that he is unstable.[25]

Why does the king go to his servant? Does he wish to make sure that his order is carried out or does he hasten in repentance to take everything back? Commentators favour the latter interpretation. Elisha not only knew the changeable character of the king, but also the slightest variations of his decisions. All he needs to do is lock the door to delay the messenger and wait for the king's counter order.

After fulfilling his double prophesy Elisha predicts two things which will happen the following day: the end of the famine (7:1) and the impossibility for the officer to take advantage of it (7:2). Elisha sees clearly. What he announces precisely takes place. He not only predicts the end of the famine, but also the moment when it will happen (the following day) and indicates the price

---

[24] Elisha calls the king a "son of a murderer", perhaps in recollection of the infamous trial of Naboth (1 Kings 21). The king, just like his father (Ahab), wants to kill an innocent.

[25] Verse 33a is translated differently depending on the identity of the subject of the verbs *come down* and *say*, because the Hebrew text omits the subject of the second verb. Certain translators think it means the messenger both times (*"the messenger came down and said ..."*: KJ, NASV); others think that only the first verb refers to the messenger and that the second refers to the king (*"the messenger came down and the king said..."*: NIV, Living Bible); even others attribute the two actions to the king (*"the king came down and said"*: Good News Bible). The end of the previous verse (*"Is not the sound of his master's feet behind him?"* 6:32) and the words which follow (*"Surely this calamity is from the LORD; why should I wait for the LORD any longer?"* 6:33) lead one to think that the king is present in person. For TOB (note), "the messenger speaks on behalf of, and, in this circumstance, in the presence of the king whose personal coming signifies a change of mind." Keil (p. 329) draws attention to 7:2, where the narrator specifies that the person who reproaches the prophet is the *"officer on whose hand the king leaned"*; the specification is not justified unless the person who had previously addressed Elisha had been the king. One note from SEM specifies that if read/pronounced differently, the Hebrew text, verse 33 (*"there was the* messenger, *coming down to him"*) can be interpreted as *"there was the* king, *coming down to him."*

of two basic food items. Within twenty-four hours we go from extreme distress to abundance; exorbitant prices for impure food without nutritional value (6:25) give way to derisory prices for stock liquidation (*"a seah of fine flour shall be sold for a shekel, and two seahs of barley for a shekel"* 7:1). It all seems so incredible that the royal officer[26] ridicules the prophet (*"Look, if the LORD would make windows in heaven, could this thing be?"* 7:2). Perhaps he is suggesting that even an exceptionally strong rainfall would not suffice to make the grain grow so quickly.[27]

Elisha announces the future with precision, but not in detail. For example he says nothing about the manner in which the famine will end: not a word about the sound of the chariots and horses that the Lord will cause to be heard in the Syrian camp (7:6). As for the king's officer, the prophet simply states that he will see abundant food with his own eyes, but will not be able to take advantage of it (7:2): no mention is made of the reason for this hindrance. His fatal destiny is not revealed. Elisha's prophecy for the people is not that they should act, but hope. It is certainly not a reason for speculation (see commentary 7:17-20, pp. 175-178).

The reference to the elders (6:32) has intrigued more than one commentator. It is interesting for two reasons. On the one hand Elisha's prophecy is heard by witnesses who can testify to the

---

[26] *"The officer on whose hand the king leaned"* (7:2): according to Gray (p. 472), the officer was originally the third man, the bearer of arms, who rode on the chariot beside the driver and the warrior. The position became that of an aide de camp. Thus Naaman also was one upon whom the hand of the king leaned. (5:18).

[27] Vos p. 156: "Even if God had caused a great downpour and stopped the famine, one would still have had to wait for the time of harvest." For Nelson (p. 190), "Commentators have usually thought of the doubting captain's windows in heaven as a reference to rain (cf. Gen 7.11; 8.2), but this famine has been caused by siege, not drought. A more appropriate reference is to the provision of manna through heavenly openings (Ps 78:23), which would give immediate relief." Patterson (p. 197) also thinks of windows of heaven from which flour and grain is dispensed. Keil (p. 330) suggests a great irony: God had caused a miracle from heaven with the flood, but now an even greater miracle was required (flour and grain were needed). Edersheim (p. 239) suggests that the officer excludes not only natural means, but also supernatural ones: "And yet it was by *natural* means that God would send all this supply".

reality of the prophetic words after they have been fulfilled. On the other hand, the presence of the elders, locked in a room in the middle of the capital, who receive Elisha's last instructions, recalls Jesus' last supper with the disciples in the upper chamber in Jerusalem, where Jesus announces imminent woes (Judas' treason, the disciples' denial, trial and crucifixion), but also the coming deliverance (resurrection from the dead on the third day). They were also able to testify to the reality of Jesus' witness after his resurrection.

The Desperation of the Four Lepers (7:3-5)

[3]Now there were four leprous men at the entrance of the gate; and they said to one another, "Why are we sitting here until we die? [4]If we say, 'We will enter the city,' the famine is in the city, and we shall die there. And if we sit here, we die also. Now therefore, come, let us surrender to the army of the Syrians. If they keep us alive, we shall live; and if they kill us, we shall only die." [5]And they rose at twilight to go to the camp of the Syrians; and when they had come to the outskirts of the Syrian camp, to their surprise no one was there.

At this point, the narrator inserts a long section of thirteen verses (7:3-15: almost half of the story)[28] which he could have summarised in one phrase: "Frightened by the Lord, the Syrians fled back home, abandoning all of their goods." He could have also reported only the divine intervention (7:6-7) and omitted any reference to the lepers (7:3-5, 8-15).

Why does the author devote so much space to the lepers? Their change of behaviour contains a fundamental lesson which is explained later (commentary of verses 9-10). For the time being let us note that in its structure, the story of the four lepers echoes the events in the story of the two mothers (see p. 159). The two groups suffer because of the famine and act selfishly in order to survive, but the lepers' behaviour is more acceptable than that of the women. The mothers think only of themselves and come up with the most abominable kind of murder. The

---

[28]   49% of the words.

men, pressed by the same needs as the women,[29] do not consider murder, but rather the quickest possible death for themselves. Afterwards, when they discover all of the goods the Syrians have left behind, they continue to think only of themselves for a while. However, driven by their conscience and common sense, they give up their selfishness and announce the good news to everyone (7:9).

God's Intervention (7:6-7)

> [6]*For the LORD had caused the army of the Syrians to hear the noise of chariots and the noise of horses – the noise of a great army; so they said to one another, "Look, the king of Israel has hired against us the kings of the Hittites and the kings of the Egyptians to attack us!"* [7]*Therefore they arose and fled at twilight, and left the camp intact – their tents, their horses, and their donkeys – and they fled for their lives.*

The divine intervention is fundamental, because without the Lord's assistance Samaria would have fallen into the hands of the Syrians.[30] The author places this reversal midway between the start and the end of the story (the text which precedes verses 6-7 amounts to 45% of the story, and the verses which follow make up 47%). Thus the narrator places God's intervention at the "mathematical" centre of the account.

God's intervention is surprising for several reasons. The army of the Lord, which was visible at the siege of Dothan (6:17) but did not intervene, now intervenes but remains invisible. Only the noise is perceived. The noise must have been very great because the Syrians think they are being attacked by *two* armies who have joined forces (*"Look, the king of Israel has hired against us*

---

[29] "Without a doubt, having been driven away because of the enemy invasion, the lepers had not been welcome in the city." (*BA* p. 140).

[30] For Gray, who systematically refutes any miracle, (p. 466) "The Aramaean withdrawal from Samaria, however, in so far as it may not be a minor incident exaggerated by tradition, may herald the revival of Israelite power towards the end of the reign of Joash the son of Jehoahaz" (13:17, 19). "It seems more likely that a rumour had reached them of the activity of 'the kings of the Hittites' and of Musrai, and it is not impossible that this rumour had been fomented by one of the prophets by the authority of Elisha." (p. 473)

the kings of the Hittites and the kings of the Egyptians to attack us!" 7:6); the attackers believe themselves gripped in a vice by a north-south anti-Syrian alliance. Yet the Israelites hear nothing. (The theme of silence is already emphasised in the lepers' report when they mention the absence of all noise in the Syrian camp: *"not a human sound"* 7:10). The intervention of the *heavenly army* is discreet. Elisha does not announce it and the author of 1–2 Kings indicates it indirectly, without mentioning it in the text (*"For the LORD had caused the army of the Syrians to hear the noise of chariots and the noise of horses – the noise of a great army"* 7:6). This army leaves no trace because it does not strike any Syrian. All booty from the "combat" is due to the hasty departure of the Syrians (tents, horses, donkeys, different goods).

Generally speaking the army of the Lord is characterised by its discretion: it is invisible (except when Elisha opens the eyes of his servant to encourage him: 6:16-17), and it is inaudible (except when it is frightening the enemy: 7:6-7). At Dothan it does not alter the course of the battle, whereas in Samaria it defeats the enemy without the help of any Israelite.

The Reaction of the Lepers when Faced with a Miracle (7:8–10)

⁸And when these lepers came to the outskirts of the camp, they went into one tent and ate and drank, and carried from it silver and gold and clothing, and went and hid them; then they came back and entered another tent, and carried some from there also, and went and hid it.

⁹Then they said to one another, "We are not doing right. This day is a day of good news, and we remain silent. If we wait until morning light, some punishment will come upon us. Now therefore, come, let us go and tell the king's household."

¹⁰So they went and called to the gatekeepers of the city, and told them, saying, "We went to the Syrian camp, and surprisingly no one was there, not a human sound – only horses and donkeys tied, and the tents intact."

The lepers' pangs of conscience about having to share the blessing they have received is the principal lesson of this episode. Verse 9 even lies at the centre of the story on the siege of Samaria (see structure p. 160).

The lepers think of the rest of the people after reacting selfishly at first, but understandably because they are starving and bereft of everything. The four men know they must announce the good news of salvation to all of those who are captive in the city, desperate and weak just as they have been. Perhaps the lepers were resentful towards the king and the guards who had not let them seek refuge behind the city walls. Perhaps they suffered from rejection by their community. Whatever the case, faced with this immense, unexpected and undeserved blessing, they know they have no other choice than to share the good news.

Their silence would have been a crime and subject to punishment, because not to assist a person who is near death is to be a criminal. The expression *"some punishment will come upon us"* is impersonal. Do they have in mind the judgment of men or that of God?[31] Perhaps both. The lepers know that men are accountable to God for their actions. They know that sooner or later, the inhabitants of Samaria will discover the departure of the Syrians. Time wasted before announcing the good news will endanger the lives of weakest who have long been deprived of food. Delay of information could also be of military advantage to the Syrians, because they could regroup and return. If the lepers had remained silent they risked being forever rejected by the community instead of becoming heroes.[32]

The text carries a clear New Testament missionary teaching. According to Dilday (p. 328), "outside of Matt 28:18-20 and Acts 1:8, no other text has served so often as a basis for missionary preaching". The following points are worth mentioning:

1. The entire populace is freed from death, thanks to God's intervention from on high. The inhabitants of Samaria are delivered from the Syrians, even as humanity is redeemed by the sacrifice of Christ on the cross. The situation of the

---

[31] *NCB* (p. 365) leans toward the judgment of men and Whitcomb (p. 80) towards divine judgment.

[32] The "leprosy" in question here is probably not Hansen's disease, but a simple skin affliction which resulted in exclusion from the community for a more or less longer period (see footnote 5, p. 124).

Israelites was desperate, just like the state of the sinner who is left to himself.

2. Salvation is free. The lepers and the inhabitants of the capital have done nothing, but salvation is offered to them. Salvation in Christ is offered freely to all mankind, whatever their past sins. *"For by grace you have been saved through faith, and that not of yourselves; it is the gift of God"* (Eph 2:8).

3. The extent of salvation: there is not only abundant food, but objects of value for all the inhabitants of Samaria. Christ not only offers eternal life, but also new life on earth. Sharing the Gospel never impoverishes those who do so, but rather enriches them with the joy of having helped someone else.

4. This salvation had been foretold by the prophets. Elisha and the prophets had foretold certain characteristics of Jesus' coming, particularly concerning his crucifixion.

5. The announcement of salvation must be made before dawn. Here night represents present times, and day corresponds to Christ's return. At the time of judgment, each man will be accountable for his deeds and it will be too late to be converted (cf. Rom 13:12).

6. We also note that the lepers are saved from perdition, but that they are not healed of their leprosy. In the same way he who accepts Christ's work is saved from judgment, but remains in his earthly state until death. The body of a Christian is not spared from illness during this life.[33]

7. The good news of salvation moves a person to extend charity to others. The lepers become conscious of their duty. In the same way the Holy Spirit moves Christians to share the salvation they have received. *"In this the love of God was manifested toward us, that God has sent His only begotten Son into the world, that we might live through Him. In this is love, not that we loved God, but that He loved us and sent His*

---

[33] Several synonymic and antithetical parallels between Naaman and the Israelite lepers can be pointed out. The wealthy stranger is healed without spending a penny for Israel, whereas the Israelites are not healed, but are relieved from long-term starvation and enriched at the Syrians' expense. Naaman finds physical and spiritual health in Israel, whereas the Hebrews find physical wealth in heathen territory (the Syrian camp), then return to their territory (the Israelite capital) to save their countrymen. Thus, grace and twofold salvation touch both groups.

Son to be the propitiation for our sins. Beloved, if God so loved us, we also ought to love one another." (1 John 4:9-11).

8. The good tidings are announced by the lepers, by men who are scorned by society, a symbol of the Gospel proclaimed by the humble of this world whom God has chosen as his messengers, because *"God has chosen the foolish things of the world to put to shame the wise, and God has chosen the weak things of the world to put to shame the things which are mighty"* (1 Cor 1:27).

The Reaction of the King of Israel (7:11-12)

[11]And the gatekeepers called out, and they told it to the king's household inside. [12]So the king arose in the night and said to his servants, "Let me now tell you what the Syrians have done to us. They know that we are hungry; therefore they have gone out of the camp to hide themselves in the field, saying, 'When they come out of the city, we shall catch them alive, and get into the city.'"

Once again the king lacks discernment. Upon hearing the news of the abandoned Syrian camp, the monarch thinks it is a ruse (7:12). Without the good sense of a servant who sends out scouts to verify the Syrians' departure, the besieged would have lost their chance of victory and remained in their desolate state.

The Reaction of a Servant (7:13-16)

[13]And one of his servants answered and said, "Please, let several men take five of the remaining horses which are left in the city. Look, they may either become like all the multitude of Israel that are left in it; or indeed, I say, they may become like all the multitude of Israel left from those who are consumed; so let us send them and see." [14]Therefore they took two chariots with horses; and the king sent them in the direction of the Syrian army, saying, "Go and see." [15]And they went after them to the Jordan; and indeed all the road was full of garments and weapons which the Syrians had thrown away in their haste. So the messengers returned and told the king. [16]Then the people went out and plundered the tents of the Syrians. So a seah of fine flour was sold for a shekel, and two seahs of barley for a shekel, according to the word of the LORD.

A servant suggests sending out scouts. The solution is so simple that we are surprised the king did not think of it himself.

The narrator then moves directly from the servant's counsel (7:13) to its execution (7:14), without mentioning the king's approval (normally required) because the king's change of mind, based on a minimum of good sense, does not inspire admiration from the reader.

Two chariots are sent, so that "in case one was ambushed, the other could at least report the presence of the Syrians."[34] The scouts discover the objects left on the road all along the way to the border (the Jordan river). This indicates that the noise sent by God probably continued for a long period of time. The Syrians' panic was certainly not brief, but must have accompanied the soldiers all the way to the river, a distance of about fifty kilometres, representing a day's brisk march. This obvious terror must have reassured the Israelites that the enemy would certainly not be returning to Israel soon.

The narrator mentions the price of the foods which Elisha had prophesied on the previous day (7:1). He also emphasises the truth of the prophet's words which are fulfilled to the letter.[35] The repetition of the food prices also excludes any inaccuracies from the text. The size of the miracle is not a scribal error which might have confused the two figures.

Epilogue: The Death of the Officer (7:17-20)

[17]*Now the king had appointed the officer on whose hand he leaned to have charge of the gate. But the people trampled him in the gate, and he died, just as the man of God had said, who spoke when the king came down to him.* [18]*So it happened just as the man of God had spoken to the king, saying, "Two seahs of barley for a shekel, and a seah of fine flour for a shekel, shall be sold tomorrow about this time in the gate of Samaria."* [19]*Then that officer had answered the man of God, and said, "Now look, if the LORD would make windows in heaven, could such a thing be?" And he had said, "In fact, you shall see it with your eyes,*

---

[34] *BA* p. 141
[35] The narrator also recalls the fulfilment of the word of God on other occasions (1 Kings 15:29; 17:16; 22:38; 2 Kings 9:36; 15:12; 23:16-18 cf. 1 Kings 13:31-32).

but you shall not eat of it." [20]*And so it happened to him, for the people trampled him in the gate, and he died.*

From the start the officer is of secondary importance. His presence does not affect the course of the story, and the narrator could have easily left him out. However, the opposite is the case. The author insists on telling this man's fate. He even uses it as a conclusion. Quite obviously this officer bears an important lesson.

In order to understand the story we must ask the reason for this man's presence at the city gate. What was he doing there and at that particular moment? We learn that *"the king had appointed the officer on whose hand he leaned to have charge of the gate."* (7:17). The officer was supposed to guard the city gate, which is not a normal task for an officer whose duty it was to accompany the king. The text does not specify if it was on the king's initiative or that of the officer. In the former case, the death of this man would be due to fatality: by unhappy chance, the surveillance of the gate falls to the doubting officer, who is accidentally trampled by the crowd. In the latter case the death of the officer is not linked to fate, but to his egoism and his speculative faith. This point deserves to be developed in depth.

Elisha had said to the unbelieving officer: *"In fact, you shall see it with your eyes, but you shall not eat of it."* (7:2). At the time the man had probably smiled at this threat, but the following day, when the lepers' report had spread (such news cannot remain hidden for long), the officer had certainly changed his attitude. One could think that the officer was afraid of being left out and therefore wanted to be in a pole position to benefit from the food left behind by the Syrians. He would then have interpreted the prophecy as follows: "Elisha prophesies to me that my disbelief will prevent me from being at the outer defence post to dash out and gather the goods that the Syrians have left behind. In consequence, when I leave the city to gather them, there will be nothing left for me. I will not be able to eat the food which was left behind, but I will see others eat it." Because he knew Elisha's prophecy about the price of the food, the officer could then deduce that food would be abundant. He could therefore be not only tempted to eat it, but also to take advantage of the opportunity to enrich himself. By guarding the gate of the city he could prevent people from leaving and pillaging the Syrian camp. The officer perhaps planned to collect most of the goods in the king's name in order to resell them at a higher price, in the knowledge that an overabundance of food would cause the prices to drop significantly. Instead of getting out of the crowd's way the officer wants to hold it back. This gesture costs him his life. His death is a stupid accident. Because of his greediness he thoughtlessly stands in front of the crowd which has gone wild.

If Elisha had clearly announced the death of the officer, the latter would have taken pains to avoid all danger. Having realised that the prophet's words were already fulfilled once (the famine was on the point of ending), he would have doubled his efforts to avoid the prophecy from being completed a second time. But because Elisha speaks only of the *goods* that the officer would see without being able to take advantage of then, the man neglects his own security. He thinks only of placing himself in front of the crowd to prevent it from seizing the goods he covets. He attempts to prevent the prophecy from being fulfilled, but his efforts have the opposite effect and fulfil the prophecy.

These considerations show that the Lord reveals the future not for our speculation, but to encourage us. He does not reveal everything, but only that which is essential for our faith. As Paul says, *"All Scripture is given by inspiration of God, and is profitable for doctrine, for reproof, for correction, for instruction in righteousness."* (2 Tim 3:16).

The punishment may seem severe, but is that not the fate of unbelievers? Among the different actors of the story the officer is the only one who never modifies his behaviour. A woman gives up wanting to kill her child; the lepers end up notifying the people; the king reverses his decision to kill Elisha, then changes his opinion concerning the silence in the Syrian camp. All of these people, after a bad start, end up doing what is right. The officer is the only one who perseveres in his spiritual blindness, and he is also the only one to die at the end of the story. The officer, in a sense, represents unbelievers who despite signs from the Lord persevere in their blindness. They hear the words of salvation but never take part in it.

The officer is the only person in the story who is punished. Of course the narrator does not tell all. He does not inform the reader about the fate of the two women who killed a child, but everything points to the fact that they are not condemned for this barbaric act, because the king unleashes his fury on Elisha. Within the context of this impunity the condemnation of the officer shows that the "calculating" unbelief of this man is worse than child murder. Gehazi had also sought to exploit faith on a material level, and was permanently stricken with leprosy. The adolescents of Bethel were torn to pieces by two bears for having mocked Elisha (and probably Elijah). The three judgments pronounced by Elisha all deal with contempt of faith, and two of these judgments (those marked by death) are placed at the beginning and end of his ministry, perhaps to illustrate the double cleansing of the temple carried out by Jesus: one at the beginning of his ministry (John 2:13-17) and the other at the end of his ministry (Matt 21:12-13; Mark 11:15-17; Luke 19:45-46). Jesus' fury was aroused each time by contemptuous exploitation of faith.

THE SHUNAMMITE
AND THE FAMINE
(2 KINGS 8:1-6)

[1]Then Elisha spoke to the woman whose son he had restored to life, saying, "Arise and go, you and your household, and stay wherever you can; for the LORD has called for a famine, and furthermore, it will come upon the land for seven years." [2]So the woman arose and did according to the saying of the man of God, and she went with her household and dwelt in the land of the Philistines seven years.

[3]It came to pass, at the end of seven years, that the woman returned from the land of the Philistines; and she went to make an appeal to the king for her house and for her land. [4]Then the king talked with Gehazi, the servant of the man of God, saying, "Tell me, please, all the great things Elisha has done." [5]Now it happened, as he was telling the king how he had restored the dead to life, that there was the woman whose son he had restored to life, appealing to the king for her house and for her land. And Gehazi said, "My lord, O king, this is the woman, and this is her son whom Elisha restored to life." [6]And when the king asked the woman, she told him. So the king appointed a certain officer for her, saying, "Restore all that was hers, and all the proceeds of the field from the day that she left the land until now."

This story echoes several previous stories, particularly the one which immediately precedes it (the siege of Samaria: 6:24-7:20), as well as the first story of the Shunammite (the resurrection of her son: 4:8-37).

Parallel Antitheses to the Siege of Samaria

While the two stories share the theme of famine, they are nevertheless very different.
1. During the siege of Samaria all of the people are deprived of food, whereas the Shunammite can avoid severe famine. On one hand the story describes the situation of the people; on the other hand the case of a family.

2. In the first story Elisha intervenes only when the famine is at its peak, whereas in the second, he warns the Shunammite before the catastrophe occurs, so that she can take necessary measures.
3. In the first case the famine is caused by men through the siege of Samaria; in the second it is due to natural causes.
4. In Samaria the end of the famine comes about because the Syrians return home. The Shunammite finds salvation through exile. The enemies go to the northeast of Israel, whereas the Jewess goes southwest to the land of the Philistines.
5. Elisha contents himself with announcing the end of the famine in the first case, and the start and duration of famine in the second case. He performs no miracles in the two accounts. God nevertheless intervenes to aid his people, but remains discreet. The noise which terrorises the Syrians is not heard by the inhabitants of Samaria, and the restitution of the widow's possessions appears to be a fortunate set of circumstances.
6. Both stories lead to an exceptional conclusion. The inhabitants of Samaria enter a state of plenty and the Shunammite regains her country, her property and all of the revenues from her fields (8:6).

Differences to the First Story of the Shunammite

The woman who benefits from Elisha's intervention is known to the reader, the author having previously described in detail her attachment to the prophet and the blessings he has granted to her (4:8-37). However, several differences between the two stories must be mentioned:

1. In the second story the woman is identified neither by her place of origin (Shunem, Shunammite: 4:8, 12, 25, 36) nor by her status (a woman of high rank), but by the last element of the first story: the resurrection of her child. The narrator mentions this resurrection three times in six verses, ("*the woman whose son he had restored to life,*" 8:1 and 8:5).
2. The woman does not hesitate when ordered to leave her country, whereas in the first story she seems to doubt the prophet's words (4:16, 28, 30).

3. Elisha had previously proposed speaking to the king in her favour, but she had responded that she had no need for it (4:13). This time the situation is reversed. The woman is poor and needs an advocate before the king to recover her possessions, a role which Gehazi involuntarily fulfils.

4. Gehazi once again serves as an intermediary between the woman and a high-ranking person (Elisha or the king), but this time his intervention leads to salvation (cf. 4:27, 31).

Differences to the Other Stories

In regard to the general structure of the Elisha stories (see p. 42) this story corresponds to the two concise accounts on the purification of the waters of Jericho and the curse of the children of Bethel (2:19-25). One could say that the story of the Shunammite, like that of the children of Bethel, is *atypical* of Elisha: punishment of sinners on the one hand, discreet, limited aid on the other. The story is also opposite to that of the purification of the waters of Jericho, in that the prophet's intervention at Jericho permits the people to remain in a land which had been cursed forever by Joshua, whereas the woman can leave the Promised Land and find salvation abroad, contrary to past admonitions of several prophets.

The story of the Shunammite also recalls the account of the widow of Zarephath (1 Kings 17:8-16), the other woman whose son was resurrected by a prophet. In both cases a prophet feeds a woman in another land, to the north or south of Israel. The stranger of Zarephath is a widow and the Shunammite appears to have become a widow.[1] These two accounts are located at the beginning and the end of the series on Elijah and Elisha. The circle closes with the story of the Shunammite, and the author can once again concentrate his attention on the reigns of the kings of Israel and of Judah.

The recovery of property under the benevolent direction of the king of Israel is in striking contrast to the seizure of Naboth's

---

[1] This is the opinion of Montgomery and Jones (quoted by Bergen p. 148), Robinson (p. 69), Bellett (p. 60), H.R. (p. 125). The woman is presented as the head of her family (v. 2) and upon her return she and not her husband is the one who goes to see the king.

vineyard during the time of Ahab (1 Kings 21). In the past Naboth had not only lost his land but was killed together with his sons. This was a flagrant violation of basic rights, whereas the Shunammite recovers both her goods and the proceeds of her fields, which no law required. In Naboth's time Ahab hated Elijah's presence and called him *"my enemy"* (1 Kings 21:20); during the Shunammite's time, the king loves to hear of all the great things Elisha has done (8:4).

One last comparison can be made with the famine of Joseph's time (Gen 41). The parallels are synonymous. The faithful (Joseph and the Shunammite) are warned of the coming of an abnormally long famine of seven years. They encourage their family to leave the Promised Land or are encouraged to leave it together for a foreign country (Egypt or the land of the Philistines). Finally they return to their homeland with abundance: the Israelites have dispossessed the Egyptians (Exod 3:20-22; 11:2-3; 12:35-36) and the Shunammite receives the proceeds of her fields.

The Principal Theme of the Story

The story of the Shunammite is characterised by the theme of *parting*.

1. A faithful woman must *leave the Promised Land* to survive. This is a new situation, because up to now the redemption linked to Elisha has taken place within Israel. Naaman had journeyed to the Promised Land to obtain healing. He had to plunge into the waters of the Jordan to be purified of his leprosy, none of the clear rivers of his own country being appropriate (5:10-14). He had also taken back some earth from Israel upon which to worship the Lord, the God of Israel (5:17). Regarding the foreign armies, the Syrians had been prevented from waging war against the king of Israel (6:8-10), then had twice been chased out of the country after the sieges of Dothan (6:23) and Samaria (7:6-7). Now not only is someone blessed in a *foreign country*, but that person must *leave* the Promised Land to avoid suffering.

2. The Shunammite must not only leave her country, but also *go far from the prophet* to be blessed. The woman had shown great attachment to him in the past, because she had put him

up every time he had passed through the area and had even had permanent lodgings constructed for him (4:8-10).

3. Elisha himself is *distant* in this story. He gives an order, then leaves the woman to her fate. After the famine, the Shunammite is re-established to her former situation, but the prophet is only indirectly responsible. He does not give instructions either to Gehazi or to the king to aid this woman upon her return.

4. The many contrasts to the other stories also tune the reader in to the theme of change. With the story of the Shunammite the author begins a *new stage* of Elisha's ministry, a change in the manner in which God's grace will be dispensed.

The theme *of return* is also present though as a minor theme. The woman returns to her country and recovers her possessions, and Gehazi, who was supposedly banished forever, appears to be doing quite well. In both cases it is not simply a matter of backtracking, but a return which is further enhanced with an astonishing promotion: the woman receives her possessions and also the fruit of her fields, and Gehazi seems to be holding a position of counsellor at the king's court.

The Story's Position in the Series on Elisha

On the literary level the Shunammite's story prepares Elisha's "exit", as he makes himself increasingly *rare*. The lead-in which began in the previous story culminates here. Thus, during the siege of Samaria, liberation was not instigated by the prophet but simply foretold by him. His aid is now limited to advice which permits avoiding temporary suffering, but the prophet does nothing to cancel the negative consequences of exile. In the previous story the army of the Lord had terrorised the Syrians, whereas in this one the "miraculous" dimension is reduced to coinciding circumstances which permit the woman to recover her property.

Elisha's retreat continues in the two following stories which mention the prophet: he does not anoint the king of Syria himself, but only predicts what will happen (8:7-15), then he anoints the king of Israel, but through an intermediary. After these two acts, Elisha completely disappears from the story for several chapters (from 9:4 to 13:14)[2], during the reigns of Jehu and of Joahaz, which cover more than forty-five years (see p. 31).

The Christ-centred Message of the Story

This *disappearance* of Elisha conforms to the Christ-centred ministry of the prophet. The ministry of Jesus also includes a temporary retreat. After his work of redemption on earth Jesus ascends into heaven, where he intercedes at the right hand of the Father. Rather than being abandoned, the church receives more discreet aid from the Lord. The Holy Spirit strengthens hearts and helps the faithful to witness courageously in a hostile world.

Elisha warns the Shunammite (one of the most fervent of the faithful) of the difficult times which will befall the land. She must leave and go abroad. No specific place is indicated, any foreign country will be favourable. Survival is possible in heathen lands, and that is where the Christian must also live in order to witness for the Lord, while waiting for his return.

For the Shunammite the return home will take place at the time determined by the Lord. The *seven* years (number of perfection) are the period decreed by the Lord.[3] Symbolically the return illustrates the restoration of all things which is carried out by the King of kings (represented here by the king of Israel) based on the ministry of the Messiah (represented by the works of Elisha). The king of Israel is a great admirer of Elisha, just as the heavenly Father is delighted by the commitment of his Son. Gehazi himself appears to be physically and spiritually renewed, as he does not seem to be suffering from leprosy anymore, and his intervention brings salvation.

---

[2] A total of 125 verses, which is the equivalent of two thirds of the Elisha series.

[3] The seven years recall the sabbatical year and the jubilee, i.e. the period after which debts were cancelled, slaves were freed and property was returned to its owner.

Message for the Exiles

The exiles for whom this book of 1–2 Kings was written could also find comfort in this story, because after seven years the Shunammite recovered all of her possessions. Jeremiah (the probable author of the Book of Kings)[4] had predicted an exile of seventy years for the Jewish people (ten times seven; Jer 25:11-12; 29:10) before they could return to their land. The same message of consolation can be found in Daniel Ch. 4 when king Nebuchadnezzar's power was restored after he had been humbled for seven years.[5]

The Historical Context of the Account

The typological significance of the events should not lead us to doubt their historicity. The Lord is sovereign and controls history. He gives meaning to events, often far beyond man's imagination.

Two points however could pose a problem. Firstly, the attitude of the king towards the prophet is so positive that it could arouse suspicion. Nevertheless we must not forget that Joram had shown his opposition to the idolatry of his father (3:2). His admiration of the prophet is therefore not out of place. This is even more the case of his successor Jehu, who had killed all of the prophets of Baal and who might well be the king mentioned in 8:3-6.[6]

Secondly, Gehazi's situation poses a problem due to the permanent leprosy with which he was stricken in Chapter 5. There are three possible solutions:

---

[4] See Archer, *A Survey of Old Testament Introduction*, p. 277.

[5] The grace of God towards Nebuchadnezzar foreshadows the divine grace towards Israel. The tyrant of Babylon had first been warned by Daniel to repent of his pride and injustice (Dan 4:27), then was judged and relegated to the rank of the animals for seven years. Finally, when he repented, God re-established him in his former domain. Is it not the same for Israel, the chosen people? It was also full of pride and committed evil. It also had been warned in vain by the prophets. It was also humbled during a complete period (seventy years). And had not the Lord promised to restore it if it showed humility?

[6] One must not forget that seven years pass between the order given by Elisha and the intervention of the king.

1. Gehazi's leprosy did not prevent him from leading a public life, just as Naaman had (see note 5 p. 122).[7]
2. The narrator arranged the stories of the Elisha series thematically without respecting the chronological order (see p. 31).
3. Gehazi had perhaps repented of his sin and God had pardoned his transgression. As the cycles of Elijah and Elisha emphasise the grace of the Lord, would it be surprising if the Lord had pardoned Gehazi? Certainly, the leprosy had been declared permanent, but the punishment had been linked to a rejection of grace (see pp. 132-133). If Gehazi had recognised the grace of the Lord afterwards, wouldn't he have granted it to him? The book of Jonah shows that a divine judgment can *appear* permanent without actually being so. Jonah understood very well that the predicted destruction of Nineveh would not be fulfilled if the sinful people repented *("I knew that you are a gracious and compassionate God, slow to anger and abounding in love, a God who relents from sending calamity".* Jonah 4:2). The message of 1–2 Kings underlines the same lesson. Ahab's repentance after the murder of Naboth serves to remind him of this (1 Kings 21:27-29).[8]

---

[7] Certain commentators point out that Gehazi, still under divine judgment, continues to be led by carnal desires. "Gehazi had coveted 'olive groves and vineyards, sheep and oxen, male and female servants' in the past, and thanks to his possessions, he had climbed the social ladder and was now an associate and companion of the king. Gehazi is in with the VIPs." (Smith p. 178). Perhaps he is proud of what he has experienced, but refrains from mentioning the leprosy with which he has been afflicted (Smith p. 179).

[8] Vos (p. 158) and Whitcomb (p. 75) opt for the first solution; Keil (p. 333), Marshall (p. 213) and *NCB* (p. 365) support the second; Patterson (p. 200) maintains the third.

POLITICAL CHANGES
(2 KINGS 8:7-9:10)

The period of grace comes to an end. The Lord has shown great patience towards the house of Ahab, but God's judgment cannot be postponed indefinitely. Three men had been designated at Mount Horeb to carry out this judgment. Elijah had to anoint Hazael as the next king of Syria, Jehu as king of Israel and Elisha as a prophet to take his place (1 Kings 19:15-17). The judgment was to begin with Hazael, continue with Jehu and be completed with Elisha. Elijah had not anointed either Hazael or Jehu, because he had understood the lesson on divine goodness and patience, symbolised by the soft murmur (1 Kings 19:11-12: see *Elijah between Judgment and Grace,* p. 123-126). As long as these two persons had not been anointed, the judgment could not begin. Elijah had only anointed Elisha, so as to make sure that at the appropriate time, the two kings would be anointed by his successor and the judgment would then take place. Thus, the punishment of the house of Ahab has not been cancelled but simply postponed.

Having come to the end of the time of grace Elisha must anoint Hazael and Jehu, in order to complete the divine mandate of his predecessor. The prophet of grace carries out his task, but with reticence, as we will see.

The author of 1–2 Kings devotes particular attention to the account of the house of Ahab, but he also tells the story of Judah, and he must occasionally interrupt his main account to include brief bits of information on events related to the southern kingdom. The stories of the anointments of Hazael and Jehu (2 Kings 8:7-15; 9:1-10) provide the ideal framework for the inclusion of two stories on the political *changes* in the kingdom of Judah. Indeed they predict important political changes in Syria and Israel, and a different attitude of the Lord towards the house of Ahab. Therefore, four stories on political change are presented in sequence and are organised as a chiasm. The author begins with the neighbouring kingdoms of Israel (Syria and

Judah), then ends with the house of Ahab. He writes in the following order:

A.1	Anointment of Hazael and conspiracy against Ben-Hadad, the king of Syria (8:7-15)
B.1	The reign of Jehoram, king of Judah (8:16-24)
B.2	The reign of Ahaziah, king of Judah (8:25-29)
A.2	Anointment of Jehu and fall of the house of Ahab (9:1-10:27)

Our analysis concentrates on the texts dealing with Elisha, namely the conspiracy in Syria (8:7-15) and the beginning of the fall of the house of Ahab (9:1-10), a text which closes the series on Elisha. A brief commentary on the revolt of Jehu will be given in the appendix (9:11-10:27).[1]

The "Discretion" of Elisha

The end of the Elisha series is marked by the disappearance of the prophet. Elisha is not mentioned in the two transitions concerning the kings of Judah (8:16-29), and his interventions on behalf of Hazael and Jehu are carried out in the background.

1. The reason for the voyage to Damascus is never specified, and the reader must assume that Elisha has come to anoint Hazael in order to carry out the order previously given to Elijah (1 Kings 19:15-17).
2. The narrator does not state precisely that Elisha has *anointed* Hazael, but the words of the prophet imply that an anointment has taken place. Thus, as soon as Hazael knows his divine calling, he makes sure to carry it out.
3. Elisha does nothing to heal the ailing king, but takes the trouble to reassure him concerning his illness. Nor does he do anything to warn the king of the imminent conspiracy threatening him.[2]
4. At the anointment of Jehu (9:1-10) Elisha does not even appear personally before the future king, but charges a

---

[1] This last upheaval is described in great detail (64 verses: 9:1-10:27).
[2] Elisha rather hastens Ben-Hadad's fall by informing his lieutenant of his calling.

servant to act and speak in his place. Furthermore he asks his messenger to leave immediately after the mission is accomplished (*"Then open the door and run; don't delay!"* 9:3).

Elisha is the prophet of grace, and his predecessor's ministry of judgment does not suit him. Elisha *must* anoint the two kings, but he does it as discreetly as possible. This theme of discretion prolongs the teaching of the previous account (see 8:1-6: "The Shunammite and the Famine"). Elisha is at the departure gate. The prophet of grace retires before the coming of judgment.

The "Anointment" of Hazael (8:7-15)

Ben-Hadad's Initiative (8:7-9)

[7]Elisha went to Damascus, and Ben-Hadad king of Syria was ill. When the king was told, "The man of God has come all the way up here" [8] *he said to Hazael, "Take a gift with you and go to meet the man of God. Consult the LORD through him; ask him, 'Will I recover from this illness?'"* [9] *Hazael went to meet Elisha, taking with him as a gift forty camel-loads of all the finest wares of Damascus. He went in and stood before him, and said, "Your son Ben-Hadad king of Syria has sent me to ask, 'Will I recover from this illness?'"*

"Elisha went to Damascus" For the first time in his ministry Elisha goes abroad. Neither the Syrians nor the reader are given the reason for this voyage.

Ben-Hadad has every reason to ask the prophet for help, as the latter has a good reputation among the Syrians. In the past, Elisha had healed general Naaman of leprosy (2 Kings 5) and had shown exceptional foresight and knowledge during the Syrian invasions (6:8-12). He had also shown great sympathy towards the Syrians by sending back their prisoners of war (6:22-23). Elisha is thus esteemed as competent, knowledgeable and friendly. He would certainly enlighten the king concerning his illness, and give him the necessary treatment if required. The king asks for information on the development of his illness, perhaps to take the necessary measures in case of death. More probably, this request hides another, namely one for information regarding his recovery. For politeness' sake the bar is placed on the lowest level, but far more is expected. Two kings of Israel had acted similarly: Jeroboam I had sent his wife to get information from Ahiyah regarding their dying child (1 Kings 14:3) and Ahaziah had gone to *"consult Baal-Zebub"* about his illness (2 Kings 1:2).

These voyages taken to seek the help of a healer are accompanied by valuable gifts (cf. 1 Kings 14:3; 2 Kings 5:5; 8:9). Upon his return Naaman had perhaps informed the king that Elisha had accepted money, but with reluctance (5:16, 21-23). The Syrian general had brought *"ten talents of silver, six thousand shekels of gold, and ten changes of clothing."* (5:5), the load which could be borne by one camel.[3] Ben-Hadad sends forty camel loads, an amount greatly superior to that of Naaman. The narrator does not say whether Elisha accepts the reward, but no aspect of the prophet's character would imply that he did so, even more so as he neither heals nor helps the king. The narrator omits any mention of Elisha's refusal to avoid implying the merest idea of grace, because the time of grace is over.

The Words of Elisha (8:10-13)

> [10]*And Elisha said to him, "Go, say to him, 'You shall certainly recover.' However the LORD has shown me that he will really die."* [11]*Then he set his countenance in a stare until he was ashamed; and the man of God wept.* [12]*And Hazael said, "Why is my lord weeping?" He answered, "Because I know the evil that you will do to the children of Israel: Their strongholds you will set on fire, and their young men you will kill with the sword; and you will dash their children, and rip open their women with child."* [13]*So Hazael said, "But what is your servant – a dog, that he should do this gross thing?" And Elisha answered, "The LORD has shown me that you will become king over Syria."*

Elisha must anoint Hazael as king of Syria to complete the unfinished task of his predecessor, but the task is repugnant to him as it marks the beginning of the punishment of Israel.

---

[3] According to the *Dictionnaire de la Bible* (pub. F. Vigouroux, vol. 2. col. 520-521), "A camel can carry a load of 600 kg, travelling a distance of 40 to 50 km a day." Thus, ten talents of silver weighed between 320 to 500 kg according to estimates, and 6000 pieces of gold weighed about 60 to 120 kg.

Elisha's behaviour is circumspect. When he arrives in Damascus, instead of rushing to Hazael, he waits until circumstances bring him into the presence of the future king, namely the steps taken by the king in order to be healed of his illness. During his conversation with Hazael Elisha merely answers the Syrian's questions[4]. Three times Hazael asks a question, and Elisha replies to the questions without offering any additional information. Only Elisha's tears (and perhaps his remark concerning the death of Ben-Hadad) provoke Hazael to ask the second question: *"Why is my lord weeping?"* The Syrian does not understand the prophet's sorrow. Is it to recover from his illness? In fact, the tears *silently* announce the reason for the journey. Hazael must be anointed as the one who will punish Israel. Elisha weeps for Israel's downfall, just like Jesus wept for the destruction of Jerusalem (Luke 19:41; cf. 23:28).

Because of Elisha's passivity Hazael is never literally anointed. The prophet simply announces to him that he will be the next king of Syria. The prophet's words are accompanied neither by an anointment with oil nor the laying on of hands. Nothing is said about the manner or the moment of change. Elisha simply lets the information stimulate Hazael's reflection.

Hazael Takes the Reins of Power (8:14-15)

> [14]Then he departed from Elisha, and came to his master, who said to him, "What did Elisha say to you?" And he answered, "He told me you would surely recover." [15]But it happened on the next day that he took a thick cloth and dipped it in water, and spread it over his face so that he died; and Hazael reigned in his place.

Elisha's words rapidly "bear fruit". Just as a spark sets gunpowder afire, so the prophet's words incite Hazael, who seems to have been waiting for a favourable occasion to assassinate the king the following day. It must be said that Elisha is held in great esteem by the Syrians, so it is hardly surprising that Hazael takes the Hebrew prophet at his word.

---

[4] "The plot is kept moving by a series of questions: Shall I live? Why does my lord weep? What is your servant that he should do this? What did Elisha say?" (Nelson p. 193)

Hazael's conspiracy is confirmed "in the texts of Shalmaneser III which speak of Hazael as the 'son of no-one', the designation commonly used for a usurper".[5] Hazael quickly starts a war against Israel and Judah, in which Ahaziah, king of Judah, is seriously wounded (8:28-29).

The Reign of Jehoram, King of Judah (8:16-24)

[16] *Now in the fifth year of Joram the son of Ahab, king of Israel, Jehoshaphat having been king of Judah, Jehoram the son of Jehoshaphat began to reign as king of Judah.* [17] *He was thirty-two years old when he became king, and he reigned eight years in Jerusalem.* [18] *And he walked in the way of the kings of Israel, just as the house of Ahab had done, for the daughter of Ahab was his wife; and he did evil in the sight of the LORD.* [19] *Yet the LORD would not destroy Judah, for the sake of His servant David, as He promised him to give a lamp to him and his sons forever.*

[20] *In his days Edom revolted against Judah's authority, and made a king over themselves.* [21] *So Jehoram went to Zair, and all his chariots with him. Then he rose by night and attacked the Edomites who had surrounded him and the captains of the chariots; and the troops fled to their tents.* [22] *Thus Edom has been in revolt against Judah's authority to this day. And Libnah revolted at that time.*

[23] *Now the rest of the acts of Jehoram, and all that he did, are they not written in the book of the chronicles of the kings of Judah?* [24] *So Jehoram rested with his fathers, and was buried with his fathers in the City of David. Then Ahaziah his son reigned in his place.*

The report on the king of Judah is brief: eight verses for the eight years of his reign.[6] The author mentions the grave sins of

---

[5] "The annals of Shalmanasar report: 'I conquered Hadadezzar of Damascus and a dozen princes, his allies. Hadadezzar himself perished. Hazael, son of no-one, seized the throne." J.A. Thompson: *La Bible à la lumière de l'archéologie*, p. 138). See also James B. Pritchard: *Ancient Near Eastern Texts relating to the Old Testament*, p. 280.

[6] According to Dilday (p. 338), "Having suspended his story of the kings of Israel and Judah in order to insert the lengthy account of Elisha and his miracles, the author of Kings now returns to the familiar format of the royal

the king (v. 18) and the limited punishment imposed by the Lord (v. 19-22). He also indicates a source of complementary information on the reign (v. 23). *"The book of the chronicles of the kings of Judah"* should not be confused with the canon of 1–2 Chronicles, which was written prior to the exile, after 1–2 Kings. The book of the *"Chronicles of the kings of Judah"* has disappeared, but it is possible that certain bits of information were taken up in the canonical book 1–2 Chronicles, chapter 21 of which contains corresponding information on Jehoram, confirming and detailing the data of 2 Kings 8 on the sins of the king of Judah.

Jehoram's sin consists mainly in his closeness to the house of Ahab. The king of Judah *"walked in the way of the kings of Israel, just as the house of Ahab had done"* and he marries Ahab's daughter (8:18). The close rapport between the two kingdoms, which had begun during the reign of Jehoshaphat, is reflected in the identical name of both kings. Jehoram of Judah bears the name of his counterpart in Israel, and his son Ahaziah has the same name as that of the former king of Israel.[7] On the religious level he *"made high places in the mountains of Judah, and caused the inhabitants of Jerusalem to commit harlotry, and*

---

biographies." It would be more correct to say that the author interrupts the story of Elisha to include a brief update of the history of the kings of Judah, before concluding his story on the house of Ahab.

[7] The name of Ahab's son has two spellings in the Hebrew text. The short form *Joram* occurs eleven times and the longer form *Jehoram* ten times. Moreover, the king of Juda ruling at the time of Ahab and his son is also called *Joram* or *Jehoram* (1 Kings 22:51 ; 2 Kings 1:17 ; 8:16-24). For the king of Juda, son of Jehoshaphat, the shorter form is used four times and the longer form six times. This identity of names and the difference in spelling in the Hebrew text is a source of confusion. Translators have opted for different solutions. The NIV and the Good News Bible always use the shorter form for the king of Israel (*Joram*) and the longer form for the king of Juda (*Jehoram*). The New English Bible does just the opposite: *Jehoram* is the king of Israel and *Joram* the king of Juda. Other versions present mixed solutions. Both short and long forms are used for both kings. In this commentary we follow the NIV solution.

We also note that verse 16 aligns 2 Kings 1:17 and 2 Kings 3:1 chronologically, as it mentions the co-regency of Jehoshaphat and Jehoram. But not all manuscripts contain this reference to Jehoshaphat (NBC p. 321, NCB p. 366).

led Judah astray." (2 Chron 21:11). His domestic policy is marked primarily by the assassination of his six brothers, all of whom were rich and influential (2 Chron 21:2-4).

Despite the gravity of his sin the punishment is moderate: *"Yet the LORD would not destroy Judah, for the sake of His servant David, as He promised him to give a lamp to him and his sons forever"* (8:19). This verse is one of the few in the book of Kings which mentions Judah's particular status (1 Kings 11:32-36; 15:4; 2 Kings 19:34; 20:6; see also pp. 36-39). The Lord is not only patient, as has been shown with the house of Ahab, but Judah also benefits from the unique covenant established with the house of David. A descendant of David will occupy the throne of Israel and Judah forever (2 Sam 7:15-16). The house of David can thus never be destroyed, contrary to the house of Ahab. It is an appropriate reminder when the author is about to report the eradication of the house of Ahab (Chapters 9 and 10).[8]

The alliance of God with the house of David, however, does not mean that this house cannot be humbled for a time (2 Sam 7:14), and even severely as it was during the Babylonian exile. For the time being the kingdom of Judah is merely weakened. Edom revolts against Judah (8:20, 22), but does not crush it (8:21).

The Reign of Ahaziah, King of Judah (8:25-29)

[25]*In the twelfth year of Joram the son of Ahab, king of Israel, Ahaziah the son of Jehoram, king of Judah, began to reign.* [26]*Ahaziah was twenty-two years old when he became king, and he reigned one year in Jerusalem. His mother's name was Athaliah the granddaughter of Omri, king of Israel.* [27]*And he walked in the way of the house of Ahab, and did evil in the sight*

---

[8] "Although Judah and Israel merge in sin, God has differing attitudes towards the two nations, based on God's unconditional dynastic promise to David... The fundamental difference between Israel and Judah is not their respective behaviour, therefore, but God's gracious choice of David" (Nelson p. 198).

of the LORD, like the house of Ahab, for he was the son-in-law of the house of Ahab.
[28]Now he went with Joram the son of Ahab to war against Hazael king of Syria at Ramoth Gilead; and the Syrians wounded Joram. [29]Then King Joram went back to Jezreel to recover from the wounds which the Syrians had inflicted on him at Ramah, when he fought against Hazael king of Syria. And Ahaziah the son of Jehoram, king of Judah, went down to see Joram the son of Ahab in Jezreel, because he was sick.

The information given on Ahaziah is terse, both in the book of Kings and Chronicles. The Chronicler, who normally provides abundant information on the kings of Judah, is content to repeat the text from Kings for Ahaziah, with minor touch-ups.[9] The brief sketch of Ahaziah's reign is partly due to its short duration (one year).

The author of Kings even omits the traditional ending which begins with the phrase *"Now the rest of the acts of ..., and all that he did, are they not written in the book of the chronicles of the kings of Judah?"*, perhaps because he reports the death of Ahaziah in the following chapter, or because the political upheavals of this period either destroyed or prevented the completion of a royal chronicle for the house of Ahab (Athaliah had massacred the royal family of David, so the writing of a royal chronicle on the fallen king would have been audacious).[10]

Two of the five verses devoted to Ahaziah deal with the fate of the king of Israel, who has been seriously wounded (8:28-29). Thus, even during this period of "Judean" transition, the author of Kings remains focussed on the northern kingdom. He also

---

[9] The text of Chronicles probably contains a scribal error, as Ahaziah was forty-two upon his accession to the throne (2 Chron 22:2) rather than twenty-two as indicated in 2 Kings 8:26. Gleason Archer (*Encyclopedia of Bible Difficulties*, pp. 206-207) points out that Ahaziah could not have been forty-two when his father died, because the latter was only forty at the time (he was thirty-two years old when he ascended the throne and reigned for eight years: 2 Kings 8:17).

[10] The author of Kings mentions the *royal chronicles* for all of the kings of Israel and Judah with the exception of six, who were deposed: two at the fall of the house of Ahab (Joram and Ahaziah), one at the deportation of the northern kingdom (Hosea) and three during the different sieges of Jerusalem which preceded the deportation of the southern kingdom (Jehoahaz, Jehoiachin, and Zedekiah).

draws attention to the closer ties between the two kingdoms with Ahaziah's visit to Joram, who is convalescing at Jezreel.[11]

Ahaziah's reign was short, but it took place during a crucial year (841). "Indeed in 841 B.C. Shalmaneser III of Assyria (859-824 B.C.) at last was able to break the coalition of western allies with whom he had previously fought a long series of battles (853, 848, 845). While all these complex details were part of God's teleological processes in the government of the nations and his dealing with Israel, doubtless the long-standing controversy and the growing spectre of Assyrian power could be felt in the political intrigues that brought about the death of Ben-Hadad II of Damascus and the downfall of the Omride Dynasty in Israel. Before 841 had ended Hazael would be master of Damascus (where Shalmaneser had set him up after having defeated him in battle), the pro-Assyrian Jehu would initiate the fourth dynasty in Israel (chs. 9-10), and the wicked Athaliah would sit as usurper on the throne of Judah (ch. 11)" (Patterson p. 203).

The Anointment of Jehu (9:1-10)

[1]*And Elisha the prophet called one of the sons of the prophets, and said to him, "Get yourself ready, take this flask of oil in your hand, and go to Ramoth Gilead.* [2]*Now when you arrive at that place, look there for Jehu the son of Jehoshaphat, the son of Nimshi, and go in and make him rise up from among his associates, and take him to an inner room.* [3]*Then take the flask of oil, and pour it on his head, and say, 'Thus says the LORD: 'I have anointed you king over Israel.' Then open the door and flee, and do not delay."*

[4]*So the young man, the servant of the prophet, went to Ramoth Gilead.* [5]*And when he arrived, there were the captains of the army sitting; and he said, "I have a message for you, Commander." Jehu said, "For which one of us?" And he said, "For you, Commander."* [6]*Then he arose and went into the house. And he poured the oil on his head, and said to him, "Thus says the LORD God of Israel: 'I have anointed you king over the people of the LORD, over Israel.* [7]*You shall strike down*

---

[11]   "Jezreel is a royal residence which is closer and can be reached more easily than Samaria" (*BA* p. 146).

the house of Ahab your master, that I may avenge the blood of My servants the prophets, and the blood of all the servants of the LORD, at the hand of Jezebel. [8]For the whole house of Ahab shall perish; and I will cut off from Ahab all the males in Israel, both bond and free. [9]So I will make the house of Ahab like the house of Jeroboam the son of Nebat, and like the house of Baasha the son of Ahijah. [10]The dogs shall eat Jezebel on the plot of ground at Jezreel, and there shall be none to bury her.'"
And he opened the door and fled.

Elisha proceeds discreetly. The prophet himself does not go to Ramoth, but is represented by one of his servants who is sent to anoint the king *in private*, then leave the city immediately. Why go about it in this way?

Elisha is certainly not too old to travel, as he lives until the reign of Joash of Israel more than forty years later (13:14-21); even if he was temporarily bedridden, it would not justify the servant's discretion. The latter is instructed to flee "so as to avoid any diminishing of the (prophetic) act itself. God's work is often best done and left to have its own impact".[12] Was Elisha afraid to go to the front (Ramoth was under siege by the Syrian troops: 9:14)? But it is unlikely that the prophet of *redemption* would risk his servant's life to save his own. The private anointment remains unexplained.

Two circumstances may explain the prophet's attitude. To begin with discretion was necessary, because Elisha had to initiate the overthrow of the king.[13] He himself was too well-known to travel without drawing attention. A servant therefore had to be sent to anoint Jehu in a private ceremony. The admonition to flee as soon as the mission was completed could be a security measure (to avoid the servant of Elisha being implicated in the conspiracy) or for his protection by not remaining in a region of military and political agitation.

---

[12] Patterson p. 206
[13] "It was an appropriate time, for the king lay wounded and in a weakened condition. Thus, he was removed from the army circle so that they were freer to plot a revolt. The army was mustered for war and stood ready to support their commander against the civilian establishment. And to broaden the impact of judgment on the dynasty, the king's nephew was visiting from Jerusalem and could be trapped in the assassination web." Vos p. 162

A second reason linked to his ministry could explain Elisha's discretion. Elisha is the prophet of grace, and it is repugnant to him to be the agent of a revolution which will cause the extermination of the house of Ahab. A less scrupulous servant could take care of the task for him. (Such a procedure would not have been possible for Hazael's anointment, because none of Elisha's servants were known that well by the Syrians). Elisha also asks his servant to anoint Jehu in private, then to leave immediately once the task is accomplished, so as not to implicate the prophet of grace in this action.[14]

We also note that the narrator places the words of extermination in the servant's mouth and not directly in that of the prophet. Elisha tells his servant to transmit the following words: *"Thus says the LORD: 'I have anointed you king over Israel.'"* (9:3). The servant on the other hand specifies to Jehu that he will decimate the house of Ahab. Four verses describe in detail the extent of the massacre (9:7-10). These words are almost identical to those uttered by Elijah in the field of Naboth (1 Kings 21:21-24). Did Elisha inform his servant of the words of his predecessor and did he ask him to transmit them to Jehu? Or had the servant heard them from another source (Jehu and his officer had themselves heard the words of Elijah: 9:25-26), and had he taken it upon himself to remind Jehu of them to make his mission clear? But this initiative would be surprising. At any rate it is God's word which is proven by its literal fulfilment.[15] Its origin is closer to Elijah rather than Elisha, who, in this case,

---

[14] "Elisha does not act in person and has this mission carried out by one of the sons of the prophets. Is this not striking proof of the fact that Elisha's character is one of grace and not of judgment? The word of God had to be carried out, but not to the detriment of the character of grace which the prophet embodies." H.R. p. 129

[15] Jehu executes to the letter the mandate received from God through the mouth of the servant with the exception of Jezebel's burial. After having killed her, the new king feels that a queen must have a proper burial (*"Go now, see to this accursed woman, and bury her, for she was a king's daughter."* 9:34), whereas the prophesy had stated that *"there shall be none to bury her."* (9:10). But the servants find it impossible to carry out the order, because the queen has been eaten by dogs whilst the king is enjoying a meal (9:34-37). The prophesy is literally fulfilled without being entirely dependent on Jehu's actions.

simply transmits the message of his predecessor. We note also that in the way he relates the facts, the narrator emphasises once more how Elisha's ministry of is one of grace.

The following verses (9:11-10:27) report the massacre of the house of Ahab. Elisha is no longer mentioned because the time of grace has ended.[16] The narrator refers only briefly to the prophet, just before his death (2 Kings 13:14-21), to show that grace is not lost forever, but that it has simply been put on the "back burner". Elisha is not the Alpha and Omega of grace, but only the *prophet* of grace, he who precedes and announces Jesus Christ, the true incarnation of grace.

---

[16] According to Bergen (pp. 162-166), one returns to the world of *Elijah*, but it would be better to say to return to the *world*. Jezebel and Baal are mentioned seven and nineteen times respectively in chapters 9 and 10, whereas they are practically absent in the cycle of Elisha (Baal is mentioned twice). The name of Ahab appears twenty-two times between verses 9:16 and 10:30, but only twice in the cycle of Elisha.

APPENDIX

THE FALL OF
THE HOUSE OF AHAB
(2 KINGS 9:11-10:27)

The description of the events in the book of Kings can be succinct or elaborate. The story of the house of Ahab is detailed. The author devotes sixteen chapters out of forty-seven to it, even though the period described covers only thirty-four years out of a total of four centuries. This account located at the heart of the book (see structure p. 45), is fundamental because of the ministries of Elijah and Elisha.

The *downfall* of the house of Ahab is unravelled in two chapters[1], a section which looks even more important when we realize that the two prophets are not involved (except for Elisha in the first verse, 9:1). The downfall of this dynasty is reported in greater detail than the fall of the kingdom of Israel (2 Kings 17), and even more than that of the kingdom of Judah (2 Kings 25); this latter would have been of particular interest to the exiles, who were the first to read 1–2 Kings.

Our commentary deals with the ministry of Elisha, but having devoted this present volume to that prophet and a previously written commentary on Elijah (*Elijah between Judgment and Grace*), we feel it appropriate to include several pages on these two chapters to emphasise the main points.

The descriptions are macabre. Joram is pierced by an arrow from behind which enters between his shoulders and exits his body through the heart. The lifeless body is thrown onto the field of Naboth (9:23-25). Jezebel is defenestrated, her blood spattering the walls of the palace; her cadaver is kicked by Jehu, and, finally, the corpse is torn to pieces by dogs until only the skull, the feet and the palms of her hands remain (9:33-37). The

---

[1]   More precisely from 9:1 to 10:27. See chiasm p. 202.

seventy sons of Ahab are beheaded; their heads are collected in baskets and piled at the entrance of the city (10:6-9). Forty-two brothers of Ahaziah are disembowelled (10:14) and the priests of Baal are put to the sword after having been solemnly led to a religious ceremony (10:25).

All of the king of Israel's close relations are put to death: king Joram himself (9:14-26), his wife Jezebel (9:30-37), the brothers and sons of the king of Israel (10:1-10), his nobles, cronies and ministers (10:11), the prophets of Baal (10:18-27), the king of Judah, who is allied to the house of Ahab by marriage (9:27-29) and the brothers of the king of Judah (10:12-14).

This bloodbath is not easy to develop as a sermon text, but the message of these chapters is contained in the complete eradication of the house of Ahab. God's judgment is complete and spares neither members nor friends of the royal house. Jehu makes sure that no one escapes: *"So Jehu killed all who remained of the house of Ahab in Jezreel, ...until he left him none remaining."* (10:11). The priests of Baal are assembled: *"Let no one be missing",* (10:19) and *"... all the worshipers of Baal came, so that there was not a man left who did not come".* (10:21). Jehu makes sure that no prophet of the Lord is taken into the group by mistake (10:23); he threatens to kill his soldiers if they let even one person escape: *"If any of the men whom I have brought into your hands escapes, whoever lets him escape, it shall be his life for the life of the other."* (10:24). Jehu carries out his task thoroughly. Through prompt action he prevents his intended victims from fleeing. He thus contacts the brothers of the king of Judah before they get wind of the massacres which have already been carried out (10:12-14).

The narrator repeats certain terms to better emphasise the fulfilment of divine justice. He also points out the prophetic dimension of the punishment. The fate of the house of Ahab should surprise no one, because it had been announced by Elijah. Jehu makes sure that his words are carried out: *"Know now that nothing shall fall to the earth of the word of the LORD which the LORD spoke concerning the house of Ahab; for the LORD has done what He spoke by His servant Elijah."* (10:10). In Samaria Jehu kills all those who are close to the royal family *"according to the word of the LORD which He spoke to Elijah"* (10:17). At Jezreel Jehu has Joram's body thrown onto the field of Naboth to fulfil Elijah's prophesy, which he had heard personally: *"Then Jehu said to Bidkar his captain, 'Pick him up, and throw him into the tract of the field of Naboth the Jezreelite; for remember, when you and I were riding together behind Ahab his father, that the LORD laid this burden upon him: 'Surely I saw yesterday the blood of Naboth and the blood of his sons,' says the LORD, 'and I will repay you in this plot,' says the LORD. Now therefore, take and throw him on the plot of ground, according to the word of the LORD."* (9:25-26). When he learns that Jezebel has been eaten by dogs, Jehu recalls the word of the Lord which he had momentarily forgotten: *"Therefore they came back and told him. And he said, "This is the word of the LORD, which He spoke by His servant Elijah the Tishbite, saying, 'On the plot of ground at Jezreel dogs shall eat the flesh of Jezebel; and the corpse of Jezebel shall be as refuse on the surface of the field, in the plot at Jezreel, so that they shall not say, 'Here lies Jezebel.'"* (9:36-37).[2]

The Structure of the Account

The structure of the account also deserves being mentioned. On the one hand it is well built, as it is composed of nine elements arranged in a chiasm, which testifies to the care the narrator took when he wrote this section. On the other hand the central element relates the massacre of Ahab's sons, i.e. the judgment of *blood* relatives of the king. Thus, since the murder of Naboth, the blood of the faithful had to be avenged by the blood of Ahab: *"Thus says the LORD: 'In the place where dogs licked the blood of Naboth, dogs shall lick your blood, even yours.'"* (1 Kings 21:19). The prophecy had been deferred following Ahab's repentance (1 Kings 21:27-29), then partly fulfilled at the king's death (1 Kings 22:38: see *Elijah between Judgment and Grace*). Now, with Jehu, it is finally completed.

---

[2] In 1 Kings 21:21-24, the narrator does not report the words of Elijah on the subject of "refuse" as in 2 Kings 9:36-37, probably so as not to further lengthen the long reply of the prophet.

A.1	Introduction: the words of the true prophets (9:1-14a)
B	The end of the house of Ahab (9:14b-10:17)
a 1	Justice in a chariot: the oldest son of Ahab is the first to be executed (9:14b-26)
b 2	Justice on the road: the king of Judah (9:27-29)
c 3	Justice at Jezreel: Ahab's wife (9:30-37)
d 4	Justice in Samaria, the capital: 70 sons of Ahab (10:1-10)
c 5	Justice at Jezreel: those close to Ahab (10:11)
b 6	Justice on the road: the house of Judah (10:12-14)
a 7	Justice in a chariot (alliance concluded for punishment): the remaining followers of Ahab are killed (10:15-17)
A.2	Conclusion: the death of the false prophets (10:18-27)

Comparison of Three Accounts of Downfall

The book of Kings relates three accounts of downfall: that of the house of Ahab (2 Kings 9 to 10), that of the northern kingdom (2 Kings 17) and that of the southern kingdom (2 Kings 25). Each story provides a certain type of information, but the emphasis varies considerably. Viewing the stories of downfall as caricatures, one could say that the fall of the house of Ahab was *bloody*, that of Samaria was *theological* and that of Jerusalem was *dusty*. The account of the downfall of the house of Ahab emphasises death and blood spilled everywhere; that of Samaria explains the reasons which lead to the deportation of the northern kingdom, namely the people's sin (17:7-23); the fall of Jerusalem ends with the destruction of walls and buildings (the temple, the palace and residences, large and small) and the carrying off of sacred objects and precious metals to Babylon (25:8-10, 13-17).

The following table indicates the number of verses which deal with different themes.

	persons	objects	meaning	result
The house of Ahab	62	2	7	9[3]
The northern kingdom	6	0	17	18
The southern kingdom	13	9	0	9

The author changes the emphasis in each account to avoid having to relate three macabre stories or give long theological explanations. Each story is *characteristic* of the other judgments. The blood spilled by Jehu is characteristic of the blood spilled in Samaria in 722, in Jerusalem in 586, in Jerusalem in 70 A.D. and even at the Last Judgment (cf. Rev 14:18-20). When the time of grace comes to an end nothing more can prevent judgment from manifesting itself completely.

Evaluation of Jehu's Behaviour

Jehu is a bloodthirsty man responsible for the massacre of the family of Ahab. The author of Kings provides a mixed moral and spiritual evaluation. The new monarch is not reproached for his attitude towards the former royal family. On the contrary, the massacre of Ahab's family was the will of God and Jehu is praised for having carried it out: *"And the LORD said to Jehu, 'Because you have done well in doing what is right in My sight, and have done to the house of Ahab all that was in My heart, your sons shall sit on the throne of Israel to the fourth generation."* (10:30). Jehu is rewarded with a dynasty which lasts longer than any other in Israel.[4]

The king is not reproached for having killed sinners, but for not having gone far enough in his religious reforms. Jehu had ordered the killing of the priests of Baal and had destroyed the

---

[3]　The reign of Jehu (10:28-36).

[4]　The dynasty of Omri lasted four generations, over a period of 43 years, whereas the dynasty of Jehu lasted five generations: Jehu, Joahaz, Joash, Jeroboam II, Zachariah (15:12) and 89 years (841-753 B.C.).

statues and temple of Baal in Samaria (10:18-27), but he had not led Israel to the unique worship of the Lord centred in Jerusalem: *"Thus Jehu destroyed Baal from Israel. However Jehu did not turn away from the sins of Jeroboam the son of Nebat, who had made Israel sin, that is,*

Black obelisk (see footnote 6)

from the golden calves that were at Bethel and Dan. (10:28-29; see also v. 31).[5] As a result Jehu is confronted with a number of difficulties: Hazael, the new king of Syria *"conquered them in all the territory of Israel from the Jordan eastward"* and seized the East Bank (10:33).[6]

---

[5] A century later, Hosea condemns Jehu for having spilled blood at Jezreel; *"Call his name Jezreel, for in a little while I will avenge the bloodshed of Jezreel on the house of Jehu, and bring an end to the kingdom of the house of Israel."* (Hosea 1:4). He no doubt alludes to the death of Ahaziah, king of Judah, because the mandate of punishment transmitted by Elisha only concerned the house of Ahab. Archer (*Encyclopedia of Bible Difficulties*, p. 208) thinks that "Although Jehu had only done what God commanded, he did so out of a carnal zeal that was tainted with protective self-interest."

[6] Jehu is mentioned in different Assyrian inscriptions, particularly on the black obelisk of Shalmanasar III. "There is even a picture of Jehu's entourage presenting the tribute of the Assyrian monarch. It may be that Jehu solicited the aid of Assyria to fight off the encroachments of Hazael of Syria." (Burney quoted by Dilday, p. 344). "The event of 841 B.C. can be dated precisely and it is very exact data which supports the chronology of kings in the OT" (*NCB* p. 366). "Jehu is mentioned in Assyrian inscriptions under the name of 'Ja-u-a, son of Hu-um-ri'. He was anything but a son of Omri; on the contrary, he wiped out that entire family. But the reign of Omri had been so brilliant and his name, as founder of the dynasty, was so well-known abroad that in general his successors are erroneously designated as his descendants." (*BA* p. 146). Perhaps it was simply a way of emphasising royal descent (cf. Nebuchadnezzar is the "father" of Belchatsar in Dan 5:2).

Did Jehu massacre the family of Ahab out of religious zeal or for political reasons? It was probably a combination of both. Certain commentators see Jehu only as an opportunist who profited from the discontent of the people to establish his own power.[7]

---

[7] "Jehu's revolt was nothing else but a politically motivated military *coup d'etat* which lacked any real popular support. This would explain why it was so bloody. As a usurper Jehu naturally had to exterminate all members of the Omri dynasty and their adherents in order to secure the throne... The killing of Jezebel and the other Omrides effectively broke the treaty with Tyre, and the alliance with Judah was likewise shattered by the murder of its king and 42 princes" (Ahlström: "King Jehu – A Prophet's Mistake" in *Scripture in History,* p. 58-59). Jehu would have been completely isolated, because although he was a subject of the Assyrians, as the black obelisk indicates, they did not help him with his contentions with Hazael, king of Syria. Isolated from all sides, Israel would have lost a great deal in Jehu's *coup d'etat.* Ahlström therefore concludes: "Elisha's candidate for the throne, Jehu, did not become a blessing for Israel, but just the opposite." (p. 61). Ahlström criticises Elisha, in contempt of Scripture, but he also forgets that Israel had fallen into a time of judgment. It is thus logical that Israel's situation should decline. For Savran ("1 and 2 Kings" in *The Literary Guide to the Bible,* p. 154), Jehu's behaviour in no way resembles that of a hero. He bears all the signs of a traitor, which he actually was, to the point that even Jezebel provokes him (9:31) "Her provocative challenge to Jehu... can be translated 'Is all well, you Zimri, murderer of his master?', equating Jehu with the officer who assassinated King Elah of Israel some forty years earlier, at the encouragement of a prophet ironically named Jehu ben Hanani (1 Kings 16:8-12)" (p. 154). Thus, God ends up punishing the house of Ahab for having turned its back on him, and for this purpose uses a traitor (Jehu) who (also literally) stabs his adversaries in the back.

THE LAST ACTS OF ELISHA
(2 KINGS 13:14–21)

Surprisingly, the author mentions Elisha again so far away from the other texts dealing with this prophet. The man who had retreated into the background is suddenly back on centre stage. Why speak of Elisha at this point? Certainly, the author of Kings is a historian, and Elisha dies during the reign of Joash. Chronologically, the account of the last acts of the prophet is in the right place. The author, however, was not obliged to mention the death of Elisha (he did not do so for the other prophets).[1] He could have attached these verses to the section on Elisha simply by omitting the name of the king of Israel, as in the other stories of Elisha.[2] The author often groups certain stories such as the reigns of kings. He thus passes from one reign to another, sometimes anticipating a reign or going back in time to bring the story of a neighbouring kingdom up to date.[3] Why did he set apart these verses on Elisha when he could have proceeded in a different manner?

This separation is important for several reasons:

1. It shows that the prophet lived for a long time after the destruction of the house of Ahab (more than forty-five years: see p. 17).

---

[1] *NDB* (p. 400) remarks on the death of the prophet in hindsight: "Having that much power to perform miracles did not prevent the great servant of God from 'being stricken with the illness of which he would die.' (v. 14) Because the believer must one day leave this world, it is quite possible for him to be ill and not be healed." The remark is in itself pertinent but is not helpful for the the comprehension of this text; the author does not emphasise the death of the prophet but rather the life that he gives.

[2] Exceptions: 3:1, 6 and the two transitions on the kings of Judah (8:16-29).

[3] Jehoshaphat is mentioned in 1 Kings 22:1-33, but is not introduced until 1 Kings 22:41-51; he then reappears in 2 Kings 3:1-14; Baasha is mentioned during the reign of Asa of Judah in 1 Kings 15:17-22, whereas the reign of Nadab, father of Baasha, is presented later on.

2. It is sometimes possible to regroup certain actions, but moving the announcement of the Syrian defeat and the story of Hazael's death (13:22-25) to a point before the beginning of Jehu's reign would have significantly changed the perspective of this victory.

3. Elisha's miraculous ministry is concentrated in one particular period, that of king Joram. This period of grace, the only one of its kind in the Old Testament, is followed by a long "normal" period, during which God remains relatively in the background. At the end of this period Elisha intervenes again briefly to put an end to the king of Syria's oppression and to bring a man back to life.[4] Elisha thus foreshadows the ministry of Christ. Christ also performed miracles during a limited period (the three-and-a-half years of his ministry on earth), then withdrew for a long period (the time of the Church), after which he will return to earth to put an end to sin and resurrect the dead (his second coming). Nowadays God's miracles are more discreet than during his ministry on earth. Certainly the Holy Spirit is active and non-believers are converted and have their lives changed, but miracles of a physical nature (healings, resurrections, multiplication of food, etc.) are rare; when they do occur, they are less "spectacular" than during Jesus' ministry on earth. We also note that the coming of Elisha was announced long before the start of his ministry, because four chapters separate the beginning of his ministry (2 Kings 2:14) from the first calling (1 Kings 19:19-21). In the same way Christ's coming was foretold centuries before his incarnation.

4. The structure of the Elisha account is well-balanced, because the calling of the prophet (1 Kings 19:19-21) precedes his ministry by four chapters, and the epilogue on Elisha

---

[4] The remark and the exhortation of John H. Alexander (p. 184) deserve to be mentioned: "It was as if Elisha was completely ousted for 45 years. But he remains ready for the day when God will need him when he receives Joash, the grandson of Jehu who has just become king, at his deathbed in order to transmit to him God's commands regarding the defeat of the Syrians ... Are we ready — perhaps after having played a major part in carrying out God's works — to step back, to delegate our responsibilities to others, perhaps even to disappear, but to remain vigilant until the King needs us and we can still serve as his messengers?"

(2 Kings 13:14-21) follows four chapters after his ministry.[5] This structure in the form of 1-0-1-0-1 (three appearances interrupted by two empty periods) resembles the Elijah cycle, where two chapters "interrupt" the story line of Elijah (1 Kings 20 and 22). With Elijah the sections at both ends are longer than the one in the centre (1 Kings 21) and the interruptions are brief (one chapter each) instead of long, as shown in the illustration below.

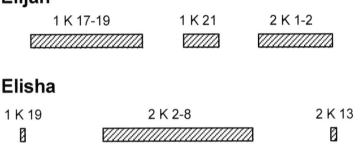

Elijah

1 K 17-19   1 K 21   2 K 1-2

Elisha

1 K 19   2 K 2-8   2 K 13

5. The end of Elisha's ministry is marked by *grace*. Hazael, who had been "anointed" by Elisha's prophecy to start the period of judgment (8:7-15) is now stopped by a new prophecy of Elisha (13:14-19). In this way the ministry of judgment which was carried out with reservation by Elisha is now "neutralised". The defeat and the death of Hazael are related in the last verses of chapter 13. The author mentions God's mercy, which is the only reason of hope for Israel: "*And Hazael king of Syria oppressed Israel all the days of Joahaz. But the LORD was gracious to them, had compassion on them, and regarded them, because of His covenant with Abraham, Isaac, and Jacob, and would not yet destroy them or cast them from His presence. Now Hazael king of Syria died. Then Ben-Hadad his son reigned in his place. And Joash [alias Jehoash] the son of Joahaz recaptured from the hand of Ben-Hadad, the son of Hazael, the cities which he*

---

5   There are 144 verses between 1 Kings 19:19 and 2 Kings 2:1 and 124 verses between 2 Kings 9:3 and 13:14.

had taken out of the hand of Joahaz his father by war. Three times Joash defeated him and recaptured the cities of Israel." (2 Kings 13:22-25).

The End of Oppression (13:14-19)

[14]Elisha had become sick with the illness of which he would die. Then Joash the king of Israel came down to him, and wept over his face, and said, "O my father, my father, the chariots of Israel and their horsemen!" [15]And Elisha said to him, "Take a bow and some arrows" So he took himself a bow and some arrows. [16]Then he said to the king of Israel, "Put your hand on the bow." So he put his hand on it, and Elisha put his hands on the king's hands. [17]And he said, "Open the east window"; and he opened it. Then Elisha said, "Shoot"; and he shot. And he said, "The arrow of the LORD's deliverance and the arrow of deliverance from Syria; for you must strike the Syrians at Aphek till you have destroyed them." [18]Then he said, "Take the arrows"; so he took them. And he said to the king of Israel, "Strike the ground"; so he struck three times, and stopped. [19]And the man of God was angry with him, and said, "You should have struck five or six times; then you would have struck Syria till you had destroyed it! But now you will strike Syria only three times."

The story must be read like the account on Elijah's ascension. The king's words are identical to those of Elisha when he saw Elijah rise to heaven: *"O my father, my father, the chariots of Israel and their horsemen!"* (2:12 and 3:14). On the other hand the narrator informs us of the prophet's fate with his first words. Concerning Elijah, he had said: *"when the LORD was about to take up Elijah into heaven by a whirlwind"* (2:1; see p. 49) and here he indicates that Elisha is near the end of his life: *"Elisha had become sick with the illness of which he would die"* (13:14). The two stories do not emphasise the departure of the prophets (Elijah's ascension or Elisha's illness), but what follows. After Elijah's departure the question was whether Elisha would be his true successor, and at Elisha's departure the question is what Israel's fate will be.

The king's tears express his sorrow, not for Elisha's death (the prophet was already old[6]), but for the loss his death represents.[7] Elisha is equivalent to a "cavalry" for Israel. Perhaps the tears also express the king's last entreaty to the prophet. Similarly to Elijah's departure, the person who shows his attachment to the prophet receives a blessing. Elisha had received the double anointment for which he had asked, and Joash receives deliverance from Syrian oppression.

The bond between the departing prophet and his visitor (or his companion) is expressed physically. Elijah left his cloak which Elisha put on, and Elisha places his hands on the hands of Joash. The symbolic dimension of the gesture is obvious: "A large number of examples drawn from ancient writings prove that the act of shooting an arrow into enemy territory was the equivalent of a declaration of war or even of taking possession."[8] The window which faces east is chosen, because the victory will take place at Aphek in the valley of Jezreel, where Ahab had had a great victory (1 Kings 20:26).[9]

The sequence of orders is surprising: Elisha tells the king to tighten the bow, then to open the window. How can he do this? Would it not be more logical to open the window before tightening the bow? But between the two injunctions Elisha *"put his hands on the king's hands"*. Does this mean that he holds the bow taut for the king while the latter opens the window? This would emphasise the symbiosis between Elisha and Joash. It is also possible that Elisha simply ordered the king to tighten his bow *by attaching the bowstring*. Bows were "loosened" after each use to prevent them from losing their elasticity. Elisha would thus be telling Joash to put his weapon in working order.[10] The prophet would then place his hands on the king's hands to

---

[6] This event takes place more than sixty years after his calling.

[7] Flavius Josephus confirms that the king views Elisha's departure as a catastrophe, because Israel will be vulnerable to the Syrians (*Antiquities* 9.8.6). Other commentators share this opinion: *BA* p. 162, Dilday p. 384, Hobbs p. 169, House p. 307.

[8] *BA* p. 162.

[9] Dilday p. 385, Vos p. 178, *BA* p. 162.

[10] W. Boyd Barrick : Elisha and the Magic Bow: A Note on 2 Kings 13.15-17 in *VT* 35 (1985) pp. 355-363.

show that victory would come to the one who holds the appropriate weapon. In other words victory would belong those who were well-armed and ready for combat. Elisha then orders him to open the window and shoot in the direction of the Syrians to predict victory over them.

After the first arrow has been shot, Elisha orders the king to take the other arrows and strike the ground with them. It is likely that the king was supposed to shoot the arrows towards the ground from the window "as if to finish off a defeated enemy."[11] When Joash stops after striking the ground only three times, Elisha is irritated, not because the king interrupts an apparently senseless action, but because the king, having understood the significance of this gesture, spares the enemy. Joash probably does not want to destroy Syria for the same reasons Ahab had: he fears Assyria and wants to use Syria as a buffer state between himself and the Assyrians.[12] Elisha does not appreciate this political manoeuvre, because true peace cannot be at the expense of the judgment of the wicked.[13]

At the end of Elisha's life it is helpful to recall the words spoken at Mount Horeb concerning his ministry: *"It shall be that whoever escapes the sword of Hazael, Jehu will kill; and whoever escapes the sword of Jehu, Elisha will kill."* (1 Kings 19:17). At first glance Elisha must *continue* the punishment of Israel initiated by Hazael and Jehu, which ill suits the character of the prophet of grace. Elisha actually *halts* the punishment of Israel when he speaks the words which will conquer Hazael, a man whom Jehu and his descendants had not been able to overcome. With Hazael's death the punishment prepared at the time of Hazael's anointment is finished. Previously, at Mount Horeb, the Lord had clearly announced the grace which would leave a remnant of the people in Israel (*"Yet I have reserved seven thousand in Israel"* 1 Kings 19:18). Thus the parallel of 1 Kings 19:17 is not synonymic, but antithetical. First the judgment of Israel is foretold (*"It shall be that whoever escapes*

---

[11] *BA* p. 163; Keil p. 377.
[12] *NBC* 324; Whitcomb p. 83.
[13] John H. Alexander (p. 186) feels that the king lacked faith by striking only three times.

the sword of Hazael, Jehu will kill"), then grace is mentioned *("and whoever escapes the sword of Jehu, Elisha will kill."*), because the person who escapes Jehu turns out to be Hazael (Jehu has been dead for several decades and Hazael continues to persecute Israel). It is up to Elisha to end this massacre.

The Final Resurrection (13:20-21)

> [20]*Then Elisha died, and they buried him. And the raiding bands from Moab invaded the land in the spring of the year.* [21]*So it was, as they were burying a man, that suddenly they spied a band of raiders; and they put the man in the tomb of Elisha; and when the man was let down and touched the bones of Elisha, he revived and stood on his feet.*

The narrator concludes the story of Elisha with a story of *life*.

1. Elisha resuscitates a second person after the Shunammite's son. He thus shows again that exceptional grace which is characteristic of his ministry, because no other man except Jesus brought more than one person back to life.[14]
2. The Israelite brought back to life had been killed by the Moabites and not by the Syrians. This means that the redemption in which Elisha is implicated is not limited to the Israelite-Syrian conflict, but also extends to other trials. Elisha is the prophet who announces complete redemption.

The parallels of this story with the ascension of Elijah carry on, because in Elisha's case, life also continues after death. In a sense Elisha does even better than Elijah, because it is not his own life that continues after death but the life of others as well. Furthermore Elisha accomplishes this miracle after his decease.[15]

---

[14] Elijah, Peter and Paul each brought one person back to life (1 Kings 17:22; Acts 9:40; 20:10).

[15] Elisha had already been dead for some time. According to various translations, the miracle occurred "the following year" (LSG, SEM), "at the beginning of the year" (TOB, DRB, KJ), "in the spring" (NIV); other translations mention Moabite raids which took place "every year". Elisha was buried in a cave which was covered by a stone (Vos p. 178). The unexpected arrival of the Moabites forced the Israelite soldiers to throw the body of their comrade into the prophet's tomb, which had quickly been opened for that reason.

The *Wisdom of Sirach* (48:13-14) considers this miracle as one of the prophet's greatest.[16]

Elisha's life ends with the act which symbolises the greatest act of the Messiah, namely his redemptive death. Jesus died on the cross for the salvation of mankind, and as a sign of this victory over death men rose from their tombs at the very instant that Jesus atoned for the sins of mankind. *"And Jesus cried out again with a loud voice, and yielded up His spirit. Then, behold, the veil of the temple was torn in two from top to bottom; and the earth quaked, and the rocks were split, and the graves were opened; and many bodies of the saints who had fallen asleep were raised; and coming out of the graves after His resurrection, they went into the holy city and appeared to many."* (Matt 27:50-53).

---

[16] Bergen (p. 169) remarks that the narrator fortunately did not indicate the location of the grave, thus preventing the tomb from becoming a shrine and place of pilgrimage. Unfortunately, the bones of the prophet became objects of veneration afterwards, and perhaps even the sepulchre. "The tomb of Elisha could still be visited at the time of Saint Jerome…the bones of the prophet were taken from the tomb by Julian the Apostate. Some which had been preserved were given to Athanasius and transported to Alexandria in 463, then later moved to Constantinople." (Mangenot: *Dictionnaire de la Bible*, vol. 2, col. 1695-1696).

ECHOES OF ELISHA
IN THE NEW TESTAMENT

Elisha is mentioned only once in the New Testament, when Luke speaks of Jesus' comparison of the inhabitants of Nazareth with the contemporaries of Elijah and Elisha: *"Then He said, 'Assuredly, I say to you, no prophet is accepted in his own country. But I tell you truly, many widows were in Israel in the days of Elijah, when the heaven was shut up three years and six months, and there was a great famine throughout all the land; but to none of them was Elijah sent except to Zarephath in the region of Sidon, to a woman who was a widow. And many lepers were in Israel in the time of Elisha the prophet, and none of them was cleansed except Naaman the Syrian.'"* (Luke 4:24-27).

Why did the authors of the New Testament not take more advantage of the typological similarity between Elisha and Jesus? "Given the many links between the two, including the fact ... that John the Baptist is so clearly identified in the Gospels with Elijah, it is intriguing that more is not explicitly made in the NT of the Jesus-Elisha connection" (Provan p. 234). It must be emphasized that the comparisons between Jesus and Old Testament heroes seek to emphasise Jesus' superiority rather than identify him with these great men. Jesus is greater than Abraham (*"Most assuredly, I say to you, before Abraham was, I AM."* John 8:58), than Moses (*"For this One has been counted worthy of more glory than Moses, inasmuch as He who built the house has more honour than the house."* Heb 3:3), than David (Acts 2:29, 34; 13:36), than Solomon (*"and indeed a greater than Solomon is here."* Matt 12:42; Luke 11:31). This perhaps explains why Jesus was not compared with Joseph, Joshua and Elisha, all of whom have remarkable similarities to him. Actually, although these three men are important, they themselves had more famous predecessors. *Joseph* played a leading role and his behaviour was exemplary, but he never reached the same level of fame as Abraham. He is not even one of the three basic patriarchs who are regularly mentioned in the expression "the God of Abraham, Isaac and Jacob" (a triad mentioned 26 times in the Bible). There are only three allusions to the life of Joseph in the Bible outside of Genesis, only one of which is in the Old Testament (Psalms 105:17; Acts 7:9-14; Hebrews 11:21-22). As for *Joshua*, he remains in Moses' shadow, and *Elisha*, even though he received double the anointment of Elijah, was never the subject of debates like his predecessor whose return was prophesied by Malachi. From an apologetic point of view it is therefore more appropriate to emphasise the superiority of Jesus compared to Abraham, Moses and Elijah than to Joseph, Joshua and Elisha.[1]

The Gospel of John and the Miracles of Elisha

The *name* of Elisha appears therefore only in Luke 4:27. It would nevertheless seem that John the Apostle used the *miracles* of Elisha as a framework on which to base part of his gospel. In fact the seven miracles of Jesus which John relates can be equated with seven miracles of Elisha.[2] This does not mean that John falsified the story, but suggests that amongst the

---

[1]   The superiority of Jesus in relation to different persons or institutions of the Old Testament comes out very clearly in Hebrews: Jesus is exalted above the celestial beings (the angels), Moses, and the high priests. These are the highest institutions and the greatest sacrifices which serve as points of comparison to show the superiority of Jesus (for example the great day of atonement). "It may be that it is precisely because both Joshua and Elisha are successors to more famous men that this kind of thinking was inhibited. There would have been a natural desire within the church to avoid the suggestion that Jesus was John's successor in any sense that detracted from his pre-eminence – particularly since this was apparently a live issue in some quarters (note the careful way in which John 1.1-42 addresses the issue). Thus it is not surprising that the typological significance of Elisha in relation to Jesus has been downplayed" (Provan p. 234).

[2]   "It can be safely said with reference to the miracles of Jesus that these find their clearest reflection and most perfect parallel, as far as the Old Testament is concerned, in the miracles of Elisha. Seven of the most outstanding miracles of Elisha can be seen echoed and fulfilled in the miracles of Jesus. The parallelism is seen most clearly in the Gospel according to St John" Gerald Bostock: "Jesus as the New Elisha" in *The Expository Times* 92 (1980) pp. 40-41.

innumerable miracles of Jesus (cf. John 21:25), the apostle used only those miracles which corresponded to the ministry of Elisha.

1. The first miracle of Jesus concerns water, just like Elisha's first redemptive miracle. Elisha purifies the spring of Jericho (2 Kings 2:19-22) and Jesus transforms water into wine at the wedding in Canaan in Galilee (John 2:1-11). The quantity and the quality of the transformed water is emphasised by the narrators. Elisha purifies the water "to this day" and Jesus transforms roughly six hundred litres of water into premium wine. The two men use "pure" objects: Elisha asks for a *new* bowl and Jesus fills jars used for *purification*. A sign of the divine covenant is symbolically present: salt is an element of the covenant (see note 4 p. 65) and the wine represents the blood of Christ which is poured out for our sins.

Just after the miracle the two men go up to the religious capital and give a sign of judgment there: Elisha goes to Bethel (place of impure worship) and curses the adolescent mockers (2 Kings 2:23-24); Jesus goes up to Jerusalem and purifies the temple by chasing out the animal vendors and money changers (John 2:13-17). Similarities also exist between events prior to the miracles: Elisha manifests his glory to the sons of the prophets by crossing the Jordan, and he then discusses the ascension of Elijah with them (2 Kings 2:14-18); Jesus receives the witness of John the Baptist at the Jordan, then calls his first disciples and tells them what they will see: *"Most assuredly, I say to you, hereafter you shall see heaven open, and the angels of God ascending and descending upon the Son of Man."* (John 1:51).

All of these analogies contribute to the comparison between Jesus and Elisha, and demonstrate Jesus' superiority over Elisha.

a. Christ not only improves the water, but changes its nature (the water turns into wine).

b. Grace is more evident in Jesus than in Elisha (who is nevertheless the prophet of grace), because those who profane the faith are not killed, but merely chased away. Jesus takes the punishment upon himself. When the Jews ask him for a sign to condemn the sinners, he does not send two bears, but announces his death and resurrection: *"Destroy this temple, and in three days I will raise it up. "* (John 2:19).

c. The miracle of the "open sky" will be seen by all of Jesus' disciples (cf. Acts 1:9-11), not limited to the sole disciple of Elijah.

2. The second miracle reported in the gospel of John is the healing of the son of a royal officer (John 4:46-54). This healing has several points in common with the resurrection of the Shunammite's son (2 Kings 4:8-37). A high-ranking person travels twenty kilometres to the west to implore the man of God's aid for their son, who is dead or on the brink of death. Doubt is implied or mentioned: the Shunammite seems to criticise Elisha (she actually expresses her confusion) and Jesus seems to criticise the father (he actually addresses the crowd). The presence or absence of the man of God lies at the heart of the story. Elisha cannot heal the child from a distance with his staff, but must go in person to the child and lie along its body; this demonstrates Christ's superiority over the Old Testament prophet.

We also note that the stories which precede these two accounts have points in common. In the book of Kings a widow who is about to lose her children meets Elisha (2 Kings 4:1-7), and in the gospel of John, Jesus encounters a Samaritan woman who lives on the fringe of society (John 4:3-42). These two women have no husband (one has just lost her husband, while the other lives with a man who is not her husband). The former is part of the community of the faithful (she belongs to the group of the sons of prophets and her husband *"feared the Lord"*) while the Samaritan is a foreigner. Elisha and Jesus offer aid by means of a "miraculous" liquid. Elisha increases the Jewess' oil to an unlimited amount and Jesus offers the Samaritan water which will quench her thirst forever (John 4:10-14).

3. The third miracle in John immediately follows on the second (John 5:1-16). Jesus heals a crippled man at the pool of Bethesda. This miracle has parallels with the healing of Naaman (2 Kings 5), which comes shortly after the story of the Shunammite. The two accounts mention the "miraculous" water into which one must immerse oneself in order to be healed: the Jordan and the pool of Bethesda. Naaman is surprised at the choice of the Jordan as the source of purification (2 Kings 5:12) and the reader of the gospel could be surprised by the crowd's

expectation in Jerusalem: *"In these lay a great multitude of sick people, blind, lame, paralyzed, waiting for the moving of the water. For an angel went down at a certain time into the pool and stirred up the water; then whoever stepped in first, after the stirring of the water, was made well of whatever disease he had."* (John 5:3-4).[3]

The *journey* of the two men is an important element of the story. Naaman undertakes a long voyage to present himself to Elisha; he then must go to the Jordan (a two-day journey); after the healing, he goes back to the prophet before returning home. Whereas the cripple has difficulty in moving only a few metres to step into the water (other sick people always beat him to it), after his healing he walks away with his mattress, then returns to the Jewish leaders to reveal his healer's identity.

There is also a contrast in social status. Naaman the Syrian is rich and surrounded by servants, whereas the cripple is Jewish, poor and isolated, as no-one ever helps him into the pool.

The illness of the two men is apparently incurable; Naaman has certainly consulted all of the Syrian healers before making the journey to Samaria, and the cripple had been suffering from his condition for *"thirty-eight years"*. Despite his illness the Syrian has remained active and integrated in society, whereas the Jew in his resignation no longer attempts anything. Elisha asks Naaman to commit himself (he must go to the Jordan and immerse himself seven times); Jesus heals the cripple by his word alone, without compelling him to enter the water.

The two stories end sadly. Gehazi betrays Elisha, and the cripple betrays Jesus, as he diverts the ire of the Jewish leaders towards him (John 5:15-16). Elisha denounces the transgressions of his servant, who walks in sin (*"Is it time to receive money and to receive clothing, olive groves and vineyards, sheep and oxen, male and female servants?"* [v.] 26), then punishes him severely (v. 27), whereas Jesus warns the cripple not to sin anymore in order to avoid a more severe punishment: *"See, you have been made well. Sin no more, lest a worse thing come upon you."* (John 5:14).

---

[3]   The water of the pool is not "miraculous" until it is stirred up, i.e. until it resembles the currents of a *river*.

4. The fourth miracle in John is the story of the multiplication of bread (John 6:1-15), the only one mentioned in all four gospels. The parallels to the multiplication of bread performed by Elisha (2 Kings 4:42-44) have already been presented (see pp. 24, 116-117). John is the only evangelist to point out that they were made of barley (John 6:9, 13), like those used by Elisha (2 Kings 4:42).

5. The fifth miracle in John is when Jesus walks on water (John 6:16-21). The parallels to the story of the floating axe head (2 Kings 6:1-7) are described on pages 26, 136-138.

6. The sixth miracle in John is the healing of a man blind since birth (John 9). The themes of sight and blindness can be connected to the miracles in the story of the siege of Dothan (2 Kings 6:8-23). Elisha opens the eyes of his servant so he can see the armies of the Lord; he then blinds the enemy. Jesus permits a man born blind to see what he has never seen before. The latter also discovers God's glory because he recognises Jesus as the Messiah (John 9:35-38). The Pharisees behave like they were blind because they do not recognise the Messiah in spite of an undeniable miracle. Jesus affirms that his coming is a judgment which renders people blind: *"And Jesus said, 'For judgment I have come into this world, that those who do not see may see, and that those who see may be made blind.'"* (John 9:39).[4]

7. The seventh and last miracle in John is the resurrection of Lazarus (John 11:1-44). The miracle corresponds to the last miracle of Elisha (2 Kings 13:20-21). In the two accounts, a dead man is raised up from the grave. Jesus' miracle is the greater of the two, because Lazarus had been in the tomb for four days, whereas the Israelite soldier had just been placed in Elisha's tomb.

---

[4] Thomas Louis Brodie ("Jesus as the New Elisha: Cracking the Code" in *The Expository Times* 93, 1981, pp. 39-42) connects the healing of the blind man to the healing of Naaman.

Conclusion

John did not "exploit" all of the possible correlations between Jesus and Elisha, but rather let himself be inspired by *certain* stories from Kings. His goal was not to glorify Elisha, but to show the greatness of Jesus' ministry. (In order to complete his task, John limited himself to seven miracles of Jesus, the symbolic number of completeness).[5]

On a more general level, the New Testament authors often used an Old Testament story in a particular manner, and referred to a particular or even marginal aspect, meanwhile ignoring the main lesson. For example at Nazareth Jesus quoted the healing of Naaman, but restricted the lesson to what illustrated his topic. The richness of Old Testament teaching is thus more vast than the lessons the New Testament draws from it. Jesus and the apostles showed how one could use the Old Testament, opening a path they encourage us to follow. According to Paul, *"All Scripture is given by inspiration of God, and is profitable for doctrine, for reproof, for correction, for instruction in righteousness, that the man of God may be complete, thoroughly equipped for every good work"* (2 Tim 3:16-17). Jesus used the whole of Scripture to teach the disciples on the road to Emmaus: *"Then He said to them, "O foolish ones, and slow of heart to believe in all that the prophets have spoken! Ought not the*

---

[5] The resurrection of the son of the widow of Nain (Luke 7:11-17) and the healing of the ten lepers (Luke 17:11-19) are two stories which present direct parallels to the two miracles of Elisha (see p. 26). We must mention here that these two stories are mentioned only in the third gospel, the only one which mentions the name of Elisha (Luke 4:27). This gospel also contains other possible allusions to the lives of Elijah and Elisha: the healing of centurion's servant (Luke 7:1-10; cf. 2 Kings 4:8-37); the request to send lightning from the sky (Luke 9:54; cf. 2 Kings 1:10, 12). It would appear that Luke was also sensitive to the typological dimensions of Elijah and Elisha. See the contributions of Thomas Louis Brodie: "Jesus as the New Elisha: Cracking the Code" in *The Expository Times* 93, 1981, pp. 39-42 and *The Crucial Bridge: The Elijah-Elisha Narrative as an Interpretive Synthesis of Genesis-Kings and a Literary Model for the Gospels*, Liturgical Press, 2000, p. 114, and the thesis of Darrell Reid James: *The Elijah-Elisha Motif in Luke*, Dissertation Southern Baptist Theological Seminary, 1984, p. 246.

Christ to have suffered these things and to enter into His glory?"
And beginning at Moses and all the Prophets, He expounded to
them in all the Scriptures the things concerning Himself." (Luke
24:25-27). The stories of Elisha can certainly serve as sermon
texts to announce Christ and illustrate his ministry.

BIBLIOGRAPHY

--------*Nouveau Dictionnaire Biblique* (revised)*,* Emmaüs, St-Légier, 1992, pp. 399-400, 1130-1132.

--------*Traduction œcuménique de la Bible,* éd. intégrale Ancien Testament, Cerf et Bergers et Mages, Paris, 1976, pp. 615-621.

AHARONI, Yohanan & AVI-YONAH, Michael: *La Bible par les cartes*, Brepols, 1991, pp. 82-85.

AHLSTRÖM, Gösta W.: "King Jehu – A Prophet's Mistake" in *Scripture in History. Essays in Honor of J. Coert Rylaarsdam*, ed. Arthur L. Merrill & Thomas W. Overholt, Pickwick Press, Pittsburgh, 1977, pp. 47-69.

ALEXANDER, John H.: *Elie, Elisée: messagers d'hier pour aujourd'hui*, Maison de la Bible, Genève, 1990, 191 p.

ARCHER, Gleason L.: *Encyclopedia of Bible Difficulties,* Zondervan, Grand Rapids, 1982, pp. 204-209.

------- *A Survey of Old Testament Introduction*, Moody, Chicago, 1964, pp. 275-282.

ARNOLD, Daniel: *Elie entre le jugement et la grâce*, Emmaüs, St-Légier, 2001, 202 p.

------- "Une guérison en deux étapes" in *Ichthus* 135 (1986) pp. 21-24.

BARRICK, W. Boyd: "Elisha and the Magic Bow: A Note on 2 Kings 13.15-17" in *Vetus Testamentum* 35 (1985) pp. 355-363.

BELLETT, J. G.: *Courtes méditations sur Elisée*, Bibles et traités chrétiens, Vevey, 1977, 95 p.

BERGEN, Wesley J.: *Elisha and the End of Prophetism* (Journal for the Study of the Old Testament Supplement Series 286), Sheffield Press, Sheffield, 1999, 200 p.

BLAKE, Ian M. : "Jericho (Ain Es-Sultan): Joshua's Curse and Elisha's Miracle - One Possible Explanation" in *Palestine Exploration Quarterly* (1967) pp. 86-97.

BOSTOCK, D. Gerald : "Jesus as the New Elisha" in *The Expository Times* 92 (1980) pp. 39-41.

BRODIE, Thomas Louis: "Jesus as the New Elisha: Cracking the Code" in *The Expository Times* 93 (1981) pp. 39-42.

------- *The Crucial Bridge: The Elijah-Elisha Narrative as an Interpretive Synthesis of Genesis-Kings and a Literary Model for the Gospels*, Liturgical Press, Collegeville, Minnesota, 2000, 114 p.

BRONNER, Leah: *The Stories of Elijah and Elisha as Polemics Against Baal Worship*, Brill, Leiden, 1968, 155 p.

BROWN, Raymond E.: "Jesus and Elisha" in *Perspective* 12 (1971) pp. 85-104.

BUIS, Pierre: *Le livre des Rois*, Galalada, Paris, 1997, 312 p.

------- "Rois (livre des)" in *Supplément au Dictionnaire de la Bible,* vol. 10, dir. L. Pirot. Letouzey & Ané, Paris, 1979, col. 695-740.

BURNS, John Barclay: "Why Did the Besieging Army Withdraw? (2 Kings 3.27)" in *Zeitschrift für die alttestamentliche Wissenschaft* (1990) pp. 187-194.

CARLSON, R.A.: "Elisée-le successor d'Elie" in *Vetus Testamentum* 20 (1970) pp. 385-405.

CARPENTER, H. J.: "The First Book of Kings" and "The Second Book of Kings" in *A Devotional Commentary*, Religious Tract Society, Manchester, s.d., pp. 182 + 184.

CARROLL, R.P.: "The Elijah-Elisha Sagas: Some Remarks on Prophetic Succession in Ancient Israel" in *Vetus Testamentum* 19 (1969) pp. 400-415.

CAZELLES, Henri, dir.: *Introduction à la Bible,* tome 2. Desclée, Paris, 1973, pp. 301-327.

COGAN, Mordechai & TADMOR, Hayim: "2 Kings" in *The Anchor Bible*, Doubleday, 1988, 371 p.

COHN, Robert L.: "Form and Perspective in 2 Kings V" in *Vetus Testamentum* 33 (1983) pp. 171-184.

CORL, J. Banks: *Elijah and Elisha within the Argument of Kings*, Thesis Dallas Theological Seminary, Micropublished by Theological Research Exchange Network, Portland, 1987.

DARBY, J.-N.: "1 Rois à Esther" in *Etudes sur la Parole,* Bibles et traités chrétiens, Vevey, 1963, pp. 5-89.

DAVIS, Dale Ralph: "The Kingdom of God in Transition: Interpreting 2 Kings 2" in *Westminster Theological Journal* 46 (1984) pp. 384-395.

DE BOER, p. A.H.: "Leah Bronner, The Stories of Elijah and Elisha as Polemics Against Baal Worship" in *Vetus Testamentum* 19 (1969) pp. 267-269.

DERCHAIN, Ph.: "Les plus anciens témoignages de sacrifices d'enfants chez les Sémites occidentaux" in *Vetus Testamentum* 20 (1970) pp. 351-355.

DEVRIES, C. E.: "Elisha" in *The Zondervan Pictorial Encyclopedia of the Bible*, vol. 2, Zondervan, Grand Rapids, 1975, pp. 290-292.

DILDAY, Russell H.: "1, 2 Kings" in *The Communicator's Commentary*, Word Book, Waco, 1987, 512 p.

DIXON, Francis: *Notes sur la vie du prophète Elisée: 12 études bibliques*, Croisade du Livre Chrétien, La Bégude, 1975, 50 p.

EDERSHEIM, Alfred: *Practical Truths from Elisha*, Kregel, Grand Rapids, 1982, 326 p.

ELLISON. H. L.: "1 and 2 Kings" in *The New Bible Commentary*, Inter-Varsity, London, 1955, pp. 300-338.

------- *The Prophets of Israel: From Ahijah to Hosea*, Paternoster, Sydney, 1969, 176 p.

ELLUL, Jacques: *Politique de Dieu, politiques des hommes*, Editions Universitaires, Paris, 1966, 237 p.

EXELL, Joseph S.: "1 Kings" and "2 Kings" in *The Biblical Illustrator*, F. Griffiths, London, 1909, pp. 329 + 342

FARRAR, F. W.: "The First Book of Kings" in *The Expositor's Bible*, Hodder and Stoughton, London, 1893, 503 p.

FEREDAY, W. W.: *Elisha the Prophet*, Pickering & Inglis, London, s.d., 119 p.

FILLION, F.: "Rois (IIIe et IVe livres des)" dans *Dictionnaire de la Bible*, pub. F. Vigouroux, vol. 5. Letouzey, Paris, 1926, col. 1145-1162.

FREEMAN, Hobart E.: *An Introduction to the Old Testament Prophets*, Moody, Chicago, 1968, 384 p.

GAUSSEN, L.: *Leçons données dans une école du dimanche sur les prophètes Elie et Elisée*, Soc. des livres religieux, Toulouse, 1870, 420 p.

GODET, Frédéric, dir.: "Les livres des Rois" in *Bible Annotée*, AT 4, PERLE Emmaüs, St-Légier, reprinted 1986, pp. 3-214.

GRAY, John: *1 & 2 Kings: A Commentary*, SCM Press, London, 1964, 813 p.

HALEY, John W.: *Alleged Discrepancies of the Bible*, Whitaker, Pittsburgh, s.d., p. 347.

HARRISON, R. K.: *Introduction to the Old Testament*, Eerdmans, Grand Rapids, 1969, pp. 719-737.

HENTSCHEL, Georg: *2 Könige*, Echter Verlag, Würzburg, 1985, 125 p.

HOBBS, T. R.: "2 Kings" in *Word Biblical Commentary*, Word Books, Waco (TX), 1985, 387 p.

HOUSE, Paul R.: "1, 2 Kings" in *The New American Commentary*, Broadman and Holman, 1995, 432 p.

JAMES, Darrell Reid: *The Elijah-Elisha Motif in Luke*, Dissertation Southern Baptist Theological Seminary, 1984, 246 p.

JENSEN, Irving L.: *2 Kings with Chronicles*, Moody, Chicago, 1968, 112 p.

JONES, Gwilym H.: "1 and 2 Kings" in *New Century Bible Commentary*, vol. 2, Eerdmans, Grand Rapids, 1930, 666 p.

JOSÈPHE, Flavius: *Antiquities* IX.2-5.

KEIL, C.F.: "1 & 2 Kings" in *Commentary on the Old Testament*, vol. 3, Eerdmans, Grand Rapids, pp. 1-523.

KILIAN, Rudolf: "Die Totenerweckungen Elias und Elisas – eine Motivwanderung?" in *Biblische Zeitschrift* (1966) pp. 44-56.

KITTEL, Rudolf: *Die Bücher der Könige*, Vandenhoeck & Ruprecht, Göttingen, 1900, 312 p.

KRUMMACHER, F.-W.: *Elisha, son of Saphat*, Georges Bridel, Lausanne, 1850, 364 p.

LA SOR, William Sanford: "1 et 2 Rois" in *Nouveau Commentaire Biblique*, Emmaüs, St-Légier, 1978, pp. 332-380.

LABARBERA, Robert: "The Man of War and the Man of God: Social Satire in 2 Kings 6:8-7:20" in *The Catholic Biblical Quarterly* 46 (1984) pp. 637-651.

LANGMESSER, August: "Die zwei Bücher der Könige" in *Praktische Bibelerklärung*, Carl Hirsch, Konstanz, s.d., 157 p.

LASINE, Stuart: "Jehoram and the Cannibal Mothers (2 Kings 6:24-33): Solomon's Judgment in an Inverted World" in *Journal for the Study of the Old Testament* 50 (1991) pp. 27-53.

LONG, Burke O.: "2 Kings" in *The Forms of the Old Testament Literature*, Eerdmans, Grand Rapids, 1991, 324 p.

------- "2 Kings III and Genres of Prophetic Narrative" in *Vetus Testamentum* 23 (1973) pp. 337-348.

------- "A Figure at the Gate: Readers, Reading, and Biblical Theologians" in G. Tucker (ed), *Canon, Theology and Old Testament*, Fortress, Philadelphia, 1988, pp. 166-186.

LUMBY, J. Rawson : "The Second Book of the Kings" in *The Cambridge Bible for Schools and Colleges*, University Press, Cambridge, 1896, 267 p.

LUNDBOM, Jack R.: "Elijah's Chariot Ride" in *Journal of Jewish Studies* 24/1 (1973) pp. 39-50.

MANGENOT, E.: "Elisée" dans *Dictionnaire de la Bible,* pub. F. Vigouroux, vol. 2. Letouzey, Paris, 1926, col. 1690-1696.

MARGALIT, Baruch : "Why King Mesha of Moab Sacrificed His Oldest Son" in *Biblical Archaeology Review* (Nov-Dec 1986) pp. 62-63.

MARSHALL, I. Howard: "1 Kings-2 Chronicles" in *Scripture Union Bible Study Books*, Scripture Union, London, 1967, 92 p.

MCCONVILLE, J.G.: "Narrative and Meaning in the Books of Kings" in *Biblica* 70 (1989) pp. 31-49.

MEYER, Ivo: "Die Bücher der Könige, die Bücher der Chronik" in *Stuttgarter Kleiner Kommentar*, 1976, pp. 6-97.

MILLARD, Alan: *1 Kings-2 Chronicles,* Scripture Union, London, 1985, pp. 45-53.

------- *Trésors des temps bibliques*, Sator, 1986, pp. 117-118.

MINOKAMI, Yoshikazu: *Die Revolution des Jehus*, Vandenhoeck & Ruprecht, Göttingen, 1989, 189 p.

MONTGOMERY, James A.: *A Critical and Exegetical Commentary on the Book of Kings*, Clark, Edinburgh, 1951, 575 p.

MOORE, Rick Dale: *God saves: lessons from the Elisha stories*, Journal for the Study of the Old Testament Supplement Series 95, Sheffield, 1990, 169 p.

MULZER, Martin: *Jehu schlägt Jehoram: Text-, literar- und strukturkritische Untersuchung zu 2 Kön 8.25-10.36*, Eos, St. Ottilien, 1992, 414 p.

NELSON, Richard D.: "First and Second Kings" in *Interpretation, A Bible Commentary for Teaching and Preaching*, John Knox, Atlanta, 1987, 273 p.

PATTERSON, Richard D., & Austel, Hermann J.: "1, 2 Kings" in *The Expositor's Bible Commentary,* vol. 4, Zondervan, Grand Rapids, 1988, pp. 3-300.

PINK, Arthur W.: *Gleanings from Elisha: His Life and Miracles*, Moody, Chicago, 1972, 254 p.

PRITCHARD, James B.: *Ancient Near Eastern Texts relating to the Old Testament,* Princeton University, 1969, 490 p.

------- *The Ancient Near Eastern in Picture Relating to the Old Testament,* Princeton University, 1969, 390 p.

PROVAN, Iain W.: "1 & 2 Kings" in *Old Testament Guides*, Sheffield Academic Press, Sheffield, 1997, 125 p.

------- "1-2 Kings" in *New International Biblical Commentary*, Henrickson, Peabody, Massachusetts, 1995, 305 p.

ROSSIER, H.: *Méditations sur le second livre des Rois,* Bibles et traités chrétiens, Vevey, 1956, 317 p.

RAWLINSON, G.: "2 Kings" in *The Pulpit Commentary,* Funk & Wagnalls, London, 1906, 504 p.

ROBINSON, J.: "The Second Book of Kings" in *The Cambridge Bible Commentary*, Cambridge University Press, 1976, 256 p.

RÖSEL, Hartmut N.: "2 Kön 2.1-18 als Elija- oder Elischa-Geschichte?" in *Biblische Notizen* 59 (1991) pp. 33-36.

SAVRAN, George: "1 and 2 Kings" in R. Alter & F. Kermode (Eds), *The Literary Guide to the Bible*, Harvard Press, Cambridge, 1987, pp. 146-164.

SCHÄFER-LICHTENBERGER, Christa: "Joschua und Elischa Ideal-Typen von Führerschaft in Israel" in M. Augustin (ed), *Wünschet Jerusalem Frieden*, Lang, New York, 1988, pp. 273-280.

------- "Josua und Elischa – eine biblische Argumentation zur Begründung der Autorität und Legitimität des Nachfolgers" in *Zeitschrift für alttestamentliche Wissenschaft* 101 (1989) pp. 198-222.

SCHMITT, Hans-Christoph: *Elisa: Traditionsgeschichtliche Untersuchungen zur vorklassischen nordisraelitischen Prophetie*, Gerd Mohn, Gütersloh, 1972, 252 p.

SHIELDS, Mary E.: "Subverting a Man of God, Elevating a Woman: Role and Power Reversals in 2 Kings 4" in *Journal for the Study of the Old Testament* 58 (1993) pp. 59-69.

SMITH, Hamilton, *Elie et Elisée*, Bibles et Traités Chrétiens, Vevey, 1991, 191 p.

SPERBER, Daniel: "Weak Waters" in *Zeitschrift für alttestamentliche Wissenschaft* 82 (1970) pp. 114-116.

STIPP, Hermann-Joseph: "Elischa-Propheten-Gottesmänner" in *Arbeiten zu Text und Sprache im Alten Testament*, Eos, St. Ottilien, 1987, 535 p.

THIELE, Edwin R.: *The Mysterious Numbers of the Hebrew Kings: A Reconstruction of the Chronology of the Kingdoms of Israel and Judah,* Paternoster, Exeter, 1966, 232 p.

------- *Chronology of the Hebrew Kings,* Zondervan, Grand Rapids, 1977, 93 p.

THOMPSON, J. A.: *La Bible à la lumière de l'archéologie*, Ligue pour la lecture de la Bible, Guebwiller, 1988, pp. 133-143.

TURIOT, Cécile: "La guérison de Naaman" in *Sémiotique et Bible* 16 (1979) pp. 8-32.

VAN GRONINGEN, Gerard: "1-2 Kings" in *Evangelical Commentary on the Bible*, ed. W.A. Elwell, Baker, Grand Rapids, 1989, pp. 231-262.

VOS, Howard F.: "1, 2 Kings" in *Bible Study Commentary,* Lamplighter, Grand Rapids, 1989, 231 p.

WHITCOMB, John C. Jr.: *Solomon to the Exile: Studies in Kings and Chronicles,* BMH Books, Winona Lake, 1971, 182 p.

WHITFIELD, Frederick: *The Saviour Prophet or Incidents in the Life of Elisha*, James Nisbet, London, 1881, 294 p.

WILLIAMS, James G.: "The Prophetic 'Father': A Brief Explanation of the Term 'Sons of the Prophets'" in *Journal of Biblical Literature* 85 (1966) pp. 344-348.

WISEMAN, Donald J.: "1 and 2 Kings" in *Tyndale Old Testament Commentaries*, Inter-Varsity, Leicester, 1993, 318 p.

WOOD, Leon: *A Survey of Israel's History,* Zondervan, Grand Rapids, 1970, pp. 315-320.

------- *The Prophets of Israel*, Baker, Grand Rapids, 1979, pp. 243-257.

WÜRTHWEIN, Ernst: *Die Bücher der Könige (1 Kön 17 - 2 Kön 25),* Vandenhoeck & Ruprecht, Göttingen, 1984, 515 p.

YANNAI, Y.: "Elisha and the Shunammite (2 Kings 4.8-37): A Case of Homoeoteleuton, or a Text Emendation by Ancient Masoretes?" in E. Fernandez Tejero (ed), *Estudios masoreticos*, Arias Montano, Madrid, 1983, pp. 123-135.

Books and articles by Daniel Arnold: see Website
www.danielarnold.org

Published in French by Editions Emmaüs route de Fenil 40, CH-1806 Saint-Légier (Switzerland)

Bible Commentaries
- Le livre des Juges. Ces mystérieux héros de la foi. (1995, 395 pages)
- Ruth à la croisée des chemins (2003, 135 pages)
- Elie : entre le jugement et la grâce. Commentaire biblique de 1 Rois 17 – 2 Rois 2 (2001, 210 pages)
- Elisée, précurseur de Jésus-Christ. Commentaire de 2 Rois 2-9 (2002, 215 pages).
- Esther: survivre dans un monde hostile (2000, 199 pages)
- L'évangile de Marc: puissance et souffrance de Jésus-Christ (2007, 503 pages)

Reference work on Ethics
- Vivre l'éthique de Dieu. L'amour et la justice au quotidien. (2010, 400 pages)

Collection of plays
- Théâtre pour Noël, volume 1 (1996, 140 pages)
- Théâtre pour Noël, volume 2 (2009, 217 pages)

Self-published in English (available on Amazon)
- Wrestling with God. Commentary on the Book of Jonah (2014).
- Elijah between Judgement and Grace. Bible Commentary on 1 Kings 17-2 Kings 2 (2015).
- Elisha Forerunner of Jesus Christ. Bible Commentary on 2 Kings 2-9 (2015).
- Esther: Surviving in a Hostile World. Bible Commentary (2015).
- The Book of Daniel. When Structures Enlighten Prophecy. A Study of Parallelisms and Progressions as Means of Communication (2016).

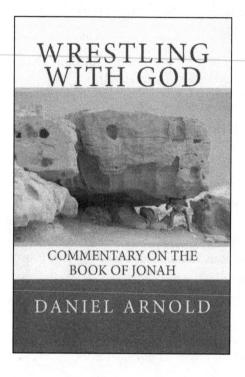

WRESTLING
WITH GOD

COMMENTARY ON THE
BOOK OF JONAH

DANIEL ARNOLD

Jonah is a fascinating book. It takes only ten minutes to read, but ten years of study cannot explain all of the questions it raises.

This commentary brings new insights into the conflict-laden relationship between God and his prophet. It explains why Jonah travels in the opposite direction from his mission field and why he sleeps in the hold of the ship when God sends a huge storm. Since actions speak louder than words, God and his prophet communicate non-verbally. Jonah is stubborn in his refusal to accomplish his mission, but God is resolute to extend his grace to bloodthirsty pagans, and he will use wind, whale, and worm to convince his reluctant prophet.

On a global level (intertextuality), the story of Jonah is an anti-flood story. God reverses the judgement that struck the ancient world. Through Jonah, God announces a salvation for all mankind that finds its full expression in Jesus-Christ.

ELIJAH between
Judgement and Grace

Bible Commentary
1 Kings 17 - 2 Kings 2

Daniel Arnold

How do judgement and grace interrelate? The eight chapters of 1-2 Kings dedicated to Elijah's ministry revolve around the theme of immediate and distant retribution.

This commentary explains how Elijah's ministry highlights God's patience during the unique time of Israel's monarchy (1-2 Kings). It explains and justifies "the theology of postponement". It draws attention to the literary features of the text and uses the narrative characteristics of the stories to underline the author's main message.

Elijah is known for his courage at Mt Carmel and his perseverance in prayer; but also for his fear before Jezebel, and his depression after failure. He is the first man implicated in a resurrection and the second to be raptured to heaven. Fundamentally, Elijah is the prophet of judgement but during his life he had to learn more about God's mercy.

JUDGES: Mysterious
Heroes of the Faith

Bible Commentary
A Global Approach

Daniel Arnold

The characters of the judges are colourful, dramatic, and often misunderstood. Should Samson be admired or despised? Each judge poses problems because the author is contented with merely narrating the facts. Generally commentators evaluate these men negatively, yet the New Testament includes the most criticized judges amongst the heroes of faith (Heb 11:32).

This commentary defends a very positive view of the judges. It analyses the book as a whole and points to various clues left by the inspired author to read positively the behaviour of these military leaders. Gideon, Jephthah, and Samson are models of spirituality.

Each story is linked to the book's themes of sin, judgement, and grace. New light is shed on Gideon's fleece, on Jephthah's vow, and on Samson's hair. Numerous spiritual and ethical lessons are enriching to the reader.

ESTHER: Surviving
in a Hostile World

Bible Commentary
A Global Approach

Daniel Arnold

The book of Esther helps the believer to live in the secular world where power, racism, and sexism crush any hope of freedom and liberation. How to survive oppression? How to refuse the unacceptable without being immediately rejected and humiliated? Confronted with the genocide of their people, Esther and Mordecai use God's opportunities with courage and faith.

This commentary analyses each chapter in the light of the whole book. Esther's strategy to undue the king's irrevocable decree is carefully analysed. With skill, intelligence, and diligence, yet without precipitation she uses her feminine charm to influence an irresponsible king to save her people.

The commentary contains an in-depth character study of the main protagonists, a presentation of the overall chiasmic structure of the book, and a detailed critique of the Greek version that adds one hundred verses to the Hebrew text.

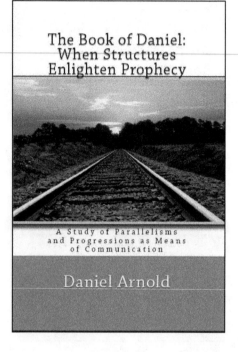

The Book of Daniel:
When Structures
Enlighten Prophecy

A Study of Parallelisms
and Progressions as Means
of Communication

Daniel Arnold

Daniel's structure is a puzzle. The work is written in two languages that divide the book into three parts (Da 1; 2-7; 8-12); there are also two genres (narrative and apocalyptic) that divide the book into two parts that do not correspond to the language structure (Da 1-6; 7-12).

This study is based on Daniel Arnold's doctoral thesis in which *Daniel* is analyzed from the perspective of parallelism and duality, which are basic paradigms of Hebrew communication. Parallelisms and progression enhance meaning. Three global structures are developed (linguistic, genre, and era).

The seven visions reveal a progression in clarity and the oppression of the faithful is expressed through the progressive hardening of kings and pagan kingdoms.

The final step of the comparative exegetical approach analyses *Daniel* from the perspective of the canon. Four antithetical perspectives are suggested: the Babel story, Joseph the patriarch, Ezekiel the contemporary exilic prophet, and the book of Revelation.

CPSIA information can be obtained
at www.ICGtesting.com
Printed in the USA
FFHW012051211019
55697229-61558FF